The
World
According
to Bumble

START THE CAR

The World According to Bumble

START THE CAR

DAVID LLOYD

HarperSport
An Imprint of HarperCollinsPublishers

HarperSport
an imprint of HarperCollins*Publishers*
77-85 Fulham Palace Road,
Hammersmith, London W6 8JB

www.harpercollins.co.uk

First published in hardback 2010
This paperback edition 2011

1

A catalogue record for this book
is available from the British Library

ISBN: 978-0-00-791022-9

Printed and bound in Great Britain by
Clays Ltd, St Ives plc

To Diana, Tags, Susan, Phil, Steven, Ben, Spike, Graham, Sharon, Joseph, Joshua, Freddie, Sarah, Enty, Sam, James and Jasmine.

Hope you enjoy it!

CONTENTS

PART 3 — IN THE BLOOD

PS ...

RICHARD GIBSON, who worked with David Lloyd on the writing of this book, is a freelance sports writer who spent ten years covering cricket for the Press Association. He has wintered with England every year since the 2001 tour of India, on which he had to be resuscitated by then England physio Dean Conway, after collapsing in the Hyderabad press box. Trekking around the globe reporting on cricket means he sees a heck of a lot of Bumble, and they naturally formed a special bond given that they hail from two of the United Kingdom's modern utopias – Accrington and Hull.

ACKNOWLEDGEMENTS

Many thanks to:
'Gibbo' – a fan of Hull City FC

And, for photography, to:
Gareth Copley – award-winning photographer (Press Association)
Michael Atherton – award-winning journalist
Dr Arthur Trumpington – bon viveur, raconteur, bullshitteur

INTRODUCTION

Thanks for buying this book. The proceeds will go to a very good cause, namely the David Lloyd Retirement Fund, and, I assure you, will be redistributed to numerous outlets, in various personal pursuits across the globe. Oh, and rest easy in the knowledge that I will have fun doing so.

Of course, you might not have put your hand in your pocket to purchase this, so, for those of you who have received it as a gift on Father's Day, on a birthday or at Christmas and want to pretend you have ploughed from cover to cover; for those of you who really like the thought of reading but never venture much further than the introduction; for those of you who normally do but find it to be the kind of book you just can't pick up after putting down; for those of you who thought you were investing in the life story of some bloke involved in top-level tennis; for those of you wanting to know no more than the secrets of my successful leisure club empire (you'll be sadly disappointed); for those of you whose concentration spans waver after a tweet or two; for those of you who have picked this up in the smallest room during a break between courses at a friend's dinner party – here is the deal. Pretty much every essential detail you need to know about me is listed below. Welcome, however briefly, to my world.

My 50 Favourite Things

Career moment (playing): My 214 not out against India, Edgbaston, 1974

Career moment (broadcasting): Yuvraj Singh's six sixes in an over off Stuart Broad, World Twenty20, 2007

Opponent: Joel Garner. He would bowl me out with a bath sponge

Team-mate: Graham Lloyd

Modern player: Can't separate Virender Sehwag and Kevin Pietersen

Cricket ground: Sydney

Football team: Accrington Stanley

Footballer: Duncan Edwards

Holiday destination: St Ives, Cornwall

Tipple: A pint of Black Sheep or Timmy T's

Meal: Chicken Madras with naan and lime pickle

Country: United Kingdom

Insect: Ladybirds are OK

Saying: 'Don't let the bastards grind you down'

Animal: Dog

Pastime: Fishing

Personal item: Motorbike

Boyhood hero: Ken Barrington

Book: *Tragically, I Was an Only Twin* – Peter Cook

Film: *Brassed Off*

Band: The Fall

Album: *Imperial Wax Solvent* – The Fall

Motorway: M6 toll road

River: Wye

Hotel: Lygon Arms, Chipping Campden

Mode of transport: Bike

Season: Spring

Beatles or Stones? Stones

Colour: Black

Decade: 1960s

Restaurant: J Sheekey, Covent Garden, London

Pub: The Hesketh Tavern, Cheadle Hulme

Advice received: 'Be yourself' – my dad

Advice given: 'If you are a politician, don't knock on my door'

Cake: Fruitcake

Flower: Rose

Number: 134

Condiment: Lancashire Sauce

Board game: Cluedo

Gadget: Chainsaw

Film star: Ray Winstone or Russell Crowe

TV soap: Emmerdale

Politician: Not one of them cheating, conniving, low-down dregs of the earth

Cricket tour: New Zealand

City: Manchester

Car: Audi

Memory: Loss of

Piece of trivia: Monaco's army is smaller than its symphony orchestra

Comedian: Tommy Cooper

Joke: My granny started jogging in 1998 … we have no idea where she is now.

PART ONE

IN THE
BOX

Chapter 1

THAT BLOKE OFF THE TELLY

Being on television inevitably means you get recognised by people when you are out and about. It is something you become accustomed to, and I have never really had a problem with it, although I did once get freaked out when a bloke came straight out with 'You're David Lloyd, aren't you?' Because when I say I am recognised, I genuinely am – only never as myself. I have had Rasputin (he had a massive beard, didn't he?), Tony Blair and Alan Titchmarsh over the years. Nice to know I have made such a good impression.

To be fair, at least it is normally another famous face from the world of cricket that I get. Although with my specs on I also encountered one of the more bizarre shouts. An Australian bloke walked up to me in a pub in Manchester and did a double take. 'Hey, I know you, you look like one of the Proclaimers,' he said, his forehead crumpling in thought. 'What do you mean, one of the Proclaimers?' I protested. 'I either look like both of them or none of them. They're bloody identical twins! Or they were the last time I looked.'

It is not as though this identity crisis has hit me solely since I hooked up in the Sky commentary box, either. Now I come to think of it, it has followed me around since my playing days. When I signed for Cumberland in early 1985, I was asked to do a local radio interview over the telephone. We went through the usual rigmarole of how the move had come about, what offers had surfaced elsewhere, how I saw the side's chances that summer and what role I would fulfil within it.

It was a pleasant enough chat, and the interviewer wound down with a final question: 'Do you think you will adapt to the Cumbrian north-west weather again quickly after spending so much time in the Caribbean?' The silly sod had got me mixed up with my brother Clive. I put him right, of course, and following a lengthy pause I heard his muffled voice relay the information to his producer: 'Hey, they've only gone and signed the wrong one!' I had some great times with Clive at Old Trafford, he has been a great pal, and he still lives down the road, but fancy getting a pasty bloke like him mixed up with a bronze Adonis like myself!

Nowhere are people more cricket daft than India, and appropriately it is there that I have experienced some of the daftest shouts. One chap in Rajkot was overjoyed when I agreed to pose with him for a picture at the airport. 'You are my most good commentator Sky Sport,' he told me, through clenched teeth, as we grimaced for the first snap. After seven more shots, I made my excuses and left. 'Thank you, Mr Paul Arlott,' he said. 'For being my friend.'

Now they don't get a great deal of international cricket in Rajkot, I grant you, so the locals tend to get excitable when a game comes to town. After England were trounced there in

4

the winter of 2008–9, I was asked for more photos at the ground. I was only too happy to oblige until the chap pointing the camera said: 'Excuse me, Mr Duncan Fletcher, look this way please.' There must have been a particularly virulent strain of this eye infection going around, as later that evening came a knock at my hotel door. Three chaps were standing outside and greeted me with: 'You are our favourite umpire, Mr Hair.' And you can imagine the levels of my paranoia when even the hotel staff weighed in. Upon checking out next morning, the receptionist said to me: 'Thank you for staying with us in Rajkot, Mr Bruce Yardley.' I was glad to get out.

This was enough to put a chap permanently on edge. In Bangalore, one autograph hunter instructed me: 'Please sign this, Tony Greig.' So I did exactly that to get my own back. OK, Greigy was a former England captain, but he is six foot four and speaks with an unmistakable South African accent. I undoubtedly preferred the next error, as I left the ground in Chennai during a pre-Christmas Test match. 'You are most famous English Mike Brearley,' I was unequivocally told. I gave myself the once over, confirmed in my own mind I was not, but appreciated being thought of on the same intellectual level. If you are involved in mistaken identity it's always better if it paints you in a decent light.

And you can also have some fun. Whenever we are in Leeds for a Test match, I make a dash for the Princess of Wales pub and sink a pint or three. A group of us were in there one year when a rather big Yorkshire lass, bedecked with tattoos from head to toe, sauntered up and barked: 'You're the commentator, aren't you?' She was quite an intimidating sight – supping a pint like a rugby front-rower between sentences – so I meekly replied, 'Yes, I am.'

'I just wanted to say I love you on *Test Match Special*, Jonathan,' she continued. Jolly nice of her to say so, I thought, as I subtly brought up Agnew's number on my phone, passed it on to her and suggested she give me a call any time she needed tickets.

Chapter 2

Ten Minutes to Decide — the Ultimate Job Ultimatum

Sky Sports is a truly great company to work for, one that I am genuinely proud to be a part of, and one that I look forward to putting in a shift for each and every day. There is a real energy about the entire production department, and that rubs off on our commentary team, without a doubt. The production crew are incredibly youthful – particularly given the extreme responsibility that goes with the jobs that they do – but they are exceptional in their fields and help to keep me feeling young at heart. They are well marshalled by Paul King and Bryan Henderson, executive and senior producer respectively, and Mark Lynch, as good a senior director as there is in the field, and there is a real buzz from the top all the way down to the office staff and runners.

These people are as keen as hell and they dance around television, knowing every single technical step along the way. It's a very tight unit and wherever we are in the world there is a real sense of being a team. A team that works hard and plays hard. They do their time and are great fun to be with after hours. Good relationships between commentators and the production team are essential, and I speak on behalf of us all, I am sure, when I say that we are very comfortable with them directing us. We know exactly what they are about, and we all benefit from their expertise, commitment and enthusiasm. It is a thoroughly modern organisation, and Sky's cricket has involved some of their best people.

Sky's cricket coverage is still relatively young, well, certainly in comparison with that great institution *Test Match Special*. I felt equally privileged to have worked on that programme for a number of years and I thoroughly enjoyed my radio work. What a great position to be in, describing the game to thousands of people, who are doing thousands of different things as they listen. Radio has always been a great medium for cricket, and *TMS* embodies the most essential requirement of sporting commentary. The trick has always been to get the person you are addressing to feel as though they are sitting next to you, whether they are in their living-room, in a pub or driving in their car. That is something the *TMS* team have successfully achieved throughout the decades and will continue to do in their own individualistic style. They do so now through Jonathan Agnew, Christopher Martin-Jenkins, Henry Blofeld and Victor Marks, and that will be carried on by the next regime and the one after that.

I have never subscribed to the rose-tinted view that there will never be another John Arlott or another Brian Johnston.

Sure, they were one-off characters, national treasures, wonderful broadcasters, and yes, they are missed. But we have also come to love those that have taken their place. New guys will emerge, just as Aggers has, for example. His part in Johnners's irresistible 'leg-over' moment, when Ian Botham was dismissed hit wicket in the 1991 Oval Test against West Indies, showed perfectly how one generation could merge into the next. We can all get nostalgic, but the show goes on and the bottom line is that it is still brilliant. The formula that Johnners so revered – he made *TMS* sound like a group of mates getting together for a chat at the match – has not been lost.

I was part of that group for ten years or so, from the late 1980s, working alongside the irrepressible Fred Trueman and Trevor Bailey. They were priceless times. There was never a dull moment. Nor is there now, and I have a real respect for their commentary team. Yes, there is always a joust between the BBC and Sky because of our different agendas, but I would like to think it is a good-natured one and comes with a mutual respect and understanding from each side that, competitive rivalry notwithstanding, you are talking about two bloody good productions. We spend our lives in the same venues, the same hotels, travelling the same motorways, or sitting in the same aeroplanes, and I would say that between us we give the British public what they seek in terms of cricket coverage.

When I initially moved into broadcasting I was still on the umpiring circuit, and had half an eye on making the international panel of officials which was rumoured to be on its way into the sport. In fact, it was Sky's decision to begin screening cricket that first took my life in a different direction, away from involvement on the field of play, and when I was subsequently approached by then *TMS* producer Peter Baxter it gave me licence to do what I have always enjoyed – to talk passionately about the game, and have some laughs along the way. After all, sport is there to be enjoyed first and foremost, and conveying that always came naturally enough to me. As it happened, the next stage of my life, as a full-time coach, was only just around the corner, but the stints on television and radio whetted the appetite.

Upon leaving the commentary box to don the tracksuit, I left the door ajar for a return. That much became clear when my time as England coach concluded in the summer of 1999. The truth is, I knew it was time for me to step aside, but I had no idea what I was going to do after handing in my resignation to my bosses at Lord's. Deep down I thought I would get back into coaching with a county club, but there was no obvious opening for me. There was nothing at Lancashire, which was understandably my first choice, because they already had Dav Whatmore in position. I had enjoyed a really good spell at Old Trafford as coach previously, but someone else was in that job on their own merits, which meant spending some time studying the county circuit to weigh up where an opportunity might present itself. Not many days had passed, however, when I received the phone call that was to change my life once more. I had always loved being involved in broadcasting, I had done loads over the years, but the voice at the other end was offering me something a bit different: the chance of a permanent appointment.

The Australian accent greeting me at 8.50 a.m. on the morning of my England resignation press conference belonged to John Gayleard, then head of Sky's cricket team.

'Come and work for us,' he said. 'Our offer is on its way through to you. Oh, and by the way, we want your answer within ten minutes.' It was the age of the fax – seems so long ago now, doesn't it? – and this contract offer that landed on my desk needed signing and returning before the paper it was written on had cooled down. Sky wanted an immediate response because, spotting the opportunity for some publicity, they had decided to jump on the back of my departure from the national job. Their cameras were all set up down the road at Old Trafford to cover the announcement, which was just one and a half hours away, and they wanted to follow it with one of their own: 'By the way, he now works for us.' Of course, I accepted. So one minute I was sitting there in my England blazer, doing my thank you and goodbye with Ian MacLaurin, and the next I was taking up the microphone and jumping fence. Almost literally.

During our hurried conversation that morning I asked John for a break, for a period of time specifically for some kind of reflection. Just to weigh up what had happened and where I was. 'You're in from next week' was the terse reply. 'You start straight away.' So that was that. Like most Australians, Gayleard was forthright. He told me how it was going to be, and I was in no real position to argue. I later reflected that his instructions were not for his benefit at all but for mine, and I appreciated that. I think he could tell I was hurting in the aftermath of my England exit but guessed that any licking of wounds would be better done while my mind was fully engaged in a new environment, working for a new team.

I immediately knew he was right when I first strolled into the commentary box. There was not a lot of time for me to prepare, and they were hardly ready for my arrival either – the first jacket I wore was one that Ian Botham had rejected, so you can imagine the size of this darn thing. I was tasked with hauling around the equivalent of a Karrimor tent on my shoulders until I eventually got my own.

I work for Sky between 150 and 170 days a year, depending on what is on, and do lots of other stuff, within the media primarily, as a spin-off from that. In fact, some of the time when you may think I'm on Sky duty, I am technically working for other companies. When I am away commentating on an International Cricket Council event, for example, I am actually on duty for ESPN. And although the assignments stem from my profile with Sky, I can be working for all manner of different stations, people and directors: Ten Sports, Zee, Nimbus and TWI among them. It means being adaptable, and for any number of reasons. You have to slot in as seamlessly as possible and, believe me, you get to see exactly how good Sky are when you are working for rival television networks. Some of them fly by the seat of their pants in comparison and, without being too parochial about it, are left trailing in our wake. Few would be able to argue against that assessment, although I have to say that Australia's Channel 9 are right up there as well in the slickness of their production.

All in all, I have not looked back since I squiggled my signature and thrust that offer of employment back through my old fax machine. I simply love what I do. In broadcasting, your enthusiasm has to be unleashed, and that is not a problem as far as I am concerned because my enthusiasm for the game has rarely waned. I never see a day's work as a chore. People are depending on you to entertain them. Sure, parts of matches can be a bit dull and sometimes you have to let a couple of turgid hours of cricket speak for themselves. Less can be more occasionally, and you have to get the balance of allowing games to drift along at some stages and forcing the pace at others. There are always going to be those periods that lend themselves to Johnny making a brew or Hilda feeding the budgie, but there are obviously other times when the action has to be revved up – more often than not when a wicket falls to alter the balance of the contest or in against-the-clock situations when teams are chasing victory. Thankfully getting excitable comes as second nature to me and I have always heeded the advice of the great broadcasters I have worked with. Their common opinion has been that you have to get the viewer feeling that they are with you, and part of the excitement, part of the drama.

The other advice I always bear in mind while on commentary duty came from my dad. As a child, I received a strict church upbringing. In our household, my dad, who was a lay preacher, was very quiet. It was my mother who was the dominant one, the disciplinarian; she used to hit me with a frying pan, belts, anything she could get her hands on. Whereas I cannot remember my dad ever laying a finger on me. He just pointed me in the right direction. The one thing I always remembered was his instruction to 'Be yourself. Always be yourself. You might not always be right – there is nothing wrong with being wrong – but be yourself.' David senior was 90-odd when he died but, whatever the situation that confronted me, I always turned back to that same, long-standing guidance.

On air I have tried to keep to those guidelines. I have never been afraid of sailing close to the wind when it comes to innuendo, and I have always believed that you instinctively know where to draw the line between fun and bad taste. When I was England coach, dealing with players with families, mortgages and other responsibilities, the one thing I always said to them – we all know what blokes are like, we are all the same when we get together, whether we be sportsmen, press men, whatever; we want a lot of fun, occasionally act a bit over the top, or be a bit laddish – was never to do anything that would prevent your mother and father standing up and proudly declaring to all and sundry: 'That's my lad.' It was as simple as that. As parents, you want to be able to say: 'Yep, that's our George … the one with his arse hanging out.' I am all for being outrageous on occasion, but you have to keep it affectionate.

For example, I hope I don't behave differently on camera from how I act off it. My view is that I am the same man and that I am pretty natural at what I do. Talking about cricket has always come pretty easily, put it that way, but neither am I afraid to say things out loud that come into my head. It is not always pre-planned but I never regret what I say, even though it can be close to the bone occasionally. During the Ashes in 2009, one of the cameras panned to a young lass, who had the biggest chest you've ever seen, walking in front of the stand with a couple of pints in hand. 'Oooh, I wouldn't mind two of those,' I said. To me, genuinely funny innuendo is born of innocence.

When we are working, we will normally get a nudge from our crew to warn us that they are about to pan around the crowd. But when you are abroad, and therefore taking another company's pictures, you haven't a clue what is around the corner. Such was the case in the Durban Test of 2009–10 as SABC went into a random surf of the stands. The camera focused on a young lady, who at that very second produced an enormous sausage from a picnic tray concealed between her legs. Instead of panning away to something else, they kept on this 12-inch pork truncheon. What on earth does a bloke say when confronted by that image? You're in a no-win situation. 'Well, sorry, I have lost my train of thought,' I declared, as this thing wobbled this way and that. Sometimes you get into giddy schoolboy mode and this was one such occasion. The double entendre continued later when, sat alongside Michael Atherton, they zoomed in on a couple of blokes who had carved out a watermelon and plonked the outer casings on their heads as hats. 'Look at these melons here,' I said, playfully. Well, the director could not have timed his cut from one image to another any better if he had been trying to stitch me up. Exactly as I said it, the camera panned around to a woman with an enormous pair of norks …

The only venue at which I tend to pre-plan a routine is at Old Trafford. I will say to Mark Lynch, the director: 'Get us an aeroplane coming in.' On cue, I will then announce: 'Here they are. They're coming to sunny Manchester on their holidays. Hundreds of 'em. Holiday season has begun, folks. In they flood from Barbados, Mauritius and Goa. They love the wet lands of Wigan, the spa town of Salford, they come here for the waters, you know. There are the two canals of Manchester as well, of course – the near canal and the far canal.'

Sir Ian Botham —
'I'll make you famous'

Our very own knight of the realm had an on-field presence that demanded royal respect. Within our environment, however, his title is less regal and he is regularly referred to as His Buffiness, His Buffikins or His Holy Buffness. Our ribbing of him is perhaps evidence of us mere mortals being able to drag him back to the real world. For on a cricket pitch, alongside his English counterparts, he was the first among unequals; capable of extraordinary feats at will. I was a witness to one such incident during my three-season stint as a first-class umpire.

It was a televised Sunday League match at Taunton between Somerset and Middlesex. With three balls to go, and 12 runs required to win, Mr I.T. Botham was facing West Indies paceman Wayne Daniel, and I was standing at the business end. 'Diamond' Daniel was halfway through his approach to the crease when Both halted him in his tracks and, prodding the pitch, looked up to me and asked: 'Who you backing in this one?' I told him in short that a dozen required off three was a good contest, but the *Songs of Praise* theme tune was about to hit its first bar, so, if he didn't mind awfully, could we get on with it?

The first of the three balls to come down, a full-toss angled in from wide of the crease, was dispatched into the car park. Now, with the requirement reduced to six from two balls, had he asked me again who I was backing, I would have been starting to favour the batting side's chances. Only a man of the most supreme ability would have dared to do what Beefy did next – he went and blocked one on purpose, just to enhance the sense of theatre. Middlesex's senior players gathered around their fearsome fast bowler, waiting at the end of his run-up, to discuss where to bowl and where to position the field. The latter part of their deliberations turned out to be irrelevant, however, as another full bunger sailed out of the ground. The crowd went berserk, even the opposition must have appreciated his bombast, and, as I dismantled the stumps at the bowler's end, I felt the full force of his willow across my backside. 'You stick with me, pal, I'll make you famous!' he declared.

What a player he was. Absolutely brilliant. Without question the best cricketer our country has ever produced. This was a bloke who could turn games on their head with bat, ball or slip catching. He dealt in moments of inspiration. He played on instinct. He didn't think too much about it, just got on and did it. And how he did it!

Shane Warne is from the same mould, and when playing cricket followed exactly the same rules. For Beefy and Warney the coach is what you use for travelling to the ground. There would be no interest for them in being told what to do or even being offered some well-meaning advice. Whereas others need a figure to point them in the right direction, these cricket geniuses had all the answers already. Their actions were always louder than any words. Botham's ability has no doubt shaped his thinking on how players should deal with their own losses of form. His answer would always be to carry on your own merry way: to get out of a rut he would recommend a couple of glasses of wine, a day out fishing or a game of golf, not extra practice. You might lose form, he would argue, but what was lost could easily be recovered. For him there was not a great deal of thought required.

Because that was what worked for him – he could come back to the nets, give it a thrash and he'd be off on form again. Others might see a more technical necessity, but he kept things very simple indeed. Of course, his fantastic ability made it that much easier for him to have that attitude, but it was a great way to be – an enviable way. Start talking about trigger movements and he would shoot you down in laughter. Let's face it, we are always on the look-out for a new Botham, just as Australia will search fruitlessly for a new Warne. In all the time that they played, and since their departures, the search for a replica has been on. But you don't unearth genius very often. For a long time now Australia have been seeking someone to bowl leg-spin for them, but no one will ever be able to match Warne.

Beefy is one of life's true alpha males, a real man's man. So you can imagine the expression on his face when, in the aftermath of the Mumbai attacks in the winter of 2008–9, we were forced to deal with heightened security on our return, which included intimate personal searches. Everything was so much tighter when we went back, and while Botham's *Daily Mirror* colleague Oliver Holt, the newspaper's chief sports writer, somehow managed to evade the stringent identification checks with a flash of his 2008 FA Cup final accreditation, Beefy was being handled in quite a different way. Let's just say the new multi-frisking was leaving nothing to chance. In fact, anything that could pass for a weapon was being given the once over before entry to the ground was permitted. So you can imagine the ire etched on English cricket's greatest-ever player's clock when this particular cupping incident took place on the opening day of the Chandigarh Test match. They carried it out with far too much enthusiasm, rather like the school nurse when she put you through that dreaded cough test in your medicals.

At times he was like a human whirlwind on the field of play. Few could match his velocity. Neither can they off it. Beefy is not an opponent you want to take on, particularly after play, because that is the time he really comes into his own. He has an unbelievable thirst. In truth, he should carry a health warning, because it's not good to spend any length of time around him. Since his playing days there have been three distinct tactics among us fellow broadcasters: you have a general policy of avoidance, you make a pre-planned exit or you take your turn – 'You're with Beefy tonight, good luck.' People have become adept at applying these over a decade and it seems to work a treat. Needless to say, avoidance has been my primary tactic, but I have also developed a hip shuffle towards the exit that those dancing queens Darren Gough and Mark Ramprakash would be proud of.

It's only when you have taken your turn that you realise there's only one bloke who can live the way he does. Now I like a beer, but I can't drink much. He doesn't, but he can. He is massively into wine, and he drinks flagons of the stuff. I can have an odd glass but it has never done much for me. He is really into his vineyards and reading labels on the bottles, whereas I simply want a good old-fashioned pint in my hand, something I have never seen him armed with. I have seen him with copious amounts of wine, but he doesn't go into pubs. He will search out wineries and I will seek pubs. We are pretty much chalk and cheese.

Whatever your chosen tipple, you have got to be able to get up for work in the morning, and so you have to get your drinking with Beefy (long game or short) down to a fine art. Have a glass with him and then clear off sharpish is the safest bet. His mates always look thirsty too, so one must keep alert. Others among the Sky crew are also into nice wines, particularly Lord Gower, but although he would probably spend more time with Beefy than anybody, he knows when to dodge in and out. He's got Beefy avoidance down to a tee.

God help you if you spend an entire evening in Botham's company – it can do horrendous things to your insides. For a long time I wondered how on earth he could get larrupped and still turn up for work the next morning as though he had been on carrot juice and cucumber slices. I discovered that his recuperative powers are catalysed by an uncomplicated concoction. There is nothing that Beefy can neck that four cans of Red Bull, three black coffees, two enormous belches and a huge fart won't fix the next morning. Once that combination has been taken in and let out, he's back to normal. It's rather like kick-starting an old motor engine. In fact, he reminds me of the 1950s-style cars that you had to crank at the front to start. Once attended to, the engine is running again and he's ready to rock.

We are all very different characters within our commentary team and that means we have some very different views. For example, the last time we were in South Africa Beefy went off for a couple of days on safari and came back with some evidence of his trip. It was when he flashed around pictures of his grandsons, standing on an impala that was best described as very dead, that I took umbrage. The photograph showed them in possession of a gun – they had shot this poor thing. I just can't do that.

'So here he is, Mr Impala, out for the day with his family, stretching their legs in the sun when …' I began.

'No, you don't understand,' Beefy told me. 'There's too many of 'em. Far too many. They have to be culled.'

I pointed out that there are a lot of Chinese people on this planet and some would argue too many. But, despite the size of their population, nobody goes around shooting them.

'You don't get it, do you?' he said.

The way I saw it was that this impala family was out having some breakfast one morning when their dad was shot and subsequently stood on. In one way Beefy was right, I suppose. I didn't get that at all.

Off screen Both and I do not have much in common, I guess, but one thing we do share is a love of fishing. On another occasion during my three years in the white coat, I turned up at New Road to officiate in a Benson & Hedges Cup match. Beefy, now with Worcestershire, popped into the umpires' room before play for a chat, during the course of which he invited me for a day out on a prime stretch of water on the River Wye. He also left me with a catalogue, telling me to pick out what I wanted and he would get any clobber sent on to me. As it happened, his friendly offer could not have been better timed, as I needed a new rod and reel.

Later in the day, he came on to bowl at my end, and announced himself with a loosener which plopped down the leg-side. My response, given the guidelines for one-day cricket, was to call and signal a wide.

'It's a what?' Botham inquired incredulously, hands on hips.

'It's a wide,' I replied. 'You couldn't have reached that with a clothes prop.'

'Clothes prop, eh?' he chuntered as he bristled past me. 'You had better get one of those for your fishing because you'll not be getting any tackle from me.'

Later that evening, as players and officials congregated outside that beautiful old bar they used to have at Worcester, I wandered over to offer him a drink. 'Let me get you one in. What are you after, Both?'

'I'll have a bottle of pink champagne,' he said. 'They know what I have at the bar, just tell them it's for me.'

'A *bottle* of pink champagne?'

'Wha's up wi' you, you tight git? I'll get you one after.'

Now what would I want with a bottle of pink champagne? Heavens above.

Michael Atherton — Captain Shabby

I have worked with Athers for large parts of his professional life, so talking cricket with him comes pretty naturally. Our chats used to take place in the privacy of a dressing-room, or team meeting-room, but now we have them in other people's living-rooms, and we are paid handsomely for the privilege. Knowing him as I have, it was no surprise to me whatsoever that he waltzed into the commentary box after retiring from the game and took up the microphone with such obvious ease. He is a bloke who does everything he sets out to accomplish with a minimum of fuss, whose professional standards are extremely high, and whose talents I believe will take him beyond commentating and cricket. He has strong opinions on the game and very good judgement, but also a capacity to expand his career into other areas. He is one of the cleverest blokes I have ever come across and is, as everyone would have to acknowledge, a brilliant writer, a factor which leads me to believe he will branch into other subjects, should he so wish, later in life.

Our working relationship goes back a long way and Athers was instrumental in my instalment as England coach, something which really did come out of the blue for me. In fact, it was not something that had seriously crossed my mind when on a January morning in 1996, as I picked him up from Manchester Airport following an underwhelming England tour of South Africa, he told me I had to get involved with the national senior side's coaching set-up. At the time I was juggling my work as first-team coach at Lancashire with various other coaching posts across England's age-group teams, occasional appearances on *Test Match Special* and a smattering of after-dinner speaking engagements. He was clearly batting for my promotion but, at the time, the job he was lining me up for did not even technically exist. In those days Raymond Illingworth acted as both chairman of selectors and England manager.

But Athers, much more progressive in his thinking as England captain than his public persona let on, was an advocate of modernisation. He no longer saw the benefit of that dual role and urged me to make myself available for a coaching position. Within a couple of months, following a disastrous World Cup, English cricket was the subject of an internal investigation. During the inquest into what exactly had been going wrong, Raymond relinquished the hands-on side of the job. The new position advertised by the Test and County Cricket Board, as it was then, was specifically on-field, bypassing the political side of things I did not care for, and therefore suited me down to the ground. In April that year I agreed to an initial six-month deal as England coach, forming an alliance with Atherton as England captain.

Professionally for three years we were as good for each other as we are now off-screen. I have developed a very good friendship with Athers, and – although he occasionally stops mid-sentence or mid-stride to wind me up by asking, 'What on earth am I doing with you? You are just an old fella. A fella old enough to be me dad' – we spend a lot of time in each other's company. I have known him since he was a Manchester Grammar schoolboy, playing in the same Lancashire age-group team as my eldest lad Graham, so I guess he has got a point. During his junior days I would be there, chatting to his mum and dad as a fellow parent. I was there when he was developing as a cricketer at Lancashire during his Cambridge University days. I was as close to Athers as I was to any player during my time as a coach at both domestic and international level. He had just always been there. And that familiarity, and our understanding of each other, meant our captain–coach relationship functioned smoothly.

Above and beyond our friendship I have never swayed from my belief that Athers was a bloody good England captain. This is not a subjective assessment either, formed because of our geographical roots or friendship, it is just a solid observation from within the dressing-room. Unfortunately, partly as a result of being his own man, he never got the credit his efforts in the role deserved.

When we were in tandem neither of us came across as we would have wanted at times, but behind closed doors we complemented each other perfectly. He knew my personality and I his. He opted for a 'give 'em nowt' approach to the press, and I occasionally said too much. Our natural characters led us to be perceived in certain ways. My passion and enthusiasm occasionally spilt over, and I would argue black was white to protect the team, while Athers actively played up to his Captain Grumpy image to get his own back at the tabloid press. In turn his portrayal to the cricket-loving public was hardly flattering at times, which affected their perception of him. Like it or not, in the positions of power we were in, your image is determined by your professional utterances, and while Athers's behavioural choice did not damage the side one iota, neither did it promote him as a warm, welcoming individual to the nation he led. Hopefully we both have the balance right in our current vocations.

Popular opinion would have been that he was surly and moody. Nothing could have been further from the truth when it came to his social interaction with his contemporaries. Nobody within the game had a bad word for him back then; and I believe that is still the case now, even though he has to be publicly critical of players on occasion both on air and in print. He had an exterior when he was England captain that could not have been further from the bloke trapped inside it. For a long time it was a case of what you saw was not what we got.

This split between his public and private images stemmed from the fact that he just couldn't be doing with the press, which is ironic, I guess, given that his post-playing career took him straight into its bosom. In defence of how he dealt with things at that time, you also have to remember that he was drugged up to the eyeballs. His back condition meant he was habitually on Voltarol tablets. Oh, and in case you were wondering, those things are not to be swallowed. They are, excuse the expression, taken up the arse. Now, to my mind, shoving those things up your bum would be enough to make anyone a bit grumpy. And the journalists in question at the time of his captaincy would now agree that on less medication he is really good fun to be around.

As captain, he had a terrific talent for mucking in as one of the lads one minute, and then flicking the switch to become more aloof as the situation demanded. He fully understood the split role necessary for him in this position of authority. He would want his team to be as happy, as competitive and as professional as possible. He would let players know when they had messed up – almost always in private – and expect them to address his criticism positively. He wanted everyone within the collective to display total commitment. Athers was not looking for brownie points outside the team environment, and he needed to be firm: his team were not as successful as those led by Nasser Hussain and Michael Vaughan in later years. The comparison is harsh, however, because his team was a struggling one, whereas those that followed were built after England had hit rock bottom and under entirely different off-field circumstances. He never got enough credit for his tenure from the public, but I can say that during my time he carried out his role with a combination of good humour and good grace. Inside the environs of Team England (the next regime officially branded it just that) he had the respect and indeed admiration of those playing under him.

The same unflustered approach to life which has been a trademark since his emergence as a schoolboy talent at Old Trafford (someone once joked he could 'block it for England' as a 16-year-old, which was ironic given his great ten-hour effort against the South Africans to save a Test match in Johannesburg in the winter of 1995–6) remained in his general attitude to the captaincy. It was what allowed him to put the blinkers on when he batted and stop fretting about the rest of the team. Through all of the highs and lows of his international career, his personality remained unaffected. The personal traits which had marked him out since adolescence, notably his stubbornness and scruffiness, were incorporated into Atherton the Captain. Sky do well to hide the sartorial *faux pas*, but day to day he is no different now.

Among our set he would win the Captain Shabby award hands down. In the summer of 2007 we all sent him up on Sky over his dress sense. A nice lady called Edith Versace had emailed in, we announced on air, remarking on how smart we all looked that summer. In this fashionista's opinion, we had all raised our game – even Atherton. She wondered: 'Have you ever thought of becoming male models?' Strange she should ask, came the reply, because we had dug up some old Lancashire club shop catalogues from the early 1990s – you know the type: county cricketers fancying themselves as Dolce & Gabbana catwalkers. Don't know about D&G, Athers looked much more like Man at C&A to me. Not sure what was going on either with the bouffant hair, or the budgie-smuggler shorts. In summary, his look was best described as 'doubtful'. But the expression on his face suggested he would be buying tickets on himself if it was a raffle.

Regardless of what he might think, he is beyond redemption when it comes to personal presentation. No matter what he wears. You can put him in the best Armani suit of all time: he will think he looks like the dog's doo-dahs; truth is, he looks like a dog's dinner. Nobody can pull off scruffy quite like him, and I guess that is quite an achievement in itself. He plays on that shabby theme all the time; I've lost count of the occasions he turns up with his shirt looking like a concertina, collar undone and hair wisping all over the place. When it comes to his attire, I am not sure he has recollected that he ever left Cambridge, because he could still pass for a student. Sometimes he will stand there and seem to be expecting reassurance. 'I look good today, don't I?' he will fish. 'No, you look like a bag of shit again, Athers.'

We have fallen out on numerous occasions over the years, but I don't recall either of us ever holding a grudge against the other. With us two we have always said what we think, agreed to disagree, or even blazed at one another, before moving on to another subject with great haste. We are completely comfortable with each other, so it would take something of seismic proportions to knock us out of kilter.

When our beloved Bertie, our faithful fox terrier, died in early 2009 I happened to be in contact with a couple of journalists in the press box in St Kitts, via Skype. Suddenly, Atherton's smiling mush appeared on my computer screen. 'Eh up, Bumble, how's things?' he asked. 'Not good,' I replied. 'Bertie's passed away. Died a couple of days ago.' Kidney disease, combined with other complications, were giving him no quality of life and it was heartbreaking to have to make that final decision. He was an absolute trooper, a great companion and well known to cricket followers around the country. It was a sad tale but – perhaps it was the tone of my voice, or the way I looked, which may have been in contrast to the solemn nature of the news I was relaying – something clearly tickled Athers, and once the giggling started he simply could not stop.

Poor old Bert had been taken from us at the age of 12, we had been down the vets for one final, suitable moment with him, and all that sod Atherton could do was laugh! Diana was so distraught, she had not gone to work for a couple of days, had failed to get out of her pyjamas and dressing gown even, and could not even spare a glance at Tags, our other dog, whose own sense of loss was evident as she traipsed around the house in a forlorn search for her pal. The entire household was absolutely mortified. We were all cut up about it, but Diana had undoubtedly taken it the worst. Yet throughout the relaying of all this information, the chuckling continued. He was pissing himself. I guess it highlighted the fact that really good pals, while caring deep down, often seem to revel in each other's misfortune. I certainly thought no ill of him, and he felt no malice towards me. But as I sat morosely in chilly Cheshire, he cackled in the Caribbean. Good old Bert's ashes now sit above the fireplace alongside my dad's and those of Judy, another of my previous dogs.

Perhaps Atherton was having the last laugh on this occasion, having come out second best to Bertie in his pomp. Now I can't actually remember him being done, but whenever Paul Allott used to pop round to our house, Bertie used to line him up for an assault, so it is eminently possible. The points of attack being either behind the ear or behind the ankle. Paul seemed to be the primary target, but a whole host of Lancashire players have been snapped at over the years. When we lived in our old house in Cheadle Hulme, Neil Fairbrother popped around for one reason or another, and as he approached I restrained little Bert by his collar, standing behind the garden gate. 'Oh, bless him,' said Neil, getting out of his car and offering a friendly, stroking arm as he wandered up. WHOOSH went Bertie's jaws, straight into the fleshy part of the hand.

Tags is also an absolute beauty, having learnt everything she knows from the master. Anyone can come into our house, and she's fine with it. She's as pleasant as can be in greeting you – in fact she'll make a right fuss. 'You're most welcome,' her behaviour tells you as you enter through the front door. There is no territorial angst, anyone can come in and plonk themselves on the sofa. She'll even come over and either sit on your knee or perch herself next to you, making a fuss of you, as though you're her long-lost buddy. Oh no, getting in the house is a placid, welcoming experience with Tags. But you bloody well try and get out again!

She will not hear of it. Our house, to her, is a bit like a secret society: once you're in, you're in. Poor Diana goes to work in smart ladies' suits and the majority of them have now got holes in the back, where Tags has had a go at her. Think about leaving and she's after you. If we have builders round, it will be all sweetness and light as they come in to assess the job. 'Isn't she a lovely thing?' would be a typical remark. But believe me, they've revised their opinion before they've got the tools out of the van. She'll be nipping their arse and clawing their legs all the way.

In fact, whenever we have someone around, it's a military operation to get them out the door unscathed; one that usually features a biscuit being strategically placed at the other end of the house, while the visitor escapes. She falls for it every time, bless her, but no sooner have I got the door shut behind us than the little rascal is launching herself through the air, chomping at the handle like Michael Jordan attempting a slam dunk. She learnt all she knows from Bertie, of course. To her this is perfectly normal behaviour. We used to have a plumber who came to the house looking like someone straight out of a Guns N' Roses tribute band. Although plumbing was his trade, his personal trademark was the builder's bum. Given a glimpse of a cheek or two, Bertie would be straight on board, indulging his taste for flesh.

Athers has always had a wicked side to his humour – and a tendency to chortle whenever others were in despair at their cricketing fortunes. Mark Butcher tells a good story of when, during the summer of 1999, in his only game as captain of the England Test team, he asked for the inclusion of all-rounder Craig White, to balance the XI. After the request was knocked back, he was forced to go in with two spinners against New Zealand at Old Trafford, and frustratingly lost the toss. Ill-equipped to dictate the pace of the game from that point onwards, and with nobody to provide new-ball pene-tration once the opening bowlers were blown, Butcher boiled over in the dressing-room. Athers sat alongside him and guffawed. Whenever certain colleagues blew a gasket, he would be off on a chortle. He would have some great jousts with Angus Fraser in the nets and enjoy witnessing the full teapot performance on the field. He has always appreciated dark humour. His laughter managed to get him through plenty of failure and frustration as England's longest-serving captain, and that was to his immense credit. He got it just about right for me because he was so natural.

But he also had a totally undemonstrative manner and went about things quietly. I lost count of the times when, as England captain, he would shun the fun-loving group on a night out in order to knock on the door of a player who was down-hearted and in need of a gee-up over dinner. The team knew it but, because of his refusal to express himself in public as he did in private, few others did. Nobody embodied better than Atherton the team spirit I wanted to see running through the side, although I would have to say Fraser was his equal in this department, displaying all the qualities you need in a sporting environment. Neither was it lost on his contemporaries just how good an international batsman Atherton was during his pomp. I always wondered how much better he could have been without the constant discomfort he felt in his lower back. There is no doubt in my mind that this restricted his performances; at times he was getting through Test matches others would not have contemplated starting. His dedication to the England cause was unerring until it reached the point at which, no longer able to mask the effects of the injury, it was too bad for him to commit to participating. However, to his credit, he rarely missed a game, and but for his condition would have averaged considerably more than the 37.69 he finished up with in his Test career.

He also always put the needs of the team first. Twice during the summer of 1997 Athers tried to resign the England captaincy and was talked out of it, first by Ian MacLaurin and then by me – because I reasoned that the side would suffer for him quitting. He had first notified David Graveney as chairman of selectors of his decision to walk away immediately after the Ashes were lost that summer, only to be moved by the persuasive tones of MacLaurin to see out the international season. Even after that stirring win at The Oval, which left the series score at 3–2, however, he was ready to jump ship. This time, Grav advised him over a drink at the then Hilton Hotel, opposite Lord's, that he should phone me before his decision was rubber-stamped.

Athers has always been his own man but, like me, has always taken fatherly advice. I have no doubt that what Alan Atherton told him privately was similar in tone to what he heard from me when he called. My passionate view was that the England team at that time was best served by continuity in the captaincy and not by making change for the sake of change. I got across the point that the man on the other end of the blower was our best man for the job. Some sections of the media called for his head – partly, I am certain, because a new captain would undoubtedly be more quotable than the dour one they knew.

His resignation at that time would have been a triumph for others, and Atherton is not the kind of man who should be remembered as one who quit. That was just not in his nature. We had also progressed the team, in my opinion, in the eighteen months we had worked together. We were heading for the Caribbean that winter with a genuinely good chance of a historic away Test series win over West Indies. Atherton deserved credit for that, if it came off. With all this put to him, he climbed down once more, but it was to be for the second and final time. After a 3–1 defeat which was the biggest disappointment of my time as coach, he stood aside.

He has always been among the elite in his field, and nothing has changed since he swapped willow for pen. His writing is excellent and the rest of us pull his leg all the time about being what I call *journalist serious*. He threw himself into the role of columnist with the *Sunday Telegraph* and coped just as comfortably when offered the position of cricket correspondent with *The Times*. And, of course, such prominent positions mean one should mix with the right company and, moreover, do so at the right establishments. In short, the most credible writers among the English press pack tend to head for the swankiest restaurants imaginable. You know you've made it when you are noshing with the Pompous Diners' Club. The kind of chaps who are very serious about their food, wine and table conversation.

The *Independent on Sunday*'s Stephen Fay, aka Captain Claret (so monikered for his rubicund complexion), *Telegraph* men Derek Pringle and Scyld Berry, and *Times* duo Simon Barnes and Alan Lee are all fully-fledged members. So as Nasser and I head off for a curry, we rib Athers about his social and culinary aspirations. His defence is always something along the lines of: 'I'm from Newton Heath. I'm just a bloke from Newton Heath.' However, while I am tearing into a naan bread and lamb rogan josh, he will be contemplating lamb shoulder, accompanied by turmeric potato, tomato *confit*, pineapple-coconut salsa with a rapidly reducing *jus*. The latter being the kind of thing Willy Wonka might have concocted to go alongside his everlasting gobstoppers.

A typical Atherton menu:

Starters

Pig's trotter, sweetbread and apricot salad
Beetroot and liquorice terrine, apple purée, pickled walnut
Chilli salt squid with nuac chum, lime, mint and coriander
Warm asparagus, goat's cheese crème, toasted hazelnut, brown
    butter vinaigrette

Mains

Slow-roasted antelope loin, aubergine soufflé, butternut and
  tomato

Magret duck breast, confit leg tortellini, pea parfait, nectarine
  and juniper

Seared beef fillet, soy braised mushrooms, pomme cigar, carrot-
  honey purée, bordelaise syrup

Pancetta-wrapped monkfish, pommes fondant, roasted pear,
  braised apple and red cabbage

Desserts

Whipped gorgonzola, mustard pear, pistachio sable

Boysenberries, bitter chocolate ganache, lemon thyme and
  buffalo yoghurt sherbet

Amarula panna cotta, smoked fudge foam, espresso ice cream.

Nasser Hussain — aka Unlucky Alf

Nasser and I have become very close friends since his retirement, not that our relationship has ever been anything other
than very cordial in the past. In fact, during our England days,
I had pushed for his inclusion in the Test team when I was
coach – and was rewarded when he scored a double hundred
in the Ashes victory at Edgbaston in 1997 – and also lobbied
for him as an opener in the 1999 World Cup. I was as happy

as anyone with the success he made of the England captaincy – and he did it his own way. When he eventually got the job it was at just the right time. For many different reasons, circumstances were on his side. Whereas previously the England team used to turn up on a Tuesday, hours after their last county appearance, now they were on the verge of central contracts and a greater level of professionalism. The job had moved on massively in two years, and Nasser used that to his advantage brilliantly and was very creative as a captain.

He can be really good fun now, but he was nothing like that as a player. The Nasser Hussain I knew built himself up through such a crescendo of concentration before each match, bubbling away for hours before reaching boiling point at the toss, that you were better off not talking to him. It was his way of preparing for the contest ahead: as an emerging player he always wanted to be on his own, and would immerse himself in the detail of getting his own game right. He wanted to prepare privately, which meant intense net sessions and extra throw-downs to fine-tune his batting. Everything was about his individual game during the period in which he was establishing himself as an international-class batsman, and the team ethic only came as he matured. For the first half of his England career he would be very snappy in preparation, and it was not until a match got under way that he calmed down. We are all different, and he was one of those players who wanted a lot of time to prepare for Test matches.

Captaincy undoubtedly increased his awareness of others, and others' respect for him. There were already significant signs of this development in his character, in fact, when his name was first bandied around for the national captaincy.

Nasser had fronted the England A tour to Pakistan during the winter of 1995–6, and the reports that came back from John Emburey and Phil Neale, who were in charge of that trip, spoke glowingly of his approach to the job and his ability as an on-field leader. In summary, they believed him to be a very good captaincy candidate for the future. However, his volatility and perceived self-centredness were to count against him after Athers stepped down as England captain in the spring of 1998.

Because of the glowing report from the A tour, there was some support for the Essex man. Unfortunately, it was not coming from the Essex corner. Sitting on the England Management Advisory Committee were two fellows from Chelmsford, Doug Insole and David Acfield and when the time came to discuss the subject of Atherton's successor at a specially convened meeting chaired by Bob Bennett, they were unequivocal in their conclusion. 'Under no circumstances should you consider our chap as captain of England,' they insisted. 'He would be absolutely awful. He is far too volatile a character.'

However, Nasser was showing distinct signs of maturing at that time, and those lingering doubts about his temperament did not prevent his elevation a little over twelve months later, following Ashes defeat and an early exit from the World Cup, which coincided with my resignation as England coach. What I would say is that it was on the 1998–9 Ashes tour that Nasser really came of age both as a Test match batsman and as an individual. It was there that you began to appreciate his awareness of the team ethos – to the extent that there was no longer any reason to doubt his captaincy credentials. Yet, even upon his appointment, I am not sure Duncan Fletcher wanted him as his leader. But whatever his initial thoughts, no one can argue about how good a partnership they made. Arguably, people soon began to appreciate that behaviour which may on the one hand be seen as insular or selfish can equally be viewed as a sign of determination and ambition.

Thankfully, for the purposes of this chapter, the position of responsibility did not completely rid him of the petulance and fiery temper for which he was renowned in his youth. As strops go, Nasser's were of a seriously high standard. We can all think back to our junior and club days and recall some great dressing-room ranters, I am sure, but this guy was an Olympic qualifier. And his best-ever barney is still available to the rest of us in the Sky Sports commentary box now. It came during the opening Ashes Test in Brisbane in 2002–3. Naturally, the first match in any series against Australia is always going to be a humdinger – you throw everything at them and they return it with interest – so Nasser was probably regretting asking the Aussies to bat first, particularly after Simon Jones's horrific injury in the field left him a bowler light.

In fact, it was Jones's knee damage that accounted for the presence of two crutches in the England dressing-room. They came into view as a cameraman panned around the Gabba's stands following Nasser's dismissal. His camera then fixed on the balcony of the dressing-room, a place of relative serenity, it appeared, with coach Duncan Fletcher gazing up at the television screen, presumably awaiting the replay of the dismissal. Duncan did not move a muscle as Nasser walked in and therefore appeared on screen, directly behind him – there was no 'Unlucky' or 'What's happened there, then?' Nothing. He just kept his eyes fixed on the monitor overhead.

Neither was Fletch moved as this bat flew across the room; he just kept staring up at that telly. Never once did he look at his captain. Nasser was remonstrating, arms akimbo, to his team-mates, pointing at the replays. Fletch did not flinch. He probably anticipated what was coming. Unfortunately, poor Simon Jones clearly didn't, and was not in a position to do anything about it anyway. To release his frustration, Nasser made a grab for the crutches and attacked them with gusto – standing on them, bending them, kicking them. Poor old Simon was just sitting with his leg up, helpless. Goodness knows what he must have thought as he contemplated a serious setback to his international career. We play that episode to Nasser every now and again to cheer him up. It is absolutely priceless television.

Nowadays he takes the rise out of everybody and has a real cutting sense of humour. He is the kind of guy you need to know in order to understand what is going on inside his head sometimes. He loves a piss-take, with a bit of niggle for good measure, and enjoys getting some stick too. But I am not sure how flattering he found physical comparisons to a certain famous Russian when the alert Jonathan Agnew spotted the likeness. Aggers's photo of Nasser interviewing Graham Onions, with the caption 'Vladimir Putin talks to President Ahmadinejad', is the funniest thing I have ever seen posted on Twitter. A cracking lookalike double.

Nasser didn't often see the funny side of things when he was playing the game, probably because he was so unfortunate when he batted. As a cricketer, he was just Unlucky Alf, so often the recipient of deliveries that nobody else got and nobody on the planet would have played. Miracle delivery, grubber, snorter – Nasser attracted them. Add to that the fact that he was never out – it was either that the pitch was wrong, it was a shit decision or the wind was blowing the wrong way – and you get the full picture. He was just 'one of them'.

His most unfortunate dismissal came in Trinidad during the 1998–9 tour of the Caribbean, when a delivery from Carl Hooper did for him good and proper. The ball literally rolled along the floor after pitching and hit him on the shoe plumb in front of off-stump. It was a stonewall lbw decision and made him look a bit of a twit. But how on earth are you meant to play a ball like that? I am sure that is what was going through his mind as he trudged off muttering, kicking at everything in his path, his bat bouncing off the floor. When he got to the dressing-room, he found Atherton, his sympathetic captain, killing himself with laughter. What else can you do when a team-mate gets one of the unplayables? We sometimes run the footage back now, during rain delays, if our discussions have taken in batting on tricky pitches, and someone will inevitably ask Nasser: 'How do you play that? What would you recommend? Commentators have always said you've got to get forward. You don't appear to have …'

'Forward? Forward? How do you get forward when it's rolled along the floor like a marble?' he flames. On some matters time has not been a great healer with Nasser.

Generally he has mellowed with age. At the time of that match at Port-of-Spain, however, his tendency to ire was at its career height, and with that in mind, his team-mates would prepare and protect themselves against the Mount Vesuvius moment. My youngest lad Ben was with us on that tour and was employed as a look-out by big Angus Fraser, who fancied a kip in the dressing-room but was only too aware of Nasser's appetite for destruction when dismissed.

'Listen, if that Hussain bloke gets out, you come and wake me up straight away. No messing,' Gus warned our lad. Now to this day I am not sure whether it was the comic nature of the demise that threw him off guard, a sense of adventure or genuine absent-mindedness, but Ben failed to carry out his task. Poor old Gus was fast asleep as the cricket equipment in Hussain's path was redistributed around the place. He awoke with a judder, an action which only served to increase the velocity of the rant. 'So, you don't want to watch me bat, huh?' Nasser raged. 'You would rather go to sleep when I'm batting. Not worth watching, aren't I?'

So, with one of his mates beside himself with laughter and another snoring as he entered the room, Nasser completely lost his cool and thrust his fist through the front of a wooden locker, an action which brought a premature close to his strop, as he could not pull his hand back out without incurring some serious damage. With splintered pieces pointing this way and that, doing so could have severed his hand, so here he was, his fury not sated but forced to contemplate one of international cricket's great injustices from a stationary position. Fraser was anything but stationary, as he hot-footed after Lloyd junior, whose ability as a nightwatchman was in keeping with others' efforts on the tour. 'Why didn't you come and wake me up, you little swine?' Gus bellowed, as he chased our Ben round the back of the stand.

I am not sure Nasser wanted to dwell on his dismissal after freeing his mitt from the hurt locker, or whether there was much mileage in doing so. Had he wanted to analyse the freakery of his downfall, it would have involved a process which seems incredibly antiquated now. Those were the days when cricket was in its initial stage of embracing technology, and players could watch themselves back on video – but this meant that we, as a touring party, were forced to lug around huge cases of VHS cassettes and three enormous television monitors. We would have tapes upon tapes of Brian Lara, Steve Waugh and Waqar Younis in action, a library of footage designed to help us assess their strengths and weaknesses, in addition to hours of footage of our own players both from net sessions and in match scenarios. Trailing this archive material around, however, was seriously hard work. Just consider the fact that with no flat TV screens this meant huge tubes and boxes. We had three steel box containers to transport around, and even then because of the limit on screens it meant players had to share. If Alec Stewart was watching his front-foot driving, he might be given the hurry-up because Jack Russell wanted to have a gander at someone's bowling, or how he kept to Phil Tufnell in the last Test. It seems unfathomable that technology has moved on so much that a decade later, if you want to prepare yourself for the pace of South Africa's Dale Steyn, you could be watching the last six deliveries he bowled in international cricket within seconds of the thought popping into your head. Press half-a-dozen buttons and you can be privately studying his last few wickets on your mobile phone.

Most of Nasser's preparations these days are to do with going somewhere for free, or at an hour which will allow him to be in bed before dark. He might have earned a reputation as a rabble-rouser as a cricketer, but he is fairly chilled in his everyday life. We wind him up something rotten about being tight, and he lives up to the reputation, but I hate to admit he can be quite generous at times. That's not to say that if he sees something for nothing, the eyes do not light up. He always enjoys things more when he's on the cadge. One of the first questions he asks when we get up to anything on days off is 'How much will it cost?' And it never ceases to amaze me how the best golf courses Nasser has ever played always seem to be the ones that offered a complimentary round or were paid for by the sponsors or hosts. If you are out for dinner with him, he will often disappear as soon as the main course is done, which means he lopes off without paying. It makes it look as if he's a blagger but, in the interests of truth and to collapse a myth, I can confirm that the settling up is done the next day. It is not the fight with the moths he is concerned about in opening his wallet at the table, he just has a habit of hitting the hay by nine o'clock.

There are rumours that he sleeps in his cap, because off screen you rarely see him without it. Indoors or out, he perpetually has that sports casual thing going on. He was wearing it one day as we drove on the freeway in South Africa, on the way back from a round of golf, when we got pulled over at a compulsory road block. Men who wear caps for the hell of it always arouse suspicion, and so when he produced his driving documents in the Afrikaaner heartland, I warned him: 'I think we're going to be here for some f——ing time, what with your name an' all.' Neither of us was quite sure what was going on, but this burly policewoman was chuntering away completely in Afrikaans. She was not in the upper percentiles of the country's intelligentsia, shall we say, and with communication at breakdown, and the process seemingly interminable, I started ordering my breakfast. 'I'll have double egg, bacon, sausage and tomato,' I began. She had waved us on before mention of the fried bread, so the distraction tactics clearly worked.

We didn't want her sifting through her records for too long, because Nasser could easily have been a feature on there. He had already crashed two vehicles on the trip – those Hertz hire jobbies which are the size of a mobile home – to earn the tour nickname Mr Magoo. One day, in Port Elizabeth, we set off from the hotel, with a little lad running alongside us, dodging through the traffic. Nothing too unusual in that: you often get cricket-mad lads who will do anything in their desperation for the signature of a former England captain. But it was not a pen he was holding up, it was part of our charabanc that had fallen off. Nasser had scraped the side of the car, and this lad was saying, 'Your trim, sir.'

As it happened, his signature was not required at the time, adding insult to injury, but it was needed later in the piece as he had to fill in a form for the car hire company to register what had happened. So imagine his surprise when we got to Durban and he discovered an even bigger motor to handle. Unperturbed by the challenge, Nasser was intent on taming the beast, only to run it straight into the garage wall of the hotel.

There are some lovely drives on a tour of South Africa, and Nasser, bless him, had volunteered to be chauffeur. It was a call of duty, in fact, that led him to turn down the privilege of playing golf at the picturesque Fancourt, a course on the Garden Route, designed by Gary Player. He took a call from Paul Collingwood, inquiring whether he would like to make up an eight, as they were one short, but to his eternal credit he did the decent thing and turned them down. That was touching, as before the £300 fee for the privilege of a private flight and eighteen holes was mentioned, he had seemed keen.

'I'm sorry, I really can't let my mates down. I'm needed to ferry them around as designated driver.' Once a team man, always a team man, I guess.

David Gower — the Lord of Cool?

Nasser has always had a reputation for having a feisty side, but it may come as a surprise to some that Lord Gower also has something of a volatile temper. He is an extremely good presenter, a very clever bloke who does everything in a typically laconic manner, and never appears to be flustered. Truth is, he never is when it comes to being on air, but off screen, boy can he blow a fuse. Beneath that chilled exterior – his style as a presenter is so reminiscent of the way he batted – there is some fire. From nothing he will erupt, then as quick as a flash the lava is cooling, and he has calmed back down again.

He has always been that way, but you remember him as a player for being a wonderfully relaxed batsman. I played against him a fair bit, and cricket for him was all about having fun. He played for sheer enjoyment, and if anything went wrong he would simply say 'sorry'. He would not be bothered, there would be an apology by way of recognition if he nicked off in a pressure situation, but he would not be overly concerned. Within seconds he would be more interested in the whereabouts of the book he'd been reading before he went out into the middle.

I recall one County Championship match in which I was officiating at Grace Road when he played absolutely magnificently, as only he could. It was a pleasure to stand and watch as he caressed, eased and touched the ball here, there and everywhere. Overnight he was 70-odd not out, and his innings was the kind that made you look forward to play resuming. Next morning, in the very first over, he had an unbelievable hack at this nondescript delivery, the ball went straight up in the air and, as he trudged off from whence he came moments earlier, all he could say was: 'Oh dear, the lights seem to have gone out.'

Things naturally came very easily to him, he was a touch player and has always been good at whatever he has put his mind to. Holding things together in that presenting role is a real knack and not something I could ever do. Some can, some can't, and I am in the latter category. What David has got – and Ian Ward also has this, by the way – is an ability to flit from being instructed to instructing with natural ease. When you sit watching them on screen, you may not realise that while they are talking, bringing people like myself into a wider debate with their questions, they also have directors and producers rabbiting in their ears.

The biggest compliment I can pay him is that he always makes me feel calm, and that is exactly what you want in my position. With him I always know where I'm going, what he wants us to talk about, why he wants to talk about it and that we will get there in a smooth ride. With the way international cricket is screened around the globe these days, you can often be working for other networks or sharing resources, and my experience of other presenters can be quite the opposite. At times you are sitting in a studio thinking, 'Crikey, where are we going now?' But Lord Gower makes me feel at ease, which is an essential part of his job.

He has made that presenting role his niche, so I don't have much interaction with him in the commentary box. Neither do I see a great deal of him outside work. While I play golf, he could think of nothing more boring. He is much more likely to set off for historical sites such as battlefields, no doubt in search of his ancestors, rather than do something as mundane as hit a golf ball around for four and a half hours. He would class that as absolute purgatory. And just as he would not engage me in conversation about a 1996 Château Margaux, I wouldn't try to persuade him to join me for a pint of Chiswick in the Lord's Tavern, among the Barmy Army. That's just not him.

Shane Warne — Entertaining in the Extreme

There are two things that connect me and the great Shane Warne: Accrington Cricket Club and Sky Sports. Few people will know that Warne played as a professional at my club during the 1990s, shortly before he made his international début for Australia. Our paths did not cross back then, as I had packed up playing at the weekend and was progressing my coaching career. But all the reports I heard around the town were that Warne was the life and soul of every party going. He used to fall off his stool at the end of a night. It was the sign that everyone had had a good one. If he didn't, people would worry something was up. He has always been Jack the lad, of course, and part of his vast appeal is that he is a guy who knows how to have fun. If there isn't any around, he goes elsewhere to find it.

There are simply not enough hours in the day for Warney; he is a real larger-than-life character. In one respect he is very similar to Beefy, always planning what he wants to do next. 'What we doing tonight? Tomorrow? Next week?' He has a busy social diary all right, but whereas others are connoisseurs of wine or beer, he is an aficionado of fast food. Yep, one in a million is Warne when it comes to this. Everything has to be just so: chips not only have to be hot but served at exactly the right temperature. He looks at chips as others would look at a glass of Cloudy Bay Sauvignon after swilling it around their palate. With pizza, he is looking for a specific consistency and depth of base. He looks at it with an expert eye and talks you through its success or failure. Oh, and he doesn't eat anything other than chips and pizza, as far as I can tell. He also smokes fags like world supplies of tobacco are about to run out, and as we usually operate at strictly non-smoking media centres these days, he will forever be dropping notes into security guards' top pockets, so he can go and have a puff out the back.

Shane is a real character and slipped seamlessly into our commentary team during the 2009 Ashes, just as I knew he would. He made a great start to his broadcasting career with Sky – he just looks the part for a start. As he ought to, given the outrageous amount of work he has had done. He's got new teeth, new hair, and goodness knows what else. With all the showbiz glamour of a man nicknamed Hollywood, however, come impeccable manners and a fantastic attitude towards the sport.

Australia will always be up there, they will always be competitive, but you just don't replace Warne, and my favourite moment of the Noughties was when he left the field at the SCG, the scene of his international début, for the final time. I sneaked out on to the field, camera in hand, and got a wonderful picture of Warne and Glenn McGrath walking off. He was just holding the ball to the adoring crowd. It is a picture I treasure and one I keep on my computer.

That picture to me symbolises what a profound effect he had on the game. You will never see the like of him again in terms of his character and ability. He was a complete and utter one-off. It is hard to pinpoint exactly what made him so good. People might say it came so easily that he did not understand, or appreciate, what he had got. But I think he did. He was such a confident lad. The only thing which suggests he ever worried – and it's so well documented that I am definitely not telling tales out of school – was the fact that he was such a chain-smoker. Yet, if he ever lived on his nerves, there was no sense of it in his career performances.

To him the art of leg-spin came so ridiculously naturally that he makes a mockery of his competition. When, during his initial summer with Sky in 2009, he did a spin-bowling demonstration at a break in the Oval Test, he did so after borrowing a pair of shorts and shoes off Michael Clarke. He must have had five fags before he went out into the middle, chain-smoking one after another. 'I 'ope it goes OK. I don't want to mess up,' he said. He hadn't bowled anywhere since last Pancake Tuesday at the IPL, and he was accompanied for the feature by two of our young English leg-spinners, Will Beer, of Sussex, and Somerset's Max Waller, their limbs loose towards the end of their seasons.

When Warne chats away as he does, the camera is his own; he has as much presence as a commentator as he did as an international performer. He knows when to look and when to look away, when to make his point and when to keep quiet. And just as in the middle, he knows how to milk the big moments, with that inherent sense of timing. This particular afternoon Nasser, who was hosting the live feature, threw him the ball in real Nasser style, as if throwing down the gauntlet to an old nemesis for the final time. 'C'mon then, show us one,' he said, abruptly, not long after he had warned the TV audience that this Aussie, fast approaching 40, had not bowled for months on end.

Well, blow me if Warne didn't rip this flippin' leg-spinner three foot. With no warm-up, no practice deliveries, his very first ball produced that trademark fizzing sound through the air.

'Ah, pretty good that,' Warne said. 'I don't think I'll bother with another.'

The jaws on these two young kids just dropped. They are two nice young leg-spinners, who can both give the ball a pleasant little spin, but Warney absolutely tore his one ball. That was enough to confirm to anyone what we already knew – he's a flaming genius.

His presence is enough to inspire a team, and I remember the way Australia reacted to his return in the 1998–9 Ashes. We had just won at Melbourne, bowling the Aussies out in what you might call English conditions, to reduce the score to 2–1, with one Test to play. But who was back for that final Test in Sydney? And they made damned sure there would be nothing in the pitch for the seamers, as they prepared what could best be described as a dustbowl for Warne, Stuart

MacGill and Colin Miller, who opened the bowling with off-cutters and then switched to spin later in the innings, to operate on. In those conditions the returning superstar might have run amok, but his presence only served to inspire MacGill, who had been phenomenal in that series, even further. He took a dozen wickets to Warne's two as we lost by 98 runs. Imagine how good a career MacGill would have had without the greatest-ever exponent of the art of leg-spin pissing on his chips.

As a character, as a mate and as a performer, Warne is absolutely top of the tree. When he waltzed into our box at Sky for the second Ashes Test of 2009 it was obvious that he had done things in television before. And it also helped that he is a complete natural. Regularly people will ask me, 'What's the best advice you've ever had?' They are normally talking about cricket and are expecting a reply like 'Keep your elbow high and play with the full face.' But I sidestep the technical stuff and tell them that the best thing to do is what comes naturally. To me, that is what Warne does. He is just so comfortable on screen, and what you see is what you get.

Certainly, Warney being himself helped me click with him on air, and it wasn't long before I got him going. We were chatting away about what we had been up to between Test matches, and Shane was recalling a memorable few days up at Archerfield in Scotland, playing golf with Beefy. 'Oh mate,' he said, and proceeded to ramble about doing this, doing that, having clearly had a spanking good time. Knowing he was a lad of great manners, however, I just knew he would come back with 'What you been up to?' Right on cue, he did so.

'Actually, I've been to LA,' I replied.

'Oh, that's great, mate, yeah, I like LA. Love it, in fact.'

'Do you? Have you been to Lower Accrington? Oh, of course you have.'

'Pardon?'

The following week, I told him, attempting to put a serious spin on things, that I was off to the USA. 'Whereabouts?' he asked.

'The Uther Side of Accrington.'

We were having a ball, bouncing off each other, and getting paid for it. But he was certainly becoming wary of my humour, so I waited for the next Test match before I snared him again.

'Been anywhere nice, Shane?' I said.

'You're not getting me with that one again, Bumble,' came back the reply.

'C'mon, where've you been?'

He relented and started telling me how he'd done this and done that.

'Great,' I said, adding a hurried, muffled 'Well I've been to T-o-u-r-k-e-e.'

'What?' he said, giving a quick glance at my lack of tan. 'You've been to Turkey?'

'No. Torquay,' I replied. 'You're not listening. And I also had a couple of days in Sw-dn.'

'Wha'd ya say? Sweden?'

'No, Swindon.'

He just put his microphone down and said: 'Get me a pint of what he's had.' During our stints we got on like a house on fire, and I was in stitches with his suggestion that we could take cricket to a new level with what one might call after-the-watershed highlights.

'I've got this management company back in Australia,' he explained. 'And I've put it to them that we could begin specialising in extreme commentary.'

'What do you mean?' I asked.

'Oh, it would be great,' he said. 'Just for the Internet, you could tell it exactly how it is, rather than have to toe the party line, like you do on TV. When the ball raps the batsman on the pad, for example, and the fielding side all go up for lbw, and the umpire gives him out, when he's clearly nicked it, you have just got to come straight to the point and say exactly what you think: "You blind c——, he's f——ing hit that!" Or, if there's a massive waft outside the off stump, a big deviation, the ball changes course and there's a huge appeal – HOWIZZEE! – when the call is answered in the negative, you could wade in with: "You're f——ing kidding, aren't you, mate? He's knocked the f——in' cover off it."' Great idea, I told him, just not sure we could do it. I have heard a few people have access to this Internet thingy these days.

Warney is just your typical Aussie bloke, no airs and graces, or side to him, just willing to call it as he sees it. Pure, unadulterated fun. We did get a taster of what he was getting at within our own family-friendly guidelines. We had only been sitting down for a couple of overs at Edgbaston when the ball was whacked through the covers for four.

'Terrific shot,' I said.

'Oh, he's twatted that,' Shane joined in.

Everything went totally quiet in the commentary box. Our producer Paul King took the opportunity to have a quiet word. 'Look, Warney,' he began, and explained the problem. 'No, we can't have that. It is not a word we can use on air.' Shane was typically apologetic. Putting his mic down, he said:

'Sorry, mate. In Australia that just means he has hit it hard.'

We made him aware of the different connotations over here, and he was kept abreast of what can and can't be said. 'Do you want me to put it right with the viewer?' he asked, full of innocent enthusiasm. 'Tell 'em what it really is? I didn't know it meant the c——.'

'No, just let it go, Shane,' came back the collective response. He is just Mr Bloke and his enthusiasm got the better of him. You can't speak highly enough of him. He is a very affectionate chap, a very infectious character. Yes, he has had off-field issues, but there is no edge to him at all. He just enjoys life to the max. He understands he has cocked up a few times, the way everybody does, but you can't speak too highly of him. As a cricketer he had few peers in history, and his treatment by the crowds around the country in the 2005 Ashes showed how he was revered. Only the very best receive such levels of abuse, and the standing ovation he received at the end of the series, and the chants of 'We wish you were English', said it all. Everyone loves a fallible hero.

The Others

Rather like a cricket team, our group features many different qualities, skills and interests but we all combine well as a unit. Charles Colvile brings us something totally different as a presenter because as a trained journalist he has that instinct for a story. When Charlie sniffs something he gets straight into it, and I think that is a terrific quality. We are all well connected, given our backgrounds in the sport, but Charlie is someone I respect greatly because of his news sense. I enjoy being around journalists – whenever I get a break during the day's play I will pop into the press box for half an hour to have a chinwag – and there are some brilliant ones in our sport.

Paul Allott, aka Walt, is our all-rounder, our utility player, because he can slip seamlessly into any of the given roles. He is equally at home as a presenter, reporting at the toss, commentating, and hosting the after-match presentation – whatever he turns his hand to he does with assurance. He is also a tremendous eater, not quite in the Jack Simmons category, but when hungry, boy, can he put away some grub. Walt is a big unit, which means he can hack it in Botham's company without spending the rest of the night in casualty, and a talented sportsman. Undoubtedly he is the best golfer among us – has been playing off very low single figures for years – and dedicates himself to fitness sprees throughout the year. In one stretch he sank four rowing machines.

Michael Holding is the nicest guy you could ever wish to meet; such a polite and gentle man. As a broadcaster he has a wonderful voice, and as a bloke I am not sure he has an enemy in the world. So it's hard to believe what a nasty bugger he could be with a cricket ball in his hand. He used to run in all day, and send it down in excess of 90 miles an hour. But his big passion is for horse racing, as long as there are no jumps involved. A flat fanatic is Mikey. He is also possibly Jamaica's greatest debater. Once he gets going off air, at the back of the commentary box, he will not let go. He reminds me so much of the Felix Dexter character in *Bellamy's People*. His capacity for debate is unbelievable, and once he is on one he does not budge from his stance. He is very trenchant in his views.

Going back to his playing days, you didn't need to tell anyone how fast he was because his reputation went before him. Everyone who faced him verified that he was like lightning, and he caused his own team-mates some problems when he played with us for seven matches at Lancashire. He took 40-odd wickets but could comfortably have had more. We had two good slip catchers in Andrew Kennedy and Jack Simmons. Well, they were good slip catchers until Michael's arrival, at least. Everything kept hitting them in the chest! At one stage Simmo sent for the 12th man, John Abrahams, moments after shelling one. Mikey was not flustered, because he knew the ball was going like an express train. But Jack, in his high-pitched Great Harwood voice, implored John: 'Fetch me my reading glasses.' He then stood there with them balancing on his hooter in a bid to clock this thing flying off the edge at great speeds.

During my umpiring days, Mikey was playing in a match for Derbyshire against Northamptonshire at Derby. Robin Boyd-Moss was batting against the new ball and got himself into a royal tangle against a throat ball on a quickish pitch. He got his hands up to defend himself and the ball struck his glove with such velocity that his thumb surround was knocked clean off and flew towards the slip cordon; Boyd-Moss's thumb, meanwhile, had gone in about five different directions. That tells you how ferociously quick he was.

Bob Willis has had his detractors but he is passionate about the game, and about English cricket, and is someone who doesn't go round the houses to get to the town. I must admit I've missed Bob since he slipped off the regular international commentary team, because he has good, strong opinions and is magnificent to work alongside. He is very intelligent and reads the game so well, you can bounce your ideas off him. Not that you can often beat him to the punch, because he calls it exactly as he sees it. To me there is nowt whatsoever wrong with that style. His following as a studio pundit for exactly that reason is phenomenal. Emails and texts are pinging around Sky's inboxes to a chorus of 'Go on Bob, get stuck into them.' The public like to see people display their passion, and he is not shy on that front. All the lads who are playing for England now make a habit of saying 'that bloody Willis', but what I would say to them is they've got to meet him, go and have a beer with him and chat. Because you can't fail to like Bob Willis – he's a great bloke, who is just doing his job.

His image may not suggest it, but he is a gentle, unassuming chap off air. He can be the happiest soul going but, whatever you do, do not get him singing. Because once he starts, you cannot shut him up. He does a very passable Bob Dylan impersonation and can trawl through his entire back catalogue, word perfect. Our Bob is a great humorist, a great wit and great fun. Whenever we have a day off, he will saunter up and ask: 'Right, what we doing then? Shall we go off for a spot of lunch? Yes, let's have a spot of lunch.' Invariably that means lunch, dinner and supper merging into one without you noticing. He can be great company.

Another bloke who always fancied himself as a bit of a pop performer, Mark Butcher, has shown himself to be very proficient with a microphone since retiring from the game. He stepped in for me when I was struck down by dengue fever on the first day of the Test series in Bangladesh. Butch was out working for BBC radio but, as a Sky regular back home, showed himself to be a great team man by stepping in when the need arose. Popular opinion was that he did a terrific job,

START THE CAR

but Nimbus clearly weren't impressed as they refused to pay him. He only discovered they were not shelling out after England's win in Chittagong had been completed. Athers texted me to suggest I should give him a 'little consideration' for standing in. Naturally, I agreed but thought that a heart-felt round of applause should suffice as my illness would have provided him with a priceless experience. You can't put a figure on that.

Geoffrey Boycott — Him from the Other Side

Contrary to popular belief, me and Geoffrey get along together OK. Yes, we have had some run-ins over the years, but we get on just fine. You don't spend decades in the game without having some seriously heated differences, stand-up rows, call 'em what you want. We have had many a spat – being two of a kind, I guess – then shaken hands and agreed to let it pass. He is, and always has been, a forthright so-and-so, and that is why he polarises opinion. People either love him or hate him: there is no middle ground. He is his own man, as everyone can tell, and quite individual in what he does, stirring up debate and clinging to one or two hobby-horses. One thing that I have never told him is that my missus, who is cricket daft, is one of those on the love side. She thinks he is absolutely brilliant on radio, listens avidly when he is on air, and I've lost count of the number of times when she has recounted a period of commentary when he is 'on one' alongside Aggers. I haven't plucked up the courage to ask: 'Do you think he's better than me?' I don't think I could bear the answer. He's told me enough times himself over the years.

Diana's fondness for Boycs is not the first affection she has felt for an England opener, of course. Discounting my own international career, my wife also recently revealed an unrequited romantic involvement with another of our surname more than thirty years earlier. To my astonishment, nay amusement, it was Andy Lloyd, known affectionately to me and many others around the English cricket circuit as Towser. Now Towser, it transpires, penned sonnets during the late 1970s expressing his affection for my good lady. However, despite them being retained as evidence by the said Mrs Lloyd, Towser denied being their composer when I quizzed him thoroughly on the subject, but freely admitted to calling her with advice to back Sea Pigeon in the 1979 Ebor.

Geoffrey and I don't spend a great deal of time together, because he is usually on air when I am, but I have often been on the wrong side of his tongue. Now Fiery has always enjoyed a gag at others' expense, and to his credit he is good at coming up with a punchline to emphasise his magnificence in comparison to your own measly existence. During our playing days, I remember chatting to him at the end of a game and asking whether he had been getting any runs. It was a question that got the customary raised eyebrow and curl of the lip. 'I always score runs,' he rapped. 'But I did have a bit of a rough time down at The Oval last week. That Geoff Arnold, with his fast-medium outswingers, bowls off stump, gets you playing at things you shouldn't be playing at. I thought I had it all worked out – played it when I should play it, left it when it was right to leave – when he produced a jaffa.

He went wider on the crease, angled the ball into me, it pitched on off stump and straightened, squared me up a bit and just as I went to leave it I got a thin edge and was caught behind.' There was a pregnant pause, and then it came. 'Of course, an ordinary player like you wouldn't have touched it.'

Another time, I got a phone call out of the blue from him. 'I've booked you and me to play in a pair at a golf day in Blackpool,' he began, barely pausing to introduce himself. 'We'll do well, I know it, but make sure you get some practice in first, I don't want you turning up cold.' He might have hung up had I not interjected: 'When is it?' As it happened, I was not available on the date in question. 'I can't do that, Boycs, I am going fishing that week,' I told him, after checking my diary. 'What do you mean, going fishing?' he asked. 'Well, I'm booked to go away on a fishing trip,' I explained. Very abruptly he finished the conversation. 'That were always your problem – fishing outside the off stump. That's why you never got any.' With that he put the phone down.

You could quite easily get a call from Geoffrey having not spoken to him for twelve months, so there was nothing much unusual in that. There was never any 'How are you? How's the wife? How are the kids? Have you been on holiday?' You just got your orders, straight to the point. 'Y' know who this is, and y'll be speakin' at ma benefit dinner in Crewe,' Geoffrey instructed me on one occasion. 'I've put ye down.' 'Oh, hello, Geoffrey,' I said. 'I don't think Crewe is in Yorkshire. Certainly wasn't the last time I checked.' 'Well, it is for this f——in' night, so get yourself down there.' So what do you do? You go. After all, you have received the royal command.

There were 427 people attending this do: it was dead simple to work out because there were 42 tables of 10, plus a top table of seven. I viewed the room and thought to myself what an earner he must be on. It would have been one cracking night for his benefit year. He had a good margin on the ticket, there was a raffle, an auction and sponsors all over the show. I was daydreaming about how much lucre might be in it for him when the club chairman stood up and said: 'I'm pleased to introduce our first speaker of the night, a Lancashire and England cricketer, David Lloyd.'

I got up, did my bit, and things went well – laughter filling the air usually being a decent sign on these occasions – so I thought I had done OK as I sat down. At which point, the chairman was back on his feet saying, 'And now the moment is here, the man you have all been waiting for.' Up gets Fiery, who somehow failed to mention the sponsors at the front, or any of the fundraising features of the evening. He didn't even say to the other 426 folk in the room, 'Thanks for coming.' The only thing he said before his arse hit the seat again was: 'The previous speaker was introduced as a Lancashire and England cricketer. Everybody in this room knows he wouldn't have played for England if I hadn't been injured.' Thank you and good night.

It is true that I made my international début in 1974 as Boycott's replacement after he withdrew, partly due to lack of form, and partly due to his relationship breakdown with then England captain Mike Denness. I had been on the periphery of selection for a couple of years, and Boycs had not helped my cause when, during the 1973 trial match at Hove (a traditional contest involving all candidates for the forth-coming Test campaign), he ran me out in the second innings before I had faced a ball. I had gone out second time around desperate to compensate for a woeful first effort that had resulted in my dismissal, lbw for nought. So, whether he was injured, out of form or out of favour, Fiery's absence undoubtedly offered me my chance, but he had arguably been involved in its delay as well.

You have to get used to his very distinctive ways, that's for sure, and I got myself acquainted with them during our time working alongside each other for British Satellite Broadcasting. I was his lackey at that time, or it certainly felt that way, driving him around the country. Whenever a game was on his side of the Pennines, he would tell me, 'You can pick me up and drop me back, see you at x o'clock.' Now I have never been the best navigator of a route, so would often veer off track while he dozed in the passenger seat. Stop for petrol and he would awake with a judder, berating you for not filling up before you set off. 'Preparation, attention to detail, it's just like batting, you have to plan ahead,' he would blather on. 'Come to think of it, you never did any of that. That's why you never scored any runs.'

In the early days of Sky commentary, Geoffrey was on with Charlie Colvile, whose enthusiasm during his stints in the box often spilt over. Whenever a wicket fell or a ball disappeared into the stands, Charlie would crank up the volume. He went absolutely potty with excitement every single time, something which his Yorkshire co-commentator was all too aware of from having tuned in at home. This was one of their first times together, and the pair were still getting to know each other – Charlie sounding out Boycott with various questions – when a wicket fell. 'GOT HIM – GREAT DELIVERY – WELL BOWLED – GEOFFREY!' That was the cue for

Boycs to summarise what had been witnessed with some expert analysis. But that was not forthcoming. Instead, Fiery, live on air, rasped: 'Don't do that, I have heard it all before and so has my cat George. Every time you shout like that he runs up the chimney and it takes days to lure him down again!'

Chapter 3

RANTING, RAVING AND REVIEWING

The press box is probably my favourite place to visit at a cricket ground. I have valued a good newspaper since I was a nipper – in the outside lavatory in Water Street where I grew up, the *Daily Sketch* or *Daily Record* cut into squares was a useful substitute for toilet paper, which was seen as a luxury we could not afford – and I believe they should play an increasing rather than a decreasing role in our everyday lives. I am fully aware of the modern-day influence of the Internet and other electronic media news outlets, but there should always be a newspaper industry.

We are extremely fortunate in cricket that we are served by so many top journalists. When I look at the travelling band that follow the England team around, I am genuinely gobsmacked at just how good some of them are. They are a pretty diverse group as well, united by one thing: a real passion for what they do and a real passion for the sport. You have to be good in your field to rise to international level, and that is what they have done, established or new, in their journalistic careers. I love mingling among these pretty opinionated so-and-so's. They've all got something to say and love a good debate on the topic of the day.

It is a real hive of industry, and one thing I would love to counsel contemporary players on is the role these writers play in our game. Contrary to opinion that has become cliché in dressing-rooms over the years, these newspaper reporters are not their enemy. Through the ages there has always been this convenient defence that the press have a certain agenda, and I certainly thought it at times throughout my career. When I was England coach I naturally wanted to fight my corner, and if someone wanted a joust I was up for it. I had some real ding-dongs with certain individuals, but there is not an ounce of ill feeling towards them now. In fact, I would like to think I have made some pretty good mates among the press, ones with whom I share many an evening supping ale, engaged in bar talk.

Such is the make-up of our national press that we become a real travelling circus for major tours. For the Ashes trips, for example, the broadsheets will have their correspondent and in some cases the number two, in addition to the dukes of their trade, the chief sports writers – you know there is an event in town when Patrick Collins, Martin Samuel, Oliver Holt and Paul Hayward turn up. These guys are terrific writers, but those at the coal face of cricket, reporting on it every day, are a wonderfully dedicated bunch of characters. Stephen Brenkley, of the *Independent*, is known as the Ombudsman because he believes no group decision can be passed without him; John Etheridge, of the *Sun*, barely missed a day of England cricket in twenty years, and the same can be said of Colin Bateman, a real dyed-in-the-wool reporter, with the *Daily Express*. That pair are no fuss but extremely good journalists. David Hopps, of the *Guardian*, is plenty of fuss but a real hoot, nonetheless. Then there are the former-cricketers-turned-journalists who get accepted after a qualification period of scorn. They don't get an easy ride to start with; nor should they. People like Steve James, Derek Pringle, Michael Atherton and Angus Fraser have followed another former England international, the *Guardian* correspondent Mike Selvey.

There is a fantastic cross-section of folk peering at matches from over their laptop screens. Between them they can write in any style you like. They are passionate about English cricket and during the course of their jobs they sometimes have to give it a bit of rattle, which more often than not actually amounts to little more than telling it exactly as it is. When I was coach I would not necessarily see it that way, but now I am on the other side it is blindingly obvious. As a player and a coach I always wanted to believe journalists had the game at heart, but sometimes I didn't understand why they always had to be so critical. I confess that I may have been too sensitive because, in actual fact, they aren't very often. They are only critical by and large when you deserve it. If you are not playing well you are going to get a lot of it. That goes with the territory.

In my short column for the *Daily Mail*, I try to be as honest as possible on the pressing issues and always try to have a bit of fun as well. Paul Newman, the *Mail*'s cricket correspondent, rounds up the week and I have my say on what made me smile and what made me frown over the previous seven days. Paul is another with a great enthusiasm for cricket – a lifelong friendship with Nasser Hussain failing to drum it out of him, surprisingly – and latterly for greyhound racing.

One night in South Africa, I met up with Paul and *Wisden* editor Scyld Berry for a curry. I was early, and so, as it happened, was Paul, phone in hand and looking agitated. He was waiting for his mother to ring with news of his dog Droopys Kelda's race at Romford. 'It's bang on,' he said, excitedly. 'Couldn't be better prepared. She'll absolutely fly in tonight.' Right on cue the phone rang. 'How's it gone, Mum?' Last.

It reminded me of another of my pals back home, Irish Tony, who had a dog which was running at a flapping track at Bolton. For those not *au fait* with flapping tracks, they are not registered venues and therefore the owners of the mutts bet against each other. Well, Tony, just like Paul, was feeling very good about his chances one evening and so had a bob or two more than usual on it and went and stood on the first bend to offer encouragement. The hare started running, the traps went up and the dogs burst forth. 'Come on, come on!' yells Irish Tony. Well, the silly four-legged beggar only ran straight to his master and licked him from shin to chin.

There are some pretty astute thinkers among our band, although if you had seen Berry running the wrong way up an escalator in Sandton shopping mall in a panic, attempting to get to the curry house on this particular night, you might contest that. They have seen some cricket over the years, understand the environment in which international teams operate, and are known to the England set-up in a professional capacity. They are pretty well qualified to make judgements on issues arising within our sport – they might not always be correct, but they have earned the right to observe and criticise.

All this brings me on to Piers Morgan. For those of you not familiar, isn't he the chap off *Come Dancing*? Now I am not sure what qualifications he has to assess the goings-on of the England cricket team, so I was astounded when he waded in over the treatment of his 'good friend' Kevin Pietersen in losing the captaincy. In Piers's *Mail on Sunday* column, poor old Peter Moores – still uncertain what he did wrong in the whole fiasco, by the way – got both barrels, as did Andrew Strauss. He reasoned that the 'buffoons at Lord's' wanted a steady hand in charge and not a rough, tough customer in the mould of Ricky Ponting or Graeme Smith.

Now, leaving KP out of this, I can give you a pretty decent character assessment of Andrew Strauss. Piers revealed that he had once had a round of golf with Strauss and found him 'funny and charming' and could imagine him 'in a plummy voice' remarking: 'I say, old chap, hope we have a fine game of cricket today.' Well, I was on hand, Piers, pal, to witness Strauss's twin hundreds in Chennai, innings which came in dramatic, morbid and emotional circumstances, so soon after the Mumbai attacks. Situations don't come much tougher than that, I can assure you. Captaining in an Ashes series brings its own pressure, but you would never have guessed it from the way Strauss batted in 2009. He has got real nerve but just happens to be eloquent too. That was not a crime last time I checked.

I have only been around professional cricket for forty-odd years, so what would I know? A little bit, I would hope. Now I am not saying you cannot have an opinion from outside, but when a TV personality with absolutely no knowledge of the work of the individual or coach in the team environment wades in with hearsay as evidence it gets my goat. Peter Moores was lambasted by a bloke famous in his own lunchtime. He did not know Moores from Adam, nor had he first-hand knowledge of his work as a coach. All this was disgraceful in my estimation. In his piece, he asked: 'Would you not rather have a Pietersen saying: "I am going to smash you lot up, Ricky lad, just like in 2005"?' For what it's worth, no. My feeling is that Pietersen is far better placed to do just that as the gunslinger, not the sheriff.

I love KP, let me make that clear. You will not find anyone who practises harder or is more dedicated to playing for England. And if there was an award for politeness in international cricket, he would monopolise it. However, he was never captaincy material for me. The star player in a team never is, and you cannot argue against Pietersen being England's star player. I have a military friend, Richard Hakes, who insists that the great, the maverick, the ego is never the leader because when the shit hits the fan they cannot empathise with others of lesser ability. It is always everyone else's fault. Being the star brings its own expectations, and there is no need to be dragged down by peripheral agendas, or the political side of the day-to-day job, whether it be running a platoon or a team.

Quite simply, some players don't need the politics of captaincy, they just need to get on and play. I am not sure Kevin was suited to hot-footing from nets to press conferences, to meetings with umpires, or talks with the ECB and the ICC. He probably didn't see it that way when he lost the position in January 2009, he may not see it that way for the rest of his days, but some things are for the best. If you look at this historically, the elite players do not make good captains. Ian Botham captained England twelve times in Test cricket and didn't win a match. There were always questions about Brian Lara when he was in charge of West Indies, while

Sachin Tendulkar also had a go at it for India, without much success. They just don't fit the role.

The best cricketer in the team often wants to take charge, and it's a natural career goal, but it is not necessarily natural from a cricket perspective. Part of captaincy is to understand the strengths, weaknesses and limitations of your team. One of the best captains England ever had, some will argue the very best, is Mike Brearley, and he still receives unbelievable respect for what he did. He would never in a million years say he was the best player in England. He wasn't, but he was the most astute.

Andrew Strauss has shown that his performances are not affected by the responsibility, in fact his return with the bat actually improves with it. He should have been appointed long before January 2009, in my opinion. For example, when the captaincy for the 2006–7 Ashes became a big issue owing to Michael Vaughan's injury absence, I thought they should have just let Andrew Flintoff be Freddie. Let him be the people's man. It was a dangerous move to burden him with the leadership, because he had enough on his plate already with bat and ball. People inevitably blame captains when things go wrong and I worried that a poor series would undermine Freddie as the darling of the crowd.

I also have to declare a liking for Jeremy Clarkson while I am on the warpath, particularly for giving that bloke Piers a slap. Sadly, it was not a seeing-to, but I am sure others will willingly follow his lead when the opportunity presents itself. Clarkson is very comfortable in his own skin and I like that. There is none of this starry-eyed crap or cooing over 'celebrities' and he is definitely no-holds-barred when it comes to politicians. In fact, if you read his newspaper column, you will discover he is one of life's great ranters. There have been some great ones over the years, and although a bloke called Adolf from Germany, who was not properly wired up, is numero uno, Clarkson would be up there. Our Jez doesn't mind getting stuck in and thinks most sportsmen are complete pricks … he certainly has a point.

In sport, we are well served for ranters, with Sir Alex Ferguson undoubtedly the doyen. The way he keeps these young, impressionable multi-millionaires in their place with a good clout around the lugs with a teacup or stray boot impresses me. To hell with political correctness for Sir Alex; giving the upstarts a good clogging has been his mantra. Reminds me of the discipline meted out by my mum with my uncle Harry's belt when I was a nipper. Uncle Harry was ex-Navy and had the thickest trouser belt worn by man. He lived five doors down from us in Accrington and was secretary of Sydney Street Working Men's Club. Whenever I got on the wrong side of Mum for such grave misdemeanours as talking to a Catholic girl, coming back from the butcher's with stewing steak instead of shin beef or climbing on to the back-yard wall to see if I could get a glimpse of my cousin Kathleen in the bath, she would send me down to Uncle Harry's for his belt. Uncle Harry had no sympathy either and routinely declared: 'Tell your mum to be quick. I have to open club up.' Never did me any harm, though. To me the equation is simple: do wrong = thwacking. None of this behavioural profiling in front of a computer, in a centrally heated room, or assessment during a trip to an outward-bound centre. Call me old-fashioned, but there was nowt wrong with the birch.

Some of the best sportsmen have been great on-field ranters. Tennis had John McEnroe, of course, with his 'You cannot be serious' rages at any official within earshot. Punters would be regularly treated for shrapnel wounds as splinters from his wooden racket flew into the stands. Nowadays McEnroe is the darling of the BBC commentary team and compulsive listening for me. He was a world champion in the making, who knew how to get there and would trample on anyone or anything that got in his way, so I was particularly interested in his observation that a 17-year-old Andy Murray would become a champion player one day. All he needed was a bit more aggression, McEnroe suggested. A smidgeon of William Wallace and a touch of Rab C. Nesbitt. I think the developing Murray has got his attitude spot on and, like McEnroe, he can play a bit too, so perhaps we really will get to see a British grand slam winner eventually.

The very best sportsmen invariably have, to borrow Australian vernacular, 'a bit of spunk about them'. And I think this is true of cricketers, as long as they play fairly and within the spirit of the game. In the vein of that great South African rugby player Schalk Burger, with that wonderful catchphrase, 'Eye, eye, that's your lot!' … or am I getting mixed up with another comedian?

Cricket is, of course, a non-contact sport, which means aggression usually takes a verbal form. It certainly does with Stuart Broad, a player I have extremely high hopes for in the next decade. Now he can go off on one at the drop of a hat, or a catch, at the raising of a finger, or a 'not out' from an umpire. These are still early days in his career, but he is already outstripping some of the greats with his strops, and the attitude is clearly in the blood. Although his father Chris is now a respected international match referee, on one memorable occasion when playing for England he showed a petulance which young Stuart will do well never to match – when given out leg before in a Lord's Ashes Test, he flatly refused to leave the arena. Given that he'd smashed his stumps down after being dismissed for 139 against the Australians in the Bicentenary Test in Sydney the previous year, this was the last straw and he was never picked again.

I rarely lost it on a cricket field, but I come into my own in real-life rants. Like when you order a rail ticket online. You get to the station and insert your credit card into the machine in a bid to retrieve your reservation, and next thing you know there is paperwork spewing out that makes the Magna Carta look like a post-it note: tickets, receipts, seat allocation, proof of purchase, the weather in Bolivia.

Oh, and what about those dipsticks that drive their clapped-out Novas and Puntos, windows down, volume up, with twelveteen base rocking the car sideways – turn it down, pal, no one in the real world is interested in Chaka Jam featuring Ra. Smell the coffee … it's all shite! Or the numpty revving a motor with an exhaust as big as the Mersey Tunnel, desperate to cut up some poor unsuspecting sod at the lights, to get to the front of the queue. In case your mum's reading this to you, your engine sounds like a Qualcast mower on heat. Or how about the berk who wears a baseball cap with the neb to the side and has clothes ten sizes too big that would look roomy on Giant Haystacks? Memo, son: you don't look cool, you don't look hard, you look a complete knob end!

Also near the top of my major irritant league are those people with behavioural ticks. Like when you are standing chatting to somebody and they start swaying side to side doing all sorts of weird exercises – groin stretches, hip rotation, neck flexes. What on earth do they think they are doing? Freaks.

Tip for you on this one: start doing exactly the same and they soon stop, believe me.

People can even get you going in the privacy of your own home these days. How infuriating is it when the phone rings, almost always just as the football kicks off or *Emmerdale* has started, and when you answer there is a wall of silence? You know what is coming next, it's Britain's most heard sentence: 'Good evening. Would I be speaking to the householder?' AAARRRGGGHHH! 'No, I just popped around to watch their telly and raid their fridge while they were out.' But refrain from this response and follow my final piece of advice. You simply say: 'No, sorry, he's in prison but should be out next week. Done eight years for fraud, you know. Can I take a name and number and get him to …' They don't call again. Finally, has anybody else gone through three tellies trying to clock that clown from the Go Compare advert?

Chapter 4

LIFE'S TWEET

Of all the technological advances since I turned to commentating full time, Twitter has to be the one that has given me the most pleasure. What a brilliant way to keep in touch with common souls on a whole host of issues – sometimes cricket gets a whirl as well. Twitter to me is your summary of life; your daily snapshot of where you and your mates (some of whom you've never clapped eyes on and are known simply as bobbydazzler74 or TheVoice) are at. 'This is happening in Truro next Tuesday, I fancy Denman in the Cheltenham Gold Cup, can you believe so-and-so reckons those roadworks on the M1 will be finished next year? Poppycock.' It's slightly strange, I suppose, in that these people are total strangers in your normal walk of life. But you chat to them every day like the best of pals.

I started tweeting on the first day of the opening Ashes Test in Cardiff in 2009, after a request from Paul King, Sky Sports cricket producer, to give it a go. The idea was that I would communicate with the viewers, much as we have done through emails in the past. Never would I have guessed what an impact this extension of that would have on my everyday life. Because of my computer illiteracy, at first Paul replied to the communications himself, but within half a day of watching what was going on I had learnt how to use the software and asked him in the politest possible terms to step aside. Cricket started me off, but it is a good vehicle for debates on all kinds of subject, and I find it extraordinary that you can use it so thoroughly for all sorts of conversations using only 140 characters at a time.

It is unbelievably addictive – if I haven't been logged on for a few hours, I want to see who is on and what is what. I love a good opinion and I don't mind offering one myself. As long as everyone who is following you takes that on board you are fine, and I am pleased to report that the majority understand. It can be a bit laddish at times, so the girls have to indulge me on occasion. Occasionally it can be a bit jokey: 'This was going on and then you'll never guess what happened … don't tell Diana.' We can have some good scrapes when we are away on the sauce. But you also get some priceless real-life observations sent on, the most memorable being a sign at a hospital in Northampton: FAMILY PLANNING ADVICE – USE REAR ENTRANCE.

Everyone knows Twitter is a social networking site (ooh, listen to me, getting down with the kids), but for hundreds of us who follow the England cricket team 365 days a year it has also become a kind of navigation system. Many of you will know the infamous Arthur, having bumped into him in or around cricket grounds over the years. At one stage, he was spotted so frequently that Jonathan Agnew and I made it into a bit of a game, competing to see him first. More often than not, his presence would elude me, but others would pipe up to alert me to his whereabouts, usually before lunch on the first day of a Test.

Many fellow Twitterites look forward to seeing him at cricket grounds around the world, although he doesn't tend to be spotted at home Test matches as much as he used to. Reported sightings are much more likely to occur in the local Sainsbury's car park, with bags (the recyclable types, I am pleased to report) full of shopping, or strolling through the leafy environs of Chifford Gippings. Since his financial windfall two summers ago he is finding that early retirement really is a full-time job. And with all that spare cash in his back pocket I suspect he would be quite a catch for a lady of a certain age. He has certainly been having a good time on his half a dozen holidays a year. In fact, I thought I caught a glimpse of him looking for wild plants in Kathmandu. And he also regularly ventures to Thailand to spend time with his young friend Yum-Yum.

Bumble's Best Bits

Rules of life #1: If you were dark glasses indoors, you are famous. If you wear them outside when it's dark, you think you're famous.

Rules of life #2: When typing rules of life, make sure there are no typos. If you WEAR dark glasses indoors …

Aussie sign in the crowd: 'Yes, their beer is warm and flat.' At least it tastes of something ...

Someone wants to know what software I'm using. I think it's gas — but it could be wind turbine.

People's Test match this one. Not too many of the prawn sandwich brigade in the house (or legends in their own lunchtime).

It's swinging. Must be something to do with the planetary alignment.

Light lunch for me. Going for the grand slam of naans tonight — keema, peshwari, garlic and plain.

11,000 followers now. Puts me up there with Ponting. Chasing Lara and Tendulkar!!!!! Thanks to you all dear pals

Pie from BBC just arrived. Beefy has eaten 9/10ths of it ...

Lovely cheese and onion sandwiches have arrived. Sir Ian seems to be guarding them. But I have used distraction tactic to pinch one.

Back on commentary now with the big man. He should be bowling. Who's guarding the sarnies?

Beefy's just announced himself. I've opened the window!

Martin Platt from Corrie in the crowd. Gail absent.

Rhydian is entertaining the crowd dressed as Billy Idol. He's belting it out. Told you there'd be a sing song.

Does anyone out there agree that Nasser is a dead ringer for Rafa Benitez?

Chapter 5

IT'S NOT WHAT YOU SAY

'Manou, Manou, do do do doo Manou, Manou, do do do doo'
— Bumble goes all Muppets on us after Graham Manou's Ashes call-up

'Set 'em up again'
— Andrew Caddick castles a West Indian batsman during the summer of 2000

'What's your name, love? You are Sally? I used to have a dog called Sally'
— Bumble's best chat-up line gets an airing on one of the npower girls

'Do you like the older man?'
— Sally on the receiving end of another

'Can we have our ball back, please?'
– Before vaulting the fence of one of the adjacent houses at Chelmsford during Graham Napier's Twenty20 assault on Sussex in 2008

'My mate's missus has left him, you know. Poor bloke, as if that wasn't enough, she's taken his Bob Marley records and their satellite dish with her. No woman, no Sky.'

'Full pint!'
– Whenever a stump gets knocked back 45 degrees or more

'The clouds are high and I think we are going to skirt the rain. I think it's just going to miss the south side and go around Reading. Reading is over here ... Er, sorry, over here'
– Geography never was his strong point

'Here's Phil and Nige ... Crime won't crack itself, you know'
– Bumble spots some policemen around the ground

'The winds are swirlin'. They're swirlin''
– In response to Nasser Hussain's ribbing that he had claimed the breeze was blowing in three different directions in the space of just half an hour

'Did you hear about the two sperm donors that went down to London to do their deeds? It ended in disaster — one missed the tube and the other came on the bus.'

'Get 'em in. I'll be there soon'
– A variation on *Start the Car!*

PART TWO

IN THE MIDDLE

Chapter 6

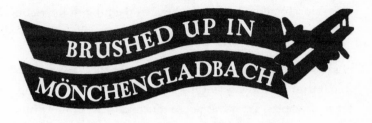

BRUSHED UP IN MÖNCHENGLADBACH

Some things in life prepare you for later events, and I look back on my five-season stretch as Lancashire captain as the period that brought me out as a person. Lancashire was quite a political club, but one that was in the midst of success when I inherited the role, thanks to the team's prowess in one-day cricket. That extended into my stewardship, with three Gillette Cup finals at Lord's, but the successful era eventually came to its end as the players aged. We had wonderful cricketers like Peter Lever, Ken Shuttleworth, Barry Wood, Clive Lloyd, David Hughes, Farokh Engineer, Jack Simmons, Frank Hayes and Harry Pilling. In fact, it was such a bloody good team that it was a travesty we did not win more.

Limited-overs cricket was our forte, key factors being our athleticism in the field and understanding of the game, but when in 1977 we finished next to bottom in the Championship it was someone else's turn to take on the mantle. Frank Hayes and then Clive Lloyd took it on, but with no greater success, and the true inspiration behind the streak of silverware had been Jack Bond, an unspectacular player but a natural leader. He loved the team, he lived the team – in some ways he was the team. Totally unselfish, he kept us pointing in the right direction, which on five occasions meant to the winners' podium.

He was something of a father figure, particularly in our initial triumphs, always setting the example and reinforcing team principles. Yet it was not so much a friend from within as the enemy across the Pennines that taught us about winning mentality. We were proud to wear the Red Rose and we inherited that tough, no-fear cricket from the Yorkshire side of the 1960s. A few of us were around at that time, as real youngsters, and witnessed their top-class players, with their 'We're f——ing better than you' attitudes. They did a nice line in intimidation and, in turn, we tried to put that across to the opposition when they rocked up to Old Trafford. It might seem strange to hear a Lancastrian admit it these days, but Yorkshire were miles better than everyone else in the Sixties, and so they just kept winning the Championship. Reputations alone would scare opponents to death. Players of the calibre of Tony Nicholson, Fred Trueman, Don Wilson, Raymond Illingworth, Doug Padgett, Ken Taylor, Jimmy Binks, Brian Close, Philip Sharpe, and an emerging lad called Geoffrey, bespectacled and with a full head of hair.

There were some serious times, of course, during my five years in charge, none more so than when our three England players of the day, Peter Lever, Barry Wood and Frank Hayes, went on strike in a pay dispute, but I look back on being captain with fondness. There were the usual ebbs and flows you would expect of any captaincy regime, but holding a position of responsibility in my twenties played an important part in my life. I was quite an introverted bloke, but Jack Bond nevertheless saw something that suggested leadership material lay within, and he mentored me for a few months in private before announcing his decision to quit.

The role enabled me to speak with confidence in public for the first time and helped my personality evolve. I was always up for a bit of fun in the dressing-room, but captaincy naturally brought greater assurance. I also enjoyed all the thinking aspects to the role – contemplating tactics, selection and so on. Generally the rest of the lads were fine with me on my promotion. Of course, some would have their moments and I would be a 'shithouse' for a couple of days in the eyes of the chosen few, but that goes with the territory. Somebody has got to make decisions that others will not appreciate, and I revelled in being their representative.

It was the making of me as a bloke, no question, as it forced me to be the spokesman for the team. Getting to finals, winning trophies, always meant introducing the group one by one to dignitaries or speaking on the team's behalf at the receptions put on to honour the club's achievements. 'Today we are proud to welcome Lancashire, with the Gillette Cup,' that kind of thing. I was petrified of that kind of scenario at first, but now I wouldn't think twice, even if it was Buckingham Palace or wherever. I would just get up and do it.

Being forced to report to the committee on your aspirations for the club, what had happened and your vision of what the next targets should be was a major change from anything I was used to. I didn't realise at the time how good that was for me – standing to address them without notes – and it was only afterwards, when I got into broadcasting, that it hit me how important that period had been for my development. It brought a guy out who you wouldn't necessarily have known resided there. I was very quiet in my youth, having been accustomed to strict discipline, and an only child. We didn't have a great deal, we just got on and did. That is how it was in those days, in northern life.

My mum worked in weaving sheds, and my dad, David senior, worked in a foundry initially, then later as an operating theatre technician in the local hospital. It was hand to mouth and a hellish tough existence. It was certainly nothing like the world as I know it now, although the house in which we lived still stands to this day. I have been back to reminisce on occasion and once took the opportunity to stop off when taking my grandchildren back to their homes in Accrington. There were five of them to be dropped off at two different houses, but I gave them a detour via 134 Water Street. 'You didn't live here, granddad? You never!' they shrieked, as I pulled up. 'Oh yeah,' I said. 'And it had an outside toilet. There was no lavvy inside.'

My county captaincy also featured a humble beginning. It came at the MCG. No, not the one in Melbourne. This was the Mönchengladbach Cricket Ground in Germany. The only cricket ground, I would wager, in the city. For some reason, our end-of-season tour in 1972, not long after one of our limited-overs successes at Lord's, amounted to a few days at an army camp and was little more than a glorified piss-up. Jack Bond was on the trip but was not intent on playing, so with me due to take over the reins permanently the following summer, I got a first taste of leading a Lancashire XI.

Well, a Lancashire two to be precise, initially, as Edward Slinger and I were the only ones present and correct in the dressing-room at the appointed time of the toss. The rest of them were holed up in their quarters, within the military housing block, nursing hangovers incurred by the partaking of several dozen *steins* of strong German lager. After winning the toss, the only course open to me in the circumstances was to bat, but instead of padding up, I was forced to rat-a-tat on the doors of my men, an action that earned the new leader his first backchat.

We were playing on a matting wicket, laid on concrete, and still only had three players as the match started. Their opening bowler was a West Indian chap by the name of Corporal Williams, a hulk of a bloke, razor sharp, super-fit and intent on decapitation. He wanted to knock people's heads off: I wanted to knock people's heads together. Of course, I had tasted some of the local brew myself, but spent the rest of the night awake, doing strategic planning, working out my fields and who was going to stand where, in my head.

We tried to shore it up against this new-ball maniac, as some of the lads started turning up in dribs and drabs. I still have flashbacks of Corporal Williams charging in now – he ran further than bloody Wesley Hall did, this fella, a tear-arse quick intent on doing some serious damage to a group of blokes all suffering from double vision. Sculling booze hours earlier was not good preparation. Cor, there was some liquid supped on that trip, the kind that left you thankful it was only one of four days' duration and not seven. We were absolutely hammered for its entirety. Both on and off the field. It was all lads together, a great team bonding week and a real good time for camaraderie. It hardly mattered that my stint in charge began with an ignominious defeat.

Our wicketkeeper was Keith Goodwin, God bless him, a man who regaled us throughout his career with stories about his own time in the military. That week he was in overdrive, saluting everybody that crossed his path. Aeroplanes and helicopters would come in to land and he would be standing there to attention, elbow stiff as hell, showing the utmost respect. That was him all over. Keith was rather an earnest chap and not someone you could take the piss out of. He just wouldn't take it.

Keith's devotion to the army was bordering on obsession. He used to have this song about Fulwood Barracks that went on for about twenty minutes, and once he started it everybody had to sit down and keep quiet. Woe betide you if you interrupted. At even the hint of unrest, he would stop, and start all over again. 'One singer, one song,' he would say, sternly. You only had to whisper to your mate and he would cut you down with a look and wind up again from the opening line. Grown men, we would have to sit bolt upright as he bellowed his way through it once more. 'To Fulwood Barracks I did went, To join the First East Lancashire Regiment.' And this would go on and on.

Ken Snellgrove, another of my former team-mates, who has since passed away, got up one time and made it all the way to the bandit. In those days they still had their one arm, and Ken had laid his hand on it without disturbing Keith's flow.

'Captain Hammond took a …'

'WHOO-DOO-CHOO,' went the machine.

'One singer, one song, Snellgrove,' Keith barked, forcing Ken to refrain from his quest for a nice set of melons. Moments later, someone else was caught talking and so Keith picked the glass ashtray up and reiterated: 'One singer, one song.'

A switch used to flick and he just went into army mode. Cross him and you were court-marshalled. Whenever he had a couple of pints, you could see the transformation taking shape, and it usually involved him gabbing to an unsuspecting stranger at the bar. 'I know a song about the army,' he would say, and suddenly any team-mates within shooting range would dive for cover. 'Christ, here it comes again.' When you got through the full rendition, he would conclude with: 'That's army life.' Great, Goody, brilliant.

Jack the Lad

The Lancashire players were at the forefront in implementing one-day skills in the early Seventies – our fielding really was as good as there was on the circuit. And our bowlers were willing to change the pace to outfox opposition batters. Modern-day slower deliveries are ten a penny – there are loads of them – out of the back of the hand, an off-spinner, whatever. There is usually some sort of signal that will go around a team when the bowler is planning to bowl one. When I was involved with England one of Darren Gough's signals was just to hitch his shirt as he turned to run in. Others would touch their badge or, if a bowler always turned one way at the end of his run, he would telegraph that he was going to send down a slower one by turning into his mark the other way. Normally left, he would approach right for the change-up. There have been so many ways of letting your team-mates know that something different is on its way. There's never been a signal so transparent, however, as the one used by my old mate Jack Simmons.

A very good, quick-through-the-air off-spinner, he used to have a lethal ball which was a darting delivery pitching on middle and leg. Straight in at the batsman's pads, and as surprise deliveries go it was very, very good. Jack never got clattered in one-day cricket. You just couldn't take liberties with him. And you certainly couldn't get under him to hit the ball aerially without inviting risk.

But in three-day cricket he used to bowl a bloody good swinger. This would come out like a flaming Exocet. Farokh Engineer would be behind the stumps and I would be at short leg. Jack would be bowling his spin but, having started in the leagues as a quick bowler, he could also get one down at real pace. All he did was get hold of the ball with a different grip. We could all see the value of this particular feature of his bowling repertoire, but given that it came down with such velocity we decided we could do with knowing it was coming. So he would get to the end of his run and chunter 'SWINGER' into the V of his sweater. Now I have never known Jack without a cough. Never. So you couldn't always tell the difference between his code and his cough. When we asked him to be a bit clearer in his bark it only added to the problem. Not only did we know, but the batter knew it was coming too. On one occasion, Farokh went back a couple of yards and I turned around the other way, so instead of facing the batsman I was showing him my arse. 'Sounds like his swinger's coming out again,' I said, making sure that not only those within earshot but everyone on the entire ground knew. The bloke in Row H was grateful, I am sure. None of this subtle touch of something, or a nod or a wink. Jack might as well have got the loud-hailer out.

We had some bloody good troughers at Old Trafford over the years, with Paul Allott prominent among them. 'Little and often,' he said to me in Barbados one winter, after polishing off a shrimp ceviche and whole swordfish for lunch. But he was an amateur compared with the great Jack. At Southport one year we had gone back on to the pitch after lunch, and I started setting the field but couldn't work out what was going on. We were one missing; we only had ten. Who's not on? 'It's Simmo,' someone said. He arrived at the boundary edge ten minutes later with a whole gooseberry pie. 'I am not cummin' on til I've fineeshed mee dinner,' he announced.

I lost count of the number of times Jack took the field with biscuits in his top pocket. He would chomp away while fielding, leaving a trail of crumbs in the slip cordon. When we went to Blackpool we would always get a wafer-thin ham salad for our lunch. 'I'm not eatin' this,' Jack would say. 'I'm goin' chip shop.' He would toddle off in his whites and spikes and sit in at Marton Fisheries up the road. They knew he was coming, so they'd have his dinner plated up. His picture, decked in his Lancashire gear, was on the wall.

Such was his capacity that his performances led to the creation of the Jack Simmons special at the appropriately named Jack's chip shop in Great Harwood. It was fish, chips and mushy peas with a steak-and-kidney pudding dunked on top. Yet, even after this mound of grub, our hero would still have room to manoeuvre. One evening I was taking him back to Great Harwood after a match, and he instructed me to drop him off at Jack's but to wait outside. I didn't have much else on, so I was happy to do as he required, intent on then running him home.

But when he got back into the car he requested that I stop short of his house. 'Drop us off under this bridge,' he said.

'Hang on. You only live a bit further, it's no bother, I'll take you up.'

'No,' Jack insisted. 'I am going to eat theese under bridge 'ere, and then when I go in she will make me some supper.'

Now that story alone qualifies him as the greatest nose-bagger I came across as a player. He was also one of the game's most wonderful characters, the life and soul of the county scene for twenty years. In addition to grub, his other interests in life were fairly straightforward, as emphasised by a gift from his team-mates in appreciation of one particularly fine, match-winning innings at Old Trafford. Graeme Fowler had wrapped up a combination of Simmo essentials – a can of lager, a packet of fags, a box of matches, a telephone and a copy of *The Sporting Life*, all sellotaped to a toilet seat. Everything he required for his lengthy vacations to the little boy's room. He would be in there for up to half an hour at a time, having a tab and scouring the paper, with his trousers around his ankles.

Mentally Disintegrating

In those days you were more likely to get a verbal bashing from your team-mates than the opposition. People often ask about the best sledging I heard while I was a player, but the truth is it never really went on. I can't remember ever being witness to anything of the sort. There were plenty of chats but never anything vitriolic or designed to undermine your opponent. Most of the great characters of the generation were too busy undermining blokes in their own dressing-room.

One of my early Lancashire outings served up a cracking Fred Trueman moment. I was batting against him in a Roses match at Bramall Lane, Sheffield. It was a damp pitch and our lads had told me: 'Whatever you do to Fred, he'll be hooping it around, so get forward. Right forward.' As an up-and-coming player you do what the senior clan tell you, so with the instructions firmly at the forefront of my mind, I got on the front foot and played the line of the ball, which was zipping past this edge and zipping past that edge with alarming regularity. After a while, Brian Close, who was positioned at short leg, stood up, adjusted his trousers and shouted: 'Fred, for f——'s sake, will you bowl straight?' Fred stood there, ruffled that Brylcreem hair of his, and replied: 'F——ing straight? How can I bowl straight, when I am swingin' it this road an' that? F——ing late an' all.' Being caught in the crossfire was a classic introduction to top-level cricket for me. I got a pair in the match but batted for half an hour in that second-innings effort, in awe of these blokes I was up against.

Most of the verbal assaults on opposition batsmen during my playing days at Old Trafford came not from the slip cordon or other close fielders but from the boundary edge. Norman Williams, or Norman the Postman as he was dubbed, had a full repertoire of put-downs for away batsmen. 'Don't close the gate, you won't be long,' he used to say, as they tramped on to the grass. Along with all the clichéd quips, such as 'Bowl him a piano, see if he can play that', he also had occasional moments of inspiration. When Derbyshire's limpet of an opener Alan Hill was in particularly defiant mood one year, he managed to spend the best part of a session compiling just four. His innings coincided with the first printing of the evening paper being delivered to the ground. Norman, who was sitting with a paper in the members' area, stopped reading and shouted out: 'Here, Hill. They've got you down as three not out in here. See if you can get to six for the final edition.' On another occasion, the nuggety Hill had managed just a couple of runs when Norman noticed the midday service arriving at Old Trafford station. 'Hey, Hill, since this match started the trains are beating you 3–2.'

Some players have no trouble getting on opponents' wicks. Pakistan's Javed Miandad was about as popular as syphilis during his time on the county circuit and so didn't need to do much to pick a fight with even the most placid opponent. In a match against Glamorgan, our 'Flat' Jack Simmons totally lost his cool following some Javed goading. Jack was completing a typically economic over when Javed patted him into the off side and threatened to steal a single. Having seized on the ball in a flash, Jack stood over it, while Javed teased him by remaining tantalisingly out of his ground. As over had not been called, the two of them were now involved in a game of dare.

'C'mun, fat Jack, throw de ball,' Javed goaded.

'Who you calling fat?' Jack blasted. 'Get back in your crease.'

This was officially a stand-off: Javed inched forward and Jack reached slowly for the ball.

In an instant, Jack picked up and hurled at the stumps, which had been left unattended by wicketkeeper Graeme

Fowler. In fact, few others on the field had paid a blind bit of notice to the duel and so, as Javed reached for his crease, the ball hurtled its way to deep backward square leg, where it passed Peter Lee, who was in the initial stages of removing his sweater, in anticipation of his next over, on its way over the rope. The thud into the advertising boards was greeted by indignation from Clive Lloyd, our captain.

'What's going on here, man?' he said.

'I'm trying to run the bastard out,' roared Jack.

Even the portliest of cricketers get the hump if you question their weight. Some you can call every name under the sun, but suggest they'd qualify for Chubby Checker's backing group and they tend to lose it big time. Shane Warne was salivating as his bunny Daryll Cullinan, a batsman he had dismissed time and again, walked to the crease in a Test match between Australia and South Africa. 'I've been waiting two years to humiliate you again,' Warne told him. 'Yeah, and it looks like you spent most of it eating,' Cullinan retorted.

Now that is surprisingly quick-witted for a South African, I can tell you. But South Africa were involved in my favourite sledging story – and forgive me, because the best sledging stories are always embellished – which occurred during their 1998 tour to England. It was a one-day international in Manchester and our side at the time included Matthew Fleming. We had first picked him during the previous winter, when we were looking for an all-action No. 8 who could bat, bowl and field; someone who was comfortable moving up and down the order; someone who, if we needed him to, could bat No. 3 as a pinch hitter; an up and at 'em kind of cricketer who could lend his hand to lots of stuff: operate in the middle overs, bowl at the death.

We had discussed the prototype on a number of occasions, and David Graveney, as chairman of selectors, came back with the name Matthew Fleming. A fairly well-to-do name as it happened, as his family were the Flemings of Flemings Bank fame. He wasn't young, in fact he had been around rather a long time, but we thought he was the kind of character who would do well as a latecomer to the international stage. Watching his batting was once described as being like watching a helicopter, with the blades whizzing round and round – it didn't look as if he had one bat in his hand, but as if he was whirling four. Every one was a winner when the ball came down. He was only looking for sixes and fours. A reporter at the local paper, the *Kent Messenger*, once wrote during a critical match report that he had batted like a millionaire. The story goes that Fleming wandered into the press box at his next opportunity, tapped this bloke on the shoulder and said, 'Multi-millionaire, if you don't mind.'

As well as being worth a bob or two and frightfully, frightfully posh, Matthew was also quite theatrical, which was no surprise given that his uncle was Ian Fleming, the creator of James Bond. He also had a colourful army past, having served on the streets of Belfast during troubled times. He was a real leader of men, and his men would run through brick walls for him. To be fair, he'd run through brick walls for you as well. He was up for the challenge, no matter what it entailed.

Although he was carded to bat at No. 8 in this particular one-day international, he was ready from ball one. His gloves, his bat and his pads were all lined up as he sat on the balcony watching our chase of 227 unfold. You could almost sense from the start of our innings that he was willing the wickets to fall, just so he could get in. Eventually, when it came to his turn, with 11 overs remaining and 58 required, the game was slipping away from us. Now there are two ways of going in to bat: you can either act cool and approach calmly, or show the opposition you are up for it and get to the crease with some haste. I always advocated getting yourself together with all your gear and getting out there, chest puffed out as if to say 'This is me', as quickly as you could. Anyone who drags his bat behind him, looking down at the floor, is out before he's got in.

Anyway, the crucial wicket falls and Fleming sets off for the crease. There's a little fellow in a white coat preparing to open the gate, but it matters not because he literally vaults it. Straight on to the field and up against rough, tough South Africa, the nastiest team on the international circuit at that time. Just as one of the opposition fielders is about to give him his first volley of abuse, Fleming cuts straight across him. 'Oh, good afternoon, the name's Fleming. I'm making my home début,' he says, in his plummiest voice. Now the South Africans are not the brightest race on the planet – their teams have never been the full picnic and are completely blinkered in humour because of the lack of stuff upstairs – so this fielder was probably already puzzled that Dominic Cork had appeared to have undergone a makeover. They were used to winding Cork up to popping point, yet here was another bloke in his place. Out in the middle, Fleming continued the chatter as Cullinan prepared to bowl his occasional off-spin. There was a lot of 'How do you do?' and 'I say!' permeating the air. When it came to facing Shaun Pollock at the other end – a bowler who could get it through at a rapid rate in those days – he asked the umpire for leg and middle and, after surveying the field, turned around and said: 'Golly gosh, slips, you are a long way back. Now, is Allan Donald … AD … is AD bowling quickly? Never mind, come along, let's play some cricket. Let's get on with this.' Nobody had said a word to him, the South Africans were all looking around bemused, but he got a couple of singles and so his innings was under way.

At the end of that over, Lance Klusener happened to be passing him. Now Lance, a bloke who had clearly seen a bit in his formative years, and whose nickname was Zulu, had already had enough of this effeminate, posh lad and his la-di-da attitude, so momentarily halted his walk to his new fielding position and blew Fleming a kiss. No response. Not even a batting of an eyelid from Fleming, who went down the pitch, chatted to Chris Lewis, his partner, and went about the customary prodding.

After another over of just a couple being scored, he crosses paths with Klusener once more. This time it is even more obvious that Klusener wants his opponent's attention as he eyeballs him, throws him another kiss and walks off. Again, no response from Fleming, who continues to look straight through him. A few more singles are taken and Klusener is at it again, standing in front of Fleming mid-pitch, slinking his hip, as if he has got two rolls of wallpaper under his arm. He puckers up, throws his head back and directs an absolute smacker from about a metre away and toddles off in a mincing manner.

Finally this drew its response as Fleming, having allowed Klusener to get about five metres away, set off in pursuit with an army-style march. 'I say old chap, were we at school together?' he asked. That has gone down as one of the great sledges. It's an absolute cracker.

Some players could not care a jot if they are taunted; others actually thrive on it. Then there are those who are so good, it's best not to upset them. Viv Richards, a man who you called Sir long before the official knighthood, was in that category. During my umpiring stint, I was officiating at Taunton when the great man came out to bat at No. 3 for Somerset against a pretty useful Glamorgan new-ball attack. Greg Thomas, who could get it through at a rate, was on at one end, and Ezra Moseley, Viv's West Indies team-mate, shared the new ball at the other. Typically, Viv swaggered out with no arm guard, no chest pad, not even a helmet. Just the customary West Indies cap.

Viv, it transpired, had had some altercation with Thomas out in the West Indies that previous winter, so there was some history here. Therefore when the ball had passed the outside edge a couple of times in the early confrontation, Thomas called out: 'It's red and round, boyo.' Goodness me, Gregory, I thought, what have you done? Like all the great players, Viv's reply came in actions, not words. His answer was authoritative and immediate. Another similarly ferocious delivery, slightly overpitched, was whacked by Viv – the noise on the bat told you how far it was going – over my head and out of the ground. There was a distinct plop as it dropped into the River Tone. He looked at Thomas and snarled: 'You know what it looks like. Go and find it.'

That was just the beginning. The Glamorgan attack had just booked in for bed and breakfast at Hotel Pongo. You knew Viv was in the mood when he stood bashing his open palm against the handle end of his bat, his snorting in between contacts adding to the rhythmical sound. And Thomas, no slouch in terms of pace, had got him into the mood. Thomas had started a fight, and soon others were feeling the full force of the retaliation, most notably off-spinner Rodney Ontong from memory. 'Look who they bring on now,' Viv said to me. 'They bring on the Ontong. I'll hit him in the river.' And he did. Repeatedly. He got 100 in just 48 balls, launching the ball time and again into what is now the Sir Ian Botham stand.

Off-putting words rarely lead directly to dismissals, I am convinced of that, but Matt Prior claimed a scalp for Graeme Swann on the 2009–10 tour of South Africa when in a warm-up contest he offered the incoming tail-ender a piece of advice. 'Never pat a burning dog,' he said. The bloke should have been out first ball, and still hadn't stopped laughing when he was dismissed by the next. And Andrew Flintoff could lay claim to an assist after telling Tino Best to 'mind the windows' at Lord's in a 2004 Test match. I would like to think the big lad was evening a score for me on this occasion. For when Tino toured England with West Indies A the previous year he took a shine to my wife during a match they played at Old Trafford. Now even allowing for obvious bias, Diana is an attractive girl, and she is used to male attention. And she had clearly left an impression on Tino because on the tour of the Caribbean, in the very match that Brian Lara scored his record-breaking 400 not out, he took the opportunity to ask after her in a most unusual manner. A wicket fell while I was commentating and Tino crouched right down next to the stumps to talk into the stump microphone. He looked up at the commentary box and said: 'Hey, man, you still with that blonde chick?' Surrounded by bemused looks, I had to explain to my colleagues that he was actually talking about my wife. It's something else when the commentators start getting sledged.

I have had some decent jousts with West Indian fast bowlers over the years, but only once can I claim to have been victorious. That was when Surrey visited Old Trafford for an end-of-season affair in the early 1980s with Sylvester Clarke in tow. In terms of pace we had nothing to hit them with, so we arranged for the groundsman Peter Marron to prepare the flattest thing you have ever seen in your life. We practised on it a couple of days before the match and it made the pitch at Chittagong look fast. On the first day it didn't get much above shin high, and knowing it wouldn't I walked out to bat without a helmet on. Having marked out his run-up, Sylvers came steaming in and there I was waiting for him on the front foot. It wasn't very often anyone did that to him, and it clearly riled him that after a good couple of overs the ball had barely carried through to the wicketkeeper, and occasionally even bounced on its way into the gloves.

He pursed his lips and said angrily: 'OK, man, I'll see you down at The Oval next year.'

'You bloody won't,' I said. 'I'll tell you a secret. I'm retiring after this game!'

Chapter 7

THE MEN IN WHITE COATS

Once you hang up those boots you are a long time retired, and although I continued to turn out for Accrington and Cumberland semi-professionally, I had lots of time to fill, and a lifetime of cricket behind me. Suddenly my past and future were looking for something to link them. I was used to dealing with cricketers, and so umpiring was one route which allowed me to keep in touch with the full-time game I had only recently departed. It was not a job for which you had to sit down and pass a test either, so my experiences over a nineteen-season career served me well.

Umpiring was not only enjoyable but also a flexible vocation, which allowed me to fit it around my playing commitments in the Lancashire League and Minor Counties Championship. Playing on the county circuit for so long also meant you knew how easy it was to get hot under the collar. I could always recognise when players were getting a bit steamy, and would have a giggle to myself about it more often than not. It also helped that I knew most of the guys competing in the matches in which I stood, and they me.

I always saw it as my job to get on their wavelength and try not to be noticed. But it was a different era of umpiring then, one in which you felt real respect from those playing. The law has not changed, in that the captain is still responsible for his team, but I am not certain that the attitude towards officials remains unaltered. Anything untoward out there in the field meant you pulled the skipper over and told him: 'Either you deal with Richard Head or I will get very interested in his behaviour.' The response, invariably, was 'Leave it with me.' Whatever the flashpoint was, I wanted to make sure it was finished and we could move on.

Of course, there are always exceptions to any rule, and sometimes circumstances meant you had to deal with perpetrators more directly. I was once umpiring a County Championship contest between Middlesex and Surrey at Lord's. The pitch on which the game was being played was a belter – as a score of 199 without loss before lunch will testify – and John Carr and Wilf Slack were hard set at the crease. I was standing at the pavilion end, and Gubby Allen, who ran English cricket for decades, was watching through his binoculars from the committee room. So when Tony Gray, the big West Indies fast bowler, unfurled an almighty appeal for leg before against one of them during that morning session and I informed him it was not out, I got rather peeved with his dramatic reaction.

He sank on to all fours and started thumping the pitch. 'Oh Jesus Christ, man,' he wailed.

I looked down at him, which can't have been something he experienced many times in his life, and said: 'Don't do that.

This game has only just begun, it is due to last three days and there is a good chance you are going to hear me say not out once or twice.'

Ian Greig, Surrey's captain, a real jolly chap, trotted over from slip and asked: 'Everything all right, Bumble?'

'No, not really,' I explained. 'I can't have him doing that every two minutes because there will be nothing left of the pitch. And that bloke behind me with the bins is watching every aspect of this game. So, I would rather him not do it anyway.' He didn't do anything like it again.

On-field officials used to be able to defuse situations, but the presence of television cameras at games has increased tenfold since the mid-1980s, and totally moved the goalposts. With two dozen cameras around a ground, occasionally incidents are seen by viewers but not by umpires. Nowadays if you get caught for malpractice you are up in front of a media jury, but in those days the umpires acted rather like friendly headmasters. Or, as in the case of Alan Whitehead, fearsome ones. He wasn't particularly popular but the players listened to what he said.

All that business with Shahid Afridi biting the ball in the one-day series in Australia in 2009–10 was crackers to me. I am not sure what he thought he was doing, or how he was going to get away with it. But I didn't have a problem with his actions per se. If an individual alters the condition of the ball, the law is quite explicit: change it. Get on with the game, no problem. People who argue it is nothing different to shining the thing are off the mark: that is allowed within the rules, but you cannot alter its condition. Why would you bite a cricket ball anyway? If you do fancy a nibble, be prepared for the consequences.

I was always a bit of an 'outer' as an umpire but – although teams would never swarm you and quiz you on why you had turned down an appeal, as now seems to be an increasingly worrying trend – one might occasionally get asked discreetly for clarification by an individual while standing at square leg next over. Somebody would perhaps sidle up and ask how the appeal had gone, whether I thought it had been close, and I wouldn't have a problem with that. But I always had my stock answer ready. And it invariably provided the last words on the matter. 'Good appeal,' I would say. 'Well worth a shout. Might have been hitting, might have been missing, so I would have to make a cultured guess to give it out. Would you like me to start guessing when you're batting?'

At that time, very occasionally, if someone had a problem we would get a knock on the door and hear: 'I was a bit disappointed, I thought I had got outside the line.' Now that was always fine. If it was my decision which had caused the disappointment, I would give my alternative view that it had nipped back and struck pad in front of off-stump. I would never hold a grudge against a player who came to see me in private. To me, that would always be the way to do it.

Players who visited us in this way might not always get what they wanted to hear, of course, and sometimes not what they had bargained for, and this certainly applied to James Whitaker during a Leicestershire game at Grace Road. Jack Birkenshaw was my partner and it was his decision that had caused the grievance. 'I was a bit disappointed, Jack, about my LB,' Jimmy began. 'Thought I might have got away with that one. Little nick on it, I felt.'

'You might have done. There might have been. I wouldn't be at all surprised,' Jack said, allowing the words to slip off the tongue in an unbelievably carefree manner. 'But this morning we arrived in Leicester, me and my colleague Mr Lloyd here, and you're here, Whitaker, of Whitakers Chocolates, and there's not a chocolate in sight. Nothing at all for me to take back to our Glo, so I just had to give you out, Jim.' Next morning, I kid you not, there were boxes of confectionery piled up in our room. That was the power we men in white coats wielded.

And you could have some real escapades on the county circuit in those days. We are only talking about twenty-odd years ago, but the era of professionalism would not have permitted the frolics I once witnessed in a match at Swansea between Glamorgan and Allan Lamb's Northamptonshire to take place. Ray Julian was the other umpire on this occasion and, after the visitors lost a wicket, he shouted over to me: 'Look who's coming in now.' The effervescent Lamb was bouncing down the eighty steps leading on to the field, and when he got within earshot Julian mischievously added: 'I bet I get him before you.'

Lamb was a real character on the field, very loud, game for a laugh, but willing to play as hard as the next man. Exactly the kind of guy to appreciate a fierce contest. Equally the kind of guy to enjoy a prank or two. So, when he was struck on the shin by one which nipped back only a few minutes into his innings, he no doubt appreciated the grin on Julian's face as the finger went up. 'There we are, told you I would get him,' Ray joked as Glamorgan's fielders celebrated another success.

Typically, though, Lamby had the last laugh. During the next interval, he pinched the pavilion keys off Eddie, the attendant, and locked us in our room. He spent the next quarter of an hour shoving lit newspapers under our door.

But his *pièce de résistance* was to leave us incarcerated as play continued. Yep, that match featured two complete overs without umpires on the pitch before Lamb relented and let us out. Unless I was mistaken there were also two mighty loud appeals. I am not sure that Hugh Morris, who played in the match, would allow that kind of thing these days.

Chapter 8

LOOSE LIPPED
BUT CARD SHARP

If I was born to do anything, it was to talk about cricket. It has been my life for more than half a century, during which time I have not changed much as a person. I don't think I am any different now from how I was when I coached England, but what I would say is that the public will have a different perception of me now compared with back then. Anybody who has seen me over more than ten years working for Sky Sports will have seen that I have a ball. Life is a lot of fun. But if I ever went back into cricket you might consider me to be a different bloke altogether, because whenever I have been involved in the game it has been unbelievably serious – if someone kicks one of mine I'll kick 'em back twice. As coach I would immediately go to the defence of the players, no matter what the situation. Because I just saw doing that as one of the first requirements of my job. I was there to defend them. If you want a bit of engagement, then you've got it here, leave them be.

I don't know whether that was my downfall as an international coach, but you can't change a character. And there are certain things I did during my tenure which I have had to live with ever since. The most obvious, and most inflammatory, example was when I attempted to take the heat off the team in Zimbabwe when we were much the better of the two sides but could not force home the advantage in the Bulawayo Test of 1996–7. I will not alter my view that we were deprived of victory by our hosts being allowed to flout the spirit of the game on a dramatic final afternoon, but the cold fact was that we did not win a match we should have won; instead we drew it with scores level. The Zimbabweans took a share of the contest by negatively bowling wide both sides of the wicket, a policy ultimately successful in thwarting our chase of 205 from 37 overs. The fact that they had resorted to this less than subtle tactic rather than attempt to make constructive or creative plays to win the game themselves left me seething. And so, when asked at the post-match press conference whether England were deserving of a draw, I let rip. 'We've flippin' murdered 'em,' I said. 'And they know it.'

Those remarks, coming on the back of some expletives at the post-match presentation ceremony, got me into bother with my bosses at Lord's regarding my conduct. They were to become the noose around my neck for the rest of my term of office. But when I made my comments to the press I maintain that I knew exactly what I was doing. I was being true to myself, acting no differently from how I would have had it been any of the teams I have ever cared passionately about. Imagine if it had been a football match. You can get mega-frustrated watching your own team, and this, to me, was just like watching my beloved Accrington Stanley versus Macclesfield. It had been the equivalent of a 0–0 stalemate when we've dominated the game, hit the bar twice and had one cleared off the line. They have done everything possible to keep the ball out of their net but done little in our half of the pitch. In the pub you'd say, 'We flippin' murdered 'em. Absolutely hammered them.' That's the message I was conveying. It was just that the bloke conveying this was the England coach and was undoubtedly expected to rein in emotion. That just ain't me.

The thing is that my outburst came on the back of some extremely testing circumstances for our touring party. To the mollycoddled players of today, the hotel, practice and changing facilities would have looked like something out of the Victorian era. The hosts did everything they could to make us uncomfortable, and in the end, when they succeeded beyond expectation, I snapped. I have since made my peace with the main players of Zimbabwe, while Dave Houghton, the coach who masterminded our catalogue of inconveniences, is now a good mate, so that's been put to bed, but the fact is that I will always have to live that down when people talk about my time as England coach. If other folk saw the situation differently from me, they saw it differently. It is similar to the situation experienced by Tony Greig during his England captaincy in the 1970s. When asked about things he has regretted, he would immediately recall telling the great West Indies team: You're gonna grovel. 'That has stuck with me forever,' he says. 'I can't get rid of that. But it was me that said it, so it's my fault.'

Different blokes react in different ways when performing the coach's role. There are no hard and fast rules to play by. South Africa's Mickey Arthur developed a reputation as the Smiling Assassin in his few years in the job, something England found themselves on the receiving end of in recent times. His tactics in the winter of 2009–10, when he began a verbal joust at the England team in an attempt to unsettle his opposite number, Andy Flower, intrigued me. Andy, being Andy, was just not playing. Mickey had got the lance out and was on the back of his trusted steed, but Andy hadn't even fed the horse. He just makes it his business not to talk about the opposition. His attitude, in his early months as coach, was that if the opposition wanted to talk about his England team, that was fine, but as far as he was concerned he wasn't going to expend any energy on it in return.

Witnessing this one-way war of words challenged me to consider how I would have reacted. Now I like Mickey Arthur a lot, I think he is a top bloke, and I wish I had been directly up against him. As far as I was concerned, he had just started a game of poker, and if I had been playing I would have finished it. England had hardly got off the plane when he had a go at Adil Rashid, or more accurately the way Rashid had been dealt with by the England management, in a blatant attempt to unsettle a young player; outed the 'mateyness' of Jonathan Trott with the rest of the South Africans; expressed his shock at the number of South Africans in the touring party; and wanted to know why the South Africans among them were playing at all? He had a go at the selectors' decision not to bring Steve Harmison on tour. He was amazed at the way that England had done this and amazed that England had done that. Why did Andrew Strauss not play in the Twenty20? His entire focus was on England.

In poker terms, the cards had been dealt and he had called. Andy Flower simply folded, but if it had been David Lloyd at the table and he had come out with anything like that about my players, I would have raised it immediately. 'If you want a game of poker, then you've got one, buddy. Now what have you got?' I would have hit him with the fact that his world-class all-rounder Jacques Kallis didn't want to bowl at all. I also found it very interesting that he felt the need to bring back a 34-year-old opening bowler, Charl Langeveldt, who retired three years previously; that his 380-wicket Test match bowler, Makhaya Ntini, was now rocking up at 132 kilometres an hour; and that South Africa had habitually failed to uncover another Harry Bromfield, the last spinner to take five wickets against England back in 1964. In this poker match, would Arthur have wanted to call, raise again or fold? I wonder.

Undoubtedly former England one-day player Jeremy Snape, his psychologist, was telling him to unsettle the opposition. Duncan Fletcher was also around the South African team as a consultant and would have known exactly what gets under the skin of England's players. They had provided the bullets and Mickey was firing them. But Andy Flower, being the way he is, was simply saying, 'Sorry, mate, I'm not interested.' To me, it was almost like the running battle in the Premier League between Rafa Benitez and Sir Alex Ferguson. Over the years, when the time has been right they have had a little pop at each other. Then it goes quiet for a while before their artillery comes out again. But in this instance, Andy had just completely blanked his opponent, as good as putting the white flag up, which highlighted to me a contentment with his own position less than a year into a job I have experience of. The attitude was simple: 'You look after yours, I'll look after mine and we'll get along fine.' But if it had been David Lloyd at the table, I would have given it him with bells on.

I could be fairly abrasive during my coaching days, but one thing I set great store by was the importance of togetherness and camaraderie within the team environment. When I left the Lancashire dressing-room for that of England in the mid-1990s, one of the first things I set out to do was turn it from being like a library into a noisy, vibrant place. Increased animation, I always found, catalyses pride and passion. So I tried all manner of things to create the right mood, including hoisting motivational placards on to the walls and blasting out patriotic anthems from the ghetto-blaster. 'Jerusalem', a tune now synonymous with the England Test team, was one of my first picks, as was 'Land of Hope and Glory', while Robert Croft was even provided with a stirring rendition of 'Land of My Fathers' to stoke his Welsh pride. Anything to make players feel relaxed, yet committed to the cause, was a good thing as far as I was concerned – card tricks, rousing speeches, famous quotations. Constructing togetherness within that environment is not easy, however, and some individuals, most notably Nasser Hussain and Mark Ramprakash, were more intent on self-preparation, albeit no less proud or keen to do well. It takes all kinds of different characters to make a team, something I learnt to respect as a coach.

A Kwik fix

My move into coaching should not have been unexpected; but nevertheless, when it arrived, it was quick. Or Kwik, to be precise. Lured into the national coaching structure by Keith Andrew, an Old Trafford committee man during my time as county captain, I was responsible for the Kwik Cricket road-shows, the vehicle designed to attract greater youth participation as the 1980s shut its doors. Our target was to get the kids in the country's 26,000 primary schools hooked on the game. Not long after that I was nigh-on full-time as a coach with the national age group sides, a role which by 1993 was combined with the main coaching role at Lancashire.

Like a number of cricketers, I took my badges while I was playing because I saw it as prudent to do so and I was always interested in coaching. Rather like umpiring, I never found coaching a chore, and coaching Lancashire proved a very happy time for me indeed. I loved it. I was extremely fortunate in that the two critical people at Old Trafford, Geoff Ogden, who was chairman of cricket, and Bob Bennett, chairman of the club, did not interfere on the playing side, they just let me get on with it. Bob merely asked to be kept in the loop as to what was going on, and that amounted to me contacting him now and again, fielding his questions and providing answers. It allowed me to concentrate on getting the job done.

Success also played a part in my mood during that period. We had a good team, an emerging team, with people like John Crawley, Peter Martin and Glen Chapple coming through. Michael Atherton, Neil Fairbrother, Warren Hegg, my lad Graham, and Gary Yates were established. Wasim Akram was a part of the furniture as overseas player. Mike Watkinson came in as a late developer, whose progress as an off-spinner, having begun his professional career as a seamer, was good enough for him to go on and play for England. He was a seriously good county performer – capable of scoring 160 in an innings and taking 11 wickets in a match. He also captained our team which released Neil Fairbrother from the burden. Neil was a very intense character, and one of the best players I have ever seen for Lancashire. In fact, if you were to pick an all-time Lancashire team I would go as far to say you could not leave Fairbrother out. He's Lancashire through and through.

In that period we all were, and we had an absolute ball. Even the groundsman, Pete Marron, was right on side with us. Some groundsmen prefer to be left to their own devices and that is their prerogative. But Marron could not do enough for us. We would have practice pitches whenever we wanted them. And he also provided the post-match social. We would finish a game, allow everyone to get out of the ground while we had a beer and showered, and as the place was emptying, Pete would wheel his portable barbecue out onto the pitch. Then we would all sit round and have a bloody good feed – a really good time. Occasionally we would clear off to the Beech, down the road in Chorlton, a dingy pub which was one of Atherton's old haunts. As it happens, the last time I popped in, for old times' sake, it was in a rather ropey state. After all, it's not often that you see motorbikes parked inside.

There was a really good camaraderie within the squad. So much so that once, when I had to administer a bollocking to Jason Gallian – for some relatively trivial matter but one that nevertheless needed addressing – I spent £57 on flaming sambuccas at the local TGI Friday's. This was the early 1990s, remember, so that represented a fairly sizeable bar bill. From what I remember that disciplining went pretty well. 'Now I've had my say, have I made myself clear?'

'Yesh, bosh.'

Genuine indiscipline did not exist within this highly motivated and successful team. In fact, the only flouting of the rules and regs had similarly comic connotations. One season Wasim Akram, as good an overseas signing as anyone has made in county cricket, was late. Not late for a match, late for a season. He was due to arrive on such a day and just didn't turn up. In fact, we named him in one team, thinking he was on his way, and had to backtrack on the day of the game. He didn't even arrive in that week, nor the next, and by the third the committee were going spare. 'Where is he?' they justifiably inquired. 'How do I know?' I said, equally justifiably. 'I am only a coach.' Truth is, none of us knew. 'Right, you've got to discipline him,' I was told. 'We will not stand for this.'

The club called a meeting on the issue and it was decided Wasim would be fined £1,000. In response, I told them I would be responsible for sorting the situation. A few days later he arrived and that meant bringing our court (more hippopotamus than kangaroo) into session. It was run under the auspices of Judge Ian *Bully* Austin – who used to sit on an elevated chair in the dressing room with a protective box on his head in place of a wig. Wasim had been told to get himself a decent lawyer because *Bully* pulled no punches as dressing room magistrate.

Now Ian had a rare ability to talk, cough and swear at the same time. 'Bahh, the court's in f——ing session ... Bring the ... urrggh ... f——ing defendant in.' So in waddles Akram with his appointed brief.

'I've been stuck in Islamabad. I could not get out,' Wasim insisted under cross examination.

'Did you ... aaagh ... or did you f——ing not say that you would ... aaachh ... be f——ing here on April 22nd? And you've not turned up until ... baargh ... May 3rd?'

As Wasim began mumbling something or other, Bully demanded: 'Answer the f——ing question.'

'I sh'd been here but delays,' Wasim replied.

The prosecution dismantled this argument by claiming that as Wasim owned Islamabad at that time, and all the aeroplanes in it, technically he would have managed to arrange a flight out at his leisure in the intervening fortnight.

His defence did not seem to wash with the rest of the team, who acted as the jury, sat in the cinema-style chairs around the dressing room. They all filed out of the room to make a decision and delivered their verdict within seconds. 'Guilty, your honour,' they barked as they snaked back into court. The sentence was suitably commensurate with the severity of the offence: Wasim either had to eat a ham sandwich or make his way to the groundsman's hut, where Marron was waiting for him, start up the sit-on roller and roll the pitch for ten minutes.

'I roll pitch,' said Wasim. Everyone was happy with this. The lads got a chortle as their world-beating superstar pal chugged back and forth in the middle, and he had escaped serious censure for his tardiness. The committee wanted to know if it had been settled. When I told them exactly how we had punished him a deadly silence fell on the committee room. 'Don't worry, it's sorted,' I assured them. It was a great way to address it for us because it got him straight back into the bosom of the team in a light-hearted manner.

I absolutely loved Wasim to bits, as all the players did. His nickname was King because whenever he crossed that white line, a king was what he was. My only other clash with him was when we were travelling down to the south coast for a County Championship match. 'Remember it's a coach trip boys,' I had told the lads a couple of days earlier, in keeping with our team rules – any journey past Birmingham meant we travelled together. 'I don't want to g'on coach,' said Wasim. 'Well it's club rules, I am afraid,' I warned him. 'We always set off on the coach together for long distances. We will be leaving at two o'clock.' So he got on the coach the next day, I was sat at the front, there was a game of cards going on at the back, the usual thing, and everything seemed fine.

We set off on time and the matter seemed to have been behind us when, with a sudden jolt, the driver pulled up on the hard shoulder of the M6. 'What the hell's going on?' I asked. 'Have we broken down?' The coach driver, looking shifty in the extreme, muttered, 'Er, no.' With that Wasim appeared at my right shoulder. 'I got on bus, now I am getting off bus,' he informed me. In a flash, he jumped off, and straight into his mate's car that had pulled up behind us. It turned out he wanted to call in at Birmingham to do a bit of business. All the other lads were in on it so they were pissing themselves. As they pointed out, he hadn't actually broken the rules because he had, as I instructed, got on the coach, and there was no rule to say you couldn't get off.

The best teams are always the happiest, I have found. Being talented obviously helps but aside from the great Yorkshire side of the Sixties which argued like buggery you find that good spirit can give you a decent platform for success. From my involvement, I found that you get the best out of players if they were happy. It is so important that team-mates respect each other. You don't have to go out socialising with each other but if you respect what the other lads do it can make a huge difference.

You are always going to have cliques in teams. People talk about avoiding them but they are so natural you are always going to get them occurring. 'I don't go out with him, he don't come out with me, but I love what he does on the field. He's great.' That's the attitude you ought to be seeking. For instance, when I first broke into the Lancashire team, greyhound racing was a fantastic night out. There used to be half a dozen of us would go, led by the older ones like Ken Higgs, Tommy Greenhough and the scorer, Mac Taylor. Others didn't like the dogs so they wouldn't come. Were we an exclusive club? No, we were just having a good time. It was just a natural thing to hang about with your mates or do what you liked doing. Some liked going to the pictures. I couldn't stand it. When you are away, somebody will have room service, somebody will have a nice meal, another will want a pint. Within a team environment it is natural for different interests and levels of friendship to prevail.

Bob Bennett was also chair of the England Management Advisory Committee, the body I reported to during my three years with the national team. My final report to EMAC concluded that other countries' teams were evolving quickly but England were not. Our opponents were further ahead in terms of preparation, rest and recuperation for their international matches. We had been seeing this in its simplest terms throughout my tenure. It first struck me during the summer of 1996 when I went out for dinner with Wasim, who was here on tour with Pakistan. He had sat out a couple of matches and so I asked him what had been up. 'I am waiting for you,' he told me. Wasim at one end and Waqar Younis at the other, both fresh as spring lambs, was enough to put a chill down anyone's spine. They were in absolute prime condition to play these Test matches against us.

Touring teams traditionally played county matches to win but as the game began to modernise through the 1990s that was no longer the case. They were coming to beat you in Test matches, nothing else mattered. So they would rest the crackerjack players while ours were getting knackered on the county circuit. It was crackerjack versus crackerbread. Goughie would roll through 50 overs for Yorkshire, turn up on a Wednesday morning and be made to practise as part of the protocol, when what you really wanted to do was tell him to go have a game of golf, a swim, relax and do nothing. We were overloading players, who were being pulled one way by their employers and another by their country. I was an advocate of a new modernised system for the players, a centrally controlled elite group, and recommended the implementation of just that in my end of tour report after losing the Ashes 3–1 down under. I promoted a cycle of rest, preparation and practise – what you and I might now easily recognise as the base ingredients of England players' contracts with their Lord's bosses. My views on sports science and nutrition had been poo-pooed by some at the time in our country, while our opponents, Australia, were market leaders in it. We needed to get fitter and stronger, analyse better and back that up with education on better lifestyle and nutrition.

Every other sport was looking to get their athletes fitter and stronger, but cricket lagged behind, as if these factors would not improve performance levels. Yet it is no accident that these blokes we see emerging now are hitting the ball miles, just like golfers. I agree that part of that would be down to improved equipment – cricket bats are now bigger and designed better – but when you see the work that is done in the gym these days it is incredible. These guys are not pumping iron, as some would suggest, to look good on the beach – I just don't buy that at all. I am working out in the same gyms as the England team, the Sri Lankans, Pakistanis and New Zealanders. Every nation's players are getting into great condition so that they can bowl faster for longer, they can dive, throw and catch, quicker, further and better. You can only promote this through proper management of the players.

Within a year the first set of central contracts were drafted – I freely admit to being envious of the drastic change in environment of which Nasser Hussain and Duncan Fletcher, as captain and coach, were the beneficiaries – and the players have been managed effectively since. Myself and Keith Fletcher and Raymond Illingworth before me were used to guys turning up knackered or with an injury, and frankly who could blame them, because they only got paid if they played. It was a real case of the tale wagging the dog for us. We were managing players with no real power over them. If I wanted a key player to rest it meant going cap in hand to the counties, through chairman of selectors David Graveney, saying 'please sir, would you mind awfully if so-and-so had a game off'. The counties were well within their rights, of course, to tell us where to stick it because they were paymasters.

Put into this context, beating that crack South African team 2–1 in the 1998 Test series was some achievement, and certainly my best as England coach. We talk about rest periods now and how players have to be fresh in order to play, so for us to compete in five Test matches against Hansie Cronje's South Africa against the backdrop of our lads playing county cricket in between was no mean feat.

However, that victory unfortunately carried a stench with it. People have claimed it was fixed because of umpire Javed

Akhtar's performances but I don't go with that at all. Any bias towards England in that series baffles me because we didn't half have some ropey decisions given against us, and if you examined the five matches, we had 13 lbws against us, exactly the same number as them. There was some really tough cricket and we just got the better of it by some bloody-mindedness and rearguard action from Angus Fraser at Old Trafford. Fraser won the Trent Bridge Test with 10 wickets and Gough cleaned them up at Headingley.

I was credited for another major change in the England team – drafting in younger players such as Ben Hollioake and Andrew Flintoff – but this does Alec Stewart an injustice. For it was actually Alec, captain at the time, who was all for getting these young lads in. I know that Andrew has since said he shouldn't have played so early because he was not ready but in my opinion he was and he should. I have no doubt that his statistical return led him to this conclusion but he got an absolute stinker at Headingley when he was caught off his pads on his way to a pair. Our team was in need of an all-rounder and if someone is good enough you get them in.

The Legend of Freddie Flintoff

Everyone within the English game has a story about Andrew Flintoff, one of the most fun and mischievous cricketers I have ever met. His drinking escapades have been well-documented but my favourite Fred fable took place at a time before he had touched a drop. He was soon to develop a thirst as a young county player, perhaps from around the age of 20, and it is one that has never really been satisfactorily quenched despite his tendency to wet, nay drench, his whistle on several occasions. Perhaps he will slow down in later life but, as my old mate CJ would gladly have told you, getting off the grog is a very gradual process. One you have to work through very carefully. With Andrew it might have been the same sort of thing. It is like putting a block of ice into hot water; it doesn't melt immediately, it just fritters away over time.

CJ once went for a check-up at the doctors, which included all the usual trappings of testing blood pressure, looking into the ears and up the nose. One thing led to another and the doctor inquired: 'Now how many units of alcohol do you consume in a week?'

'What does a unit consist of?' quizzed CJ. 'Well, half a beer or a glass of wine or a shot of a spirit,' replied the doc. 'Oh, erm, right,' said CJ, thumbing through his fingers like a hurricane through a haystack. '146 ...'

'How many?' gasped the doctor. 'Yes, 146 on a good week,' CJ declared with a cocktail of pride and conviction. 'Right, well you should be going for 26. You've got a massive problem here, or should I say your liver has.' There then ensued a full and frank discussion between doctor and patient. Over a scotch, naturally. After much deliberation on both sides it was decided that, all things being equal, the best course was to carry on with a similar level of alcoholic consumption because it would be such a shock to the system to do anything else.

Excuse me, I transgress. For the moment that Freddie made his mark on the Lancashire dressing room came when he was a teetotal teen and therefore totally sober. As far as I am concerned you will never hear a better Flintoff story than the one that took place on an end-of-season trip to Guernsey in the mid-1990s, and I was involved in it. He was 17 years old and playing in this September friendly against Hampshire. Because he was one of those without sore head, it was decided by the senior players, following a particularly good night on the tiles, that Andrew would open the batting. 'Get the lad in first,' was the shared opinion of the wise and heavy heads. Having faced up to the new ball, he soon took one in the orchestra stalls from Cardigan Connor. After treatment and significant sniggering from opposition and teammates alike, Flintoff was led from the field looking rather pale. As his coach I tried to be as supportive as possible. 'What's the matter?' I inquired. 'Awww, owww, aaaggh. It's hurting,' Flintoff, bent double, responded.

'Why, it's an absolute pleasure to be hit in the bollocks by Cardigan Connor,' I countered. 'What about me? Jeff Thomson, 1974, bowled 'em like Exocets he did. He's like a bloody off-spinner in comparison, Cardy. Anyhow, let's have a look. Get your tackle out and put it in this pint pot.' So we filled said pot with ice and left him sat with his nuts dangling in it for a while. As it happened, he was to later return to the crease and got a hundred to boot, but that's not the indelible impression he left on the Lancashire dressing room and the county game in general that afternoon.

It was time for play to resume following a tea break and young Fred was about to resume his innings. As he was preparing himself to go out, our enthusiastic off-spinner Gary Yates happended to be coming in, having been in the nets practising – what the hell he were doing practising in September, I don't know. Anyway, Gary had this persistent habit of licking his fingers – I think it must be a spinner's pandemic – and was virtually French kissing them as he strolled in, so enthused about his workout. 'Ooooh,' he said. 'I've had a long old spell and it's been coming out lovely: it's been gripping and spinning but it ain't half warm work out there … Oh, whose is that drink?' Flintoff, turning as he went out the door, and with the straightest of faces, said: 'It's mine, you can have it, I don't need it …' And the legend of Andrew Flintoff was born.

Thinking out of the box

I have always been fond of Andrew Flintoff. I was England coach when he made his début, although Alec Stewart, who was captain at the time, has to take the credit for pushing for his selection. All he achieved in the game subsequently filled me with pride because, although it came with its pitfalls, he had managed to meet the targets he set himself when I first became aware of him at Old Trafford. Unfortunately, another one of my favourite cricketers during my time as England coach did not. As a genuine fast bowler I thought Dean Headley was absolutely terrific – a really natural athlete who didn't have to work hard at all, had a fantastic engine and never stopped running in. You only have to recall the Melbourne Test match in the winter of 1998–9 when he bowled for about four hours. His shirt hung out the back of his trousers but he looked the part as an Ashes competitor. He was a great bowler against left-handers and bowled at 90 miles per hour consistently. I thought he would have been one of our best bowlers of the modern era but he broke his back at

20-odd-year-old and did not play again. That was really tough luck.

He was a smashing lad, great to be around but boy he would talk a glass eye to sleep. Partly because he was rather fond of a chat and partly because of his dulcet Brummie drone. And he would always have ideas. Boy, would he have ideas. Namely, when we were training that whatever we were doing was wrong. I remember once we were deep into a fielding drill, which included five separate stations and we had been practising at high intensity for 40 minutes, when Dean's dynamite exploded in his head. The idea behind these fielding sessions was to make them short, sharp, high intensity affairs, which didn't require much thought. It was ten minutes on the first station, typically slip catching, then ten on the next, high catches, then on to flat catches, ball retrieving and so forth. On this occasion he had come to my station for the last set. Everybody had worked hard, people even ran between the stations to keep up the intensity. I was overseeing an exercise on picking the ball up and shying at the stumps. A repetitive exercise that had been seamless up to this point. So I rolled the ball out towards the next fielder, who happened to be Headley, and as it was travelling towards him he barked: 'Can I just say something?' Suddenly the whole session had been disrupted.

'Yeah, right, want do you want?'

'I think we're aiming at the wrong stumps,' he suggested.

I am the first to admit I had a short fuse when I was coaching. My hair stood on end, my eyes rolled around in my head and pointing in the direction of what appeared to be an obvious target, I tried to spell it out to him in the simplest terms: 'Deano, I'll be rolling the f—— thing, you will be picking it up and throwing at them f—— stumps! I will decide which stumps we are aiming at.'

'I was on'y tryin' a help,' came back the West Midlands drawl. He could absolutely melt you, could Dean, and no matter what you threw back at him he would not take any offence whatsoever.

Touring Australia offers players plenty of opportunity to flout the guidelines with its numerous pubs, clubs and bars. It's a long tour and you have to expect the odd transgression, boys being boys and all that. During the 1998–99 tour, I got wind that Burswood Casino in Perth was proving a favourable night spot, so I popped down there one early evening and had a chat to the bloke on concierge, dropping him a few dollars, as I asked him to keep an eye peeled. 'This is yours,' I told him, 'on the understanding that if any of my lot turn up – you know who they all are – you let me know.' Next day I went to see him and as I approached he began his report: 'The tall lad. The the dark lad,' he said. 'Not Alex Tudor, the other one. 'No, it wouldn't be Tudor,' I said, 'he'd be a good lad would Tuds. He'd be in on time. You're talking about Headley, aren't you?'

'He came in very late, I won't tell you what time,' he said.

I had all the information I needed, so I went to Dean to confront him. 'Have a good night last night, Deano?' I asked.

'Awwright, yeah, I had a luvverly night as it happened, yeah.'

'You were in late, Dean?'

'Erm, yeah I wor a bit late, yeah.'

'And you went into the Casino. Was there any reason that you were in that casino at that time?'

'I was feeling lucky.'

'Lucky? You weren't so lucky because you were $500 down in about three minutes,' I said.

'How do you know?'

'Because I am paying the bloke to watch you.'

'Oh, there's no need to do that.'

For all his minor faults, and they actually made you more fond of him, he didn't have any on the field. Apart from one infamous spell in the Caribbean when he developed a chronic no-ball problem. Something had gone drastically wrong with his run-up and Bob Cottam, the bowling coach at the time, was sufficiently concerned for me to act. We were of the opinion that he was in need of a one-on-one session to eradicate his over-stepping, so I put my hand in my pocket and paid for use of the Kensington Club in Barbados. As it was a dedicated net for him, the only other person to come with us was Jack Russell to keep wicket. I stood as umpire to watch his front foot land and Bob stood at the start of his approach to assess what was going wrong. After about half-an-hour, Bob had got to the bottom of it. Dean's run-up was measured to precision and in order to avert any further problem in setting off, Bob got the whitewash out and painted a box in which Dean would plant his left foot. Time after time when his left foot landed within the lines, Dean hit the crease. Bingo. 'Happy Dean?'

'Yeah, I've got it.'

So we get to the one-day international a few days later, confident that there was no longer a problem. Bob had got the paint out at each end of the Kensington Oval and I took my seat on the balcony in fairly relaxed mood. I got the binoculars out and settled in to watch the opening overs with Angus Fraser, who was not playing, sat behind me. 'I'm just going to lean against this railing and watch Headley's first ball,' I explained to Gus. I had the bins on him as he was thrown the ball, and watched those seconds of preparation all bowlers go through at the start of a spell. As he set off, I screamed: 'The bastard's missed the box!' Seconds later, like clockwork, came the cry from the umpire: 'No ball.' I was so incensed I could barely restrain myself, so it was a good job Fraser had his wits about him. 'You f—— twat, Headley!' I bellowed, shaping to vault onto the middle. Fortunately Fraser pulled me back into my seat. You probably couldn't get away with that now with all the cameras around the ground. But that was Dean for you. Funnily enough, I think it was his only no-ball of the game.

Check out those wheels

Chris Lewis got caught up in some trouble after he finished playing, and paid the price by serving time in jail. But as a cricketer he had some talent. A talent that was unfathomable at times. Unfortunately, I, like others before me, failed to find the key to getting the best out of him consistently. Truth is, I suppose, he could not consistently get the best out of himself. In 1996 against India, Chris was our best bowler as we won the Test series 1–0, operating with great hostility and feared by an opposition including young batting masters such as Sachin Tendulkar and Rahul Dravid. When he slipped himself he was a real handful. There was then a gap that summer until we played Pakistan and by the time that second assignment came around he had lost form and his bowling was all over the place. Quite simply, he just wasn't the same fella.

Some cricketers are like that. Some days they're world-beaters, the next they look beaten. This might sound like a contradiction in terms given that Lewis came into that category, but he was the one player I thought was guaranteed to improve our chances in the 1999 World Cup. Alec Stewart was of the same opinion. We had canvassed the thoughts of all the opening batsmen on the county scene the previous summer and the word that came back was fairly explicit: the two bowlers they found the most trouble against were Lewis and Ian Austin, of Lancashire. Who better to listen to than the blokes stood 22 yards away? Now Chris, as a stunning fielder and more than handy batsman, was a potentially devastating package and his recall would strengthen us in every department. So, after a day-nighter in Australia early that year, Stewart and I approached chairman of selectors David Graveney on the matter, having already notified Lewis, who was in Melbourne playing club cricket, of our intention.

It was an unusual demand, coming at midnight and months from the event, but we were both of the mind that Lewis would improve the team and we wanted to integrate him back into the set-up. But Grav simply would not budge. Even though Alec and I both guaranteed our resignations should he step out of line, we could not get the proposal past first base. As far as he was concerned it was a complete non-starter and we were told not to ask again. There was too much previous and Grav was adamant that his fellow selectors Graham Gooch and Mike Gatting would not consider it. So we had to go and tell him 'sorry pal, we just couldn't swing it'. To me, Chris was not a bad lad at all. I know he has got into a lot of difficulty but I just saw him as being 'different'.

I was prepared to give Lewis a reprieve two-and-a-half years after he was unceremoniously axed for his tardiness. During the second half of that 1996 summer, he turned up 40 minutes late for a training session, for which I fined him four bottles of champagne – effectively an apology to his team-mates. Yet only a couple of weeks later he was at it again. Only this time it was a match day. A Test match day. As he lived down the road from the Oval, Lewis was allowed to stay at home, and knowing the area meant he had little excuse not to be on time. Raymond Illingworth was chairman of selectors at the time and made a habit of strolling onto the field to assess conditions and engage in general chat as our warm-ups concluded. I had to make a beeline for him on this occasion. 'There's a bit of a problem, here,' I said. 'What kind of problem?' asked Illy. 'Well, Chris Lewis hasn't arrived.'

'Where is 'e? Wha's 'is problem?' said Illingworth later, after Lewis finally arrived. He had put his tardiness down to a puncture, but Yorkshiremen are the greatest of all sceptics. 'Reeeeght,' said Raymond, with typical cunning. 'He'll be parked in that Lord Tennyson's School opposite the ground. Go and see if he's changed his wheel.' Did I hell … But the wheels had come off Lewis's international career. That was to be his thirty-second and final Test appearance, and he was not even considered for the following winter.

What's in a name?

During the 1998–9 Ashes tour we were involved in the triangular one-day series which also included Sri Lanka. On any tour there is a requirement to look after the corporate side of things, usually some dinner or other function appearances, or the donation of autographed cricket equipment. So at the start of each series there is a room put aside at the ground where the first match is to take place for mass signing sessions. Five-hundred cricket bats are laid out around this room and each team has to go in and sign these so they can be handed out to the corporate guests who are paying a lot of money for the privilege of being there. It is a really regimented thing but is an expected duty of all the international teams across the world.

A rota is usually drawn up, with each team taking its two-hour slot to complete their squiggles. At eleven o'clock Australia will go in, followed by England at 1pm and Sri Lanka at three. Each player goes round in an a clockwise fashion, picking up each bat and inking his name on it. It can be a gruelling and tedious process but it has always been part and parcel of touring. With duty completed following a final pre-match net session there was only the team meeting left before we took on the Sri Lankans the next day.

At five o'clock that night we had the meeting. Now as coach I would always lead these short, sharp gatherings, but look for the players to be proactive and offer their own opinions on how we should be looking to play and what we might expect from the opposition, both collectively and as individuals. 'We are going to hammer this lot, this is how we are going to do it, blah de blah.' So I am leading it off, ahead of Alec Stewart, who, as captain, would then talk to his team.

I have never been great on Sri Lankan names, I have to admit, and it means that before commentating on a game for Sky I will practise both recognition and pronunciation of their players. They have names that simply go on and on and on. So with the Sri Lanka game looming, I was going through a similar practice process, leading into an assessment of the strengths and weaknesses of their XI.

'Right, let's have a look at their batters,' I said. 'What do we know about their top order?' So I looked down at their list, which I had written out phonetically to help me. 'What do we know about Arjuna Ranatunga?' The little fat lad from Barnsley, Darren Gough, pipes up with: 'I'll f—— kill him. I'll knock his head off. He's frightened to death of me.' Gough, enthusiastic as ever, was reminded that there was a limit to the short stuff in one-day cricket and that it might be all about slower balls and changes of pace in this kind of contest. 'Ooh, aye, sorry boss,' said Goughie.

'Now, they might have a pinch-hitter at the top as they have done over the past few years,' I said. 'We know quite a bit about Romesh Kaluwitharana if he goes in first over here, as he did against us in the 1996 World Cup and against us last summer. What would you say about him?' Goughie was up again. 'I'll hit him. Last time I played against him, he was backing away from me and I hit him straight on the head.' I reminded him: 'No, Darren, off-cutters, slower balls, go wide of the crease, use your full repertoire.'

'Ooh, aye,' he rejoined.

So we went through this process all the way to the bowlers. 'Now let's dissect their attack and tell me what you think about it,' I said. 'What do you think about their left-arm opening bowler?' Someone from the back of the room pipes up with: 'Which one?' Fair point as it happened, as they also had Nuwan Zoysa in their squad. But I was talking about the medium-fast chap who swung it nicely and went on to take hundreds of international wickets over a 15-year career. One who went by the name of Warnakulasuriya Patabendige Ushantha Joseph Chaminda Vaas. 'Sometimes they just call him Vaas,' I joked. Getting a bit cocky, pleased as punch that I had delivered world cricket's biggest name without a false start, nor a slip through all the tongue twists and turns, I laboured the point. 'You know the one, left-arm, will bowl into the wind, hooping it this way and that, at 78 miles per hour, always at you. Goes by the name of Warnakulasuriya Patabendige Ushantha Joseph Chaminda Vaas. What do we know about him then?' A stoney silence ensued until Alan Mullally, who had been so quiet I had forgotten he was even on the tour, chimed. He stood up and declared: 'You don't want to worry about him boss, he'll still be signing all them f——ing bats.'

Whenever we had team gatherings, I always tried to get something out of the lads in the group, even the quieter members of the squad. So that would often involve addressing Al Mullall directly with: 'What do you reckon, mate? Any thoughts.' Now I am all for cricket being kept simple but his staple response took things to the extreme. 'Win the toss, have a bat, rack 'em up, get 'em in, bowl 'em out, bosh, bosh, put your jacket on, go home,' he would say in his soft Aussie hue. Simple as that, lads.

Later in that series, after we ousted Sri Lanka from the three-team event, Mullally was on the receiving end of my temper. Or rather his Bose stereo was, after we snatched defeat from the jaws of victory in the first of the best-of-three finals against Australia. Chasing a modest 233 to go 1–0 ahead, we were 198 for four in the 43rd over when Nasser Hussain was stumped by Adam Gilchrist off Shane Warne for a top-score of 58. Even so, there was only one team in it with an equation of 35 required off 46 balls with five wickets in hand. So losing two further wickets without shifting the score and eventually sliding to a 10-run defeat left me seething. It was my Sir Alex Ferguson teacup moment. This fancy music system just happened to be there, and so I gave it a thump, and it fell in bits. It was Mullally's pride and joy this thing, he just did not go anywhere without it. He carried it everywhere under his arm and he did so the next day as we flew on to Melbourne, the only problem being that it now came in numerous parts. I felt awful about it but it had just happened to be in the wrong place as I began devastating the whole dressing room.

He was a bit different to the other lads was Mullally, perhaps understandably so, given his upbringing in Western Australia. He was your typical outdoors type of bloke and during one tour of New Zealand he opted to go deep-sea fishing in Napier for the day. Well, he caught a five-foot shark on this adventure and thought nothing of bringing his catch back with him. It was probably only when he was walking down the high street with it on his shoulder that it occurred to him that he had nowhere to put it. Somehow he managed to get into Atherton's room and shoved it in his bed. Of course, a dead shark is going to give off a whiff but Athers has no sense of smell, so didn't know it was there until it was time to get some kip.

When we first called him up in 1996, he came with a reputation as one of the worst batsmen on the county circuit. He was pretty hopeless with the bat in hand but I made it my business to stress to him the importance of contributing as much as he possibly could if we were going to increase our chances of being successful as a team. 'At some stage you are going to need to get 30 for us,' I told him. 'We will be desperate for runs and I will tell you what I will do. If you get us a 30, I will buy you 30 pints of Guinness.' I was fully aware of his Irish background, of course, and always believed players responded well when faced with a challenge.

That summer we were playing Pakistan and therefore up against their hostile pace pair of Wasim Akram and Waqar Younis in their pomp. During the final Test at the Oval we lost a few wickets late on the opening day and early on the second morning, which meant that Mullally walked in with us short of 300 after winning the toss. For the next quarter-of-an-hour the ball flew everywhere. Off inside edges, outside edges, off his head, and somehow he managed to get into the 20s. When he had reached 24, he walked down the pitch, and looked up to the balcony and shouted: 'Hey, boss.' Having got my attention, he started a Gazza Euro 96-style beer-guzzling celebration. His orders to get 'em in proved premature, however, as he was cleaned up two balls later by Wasim.

Long distance fielder

As a coach of any sports team you have to be able to accommodate all kinds of characters and realise that some need to be managed differently to others. Now Phil Tufnell was a case in point here, someone who needed to be dealt with tenderly at times, a maverick with a sensitive side. Preferential treatment for one, however, breeds resentment in others and there was always a lingering backdrop to the allowances made for characters of difference. One or two could not fathom the need to treat any individual differently to the next but it is a necessity of coaching to provide each member with his own happy environment in which to flourish. Some you can leave completely to their own devices. Others need an arm around the shoulder. Then, there are those you can say or do anything to and it makes not an ounce of difference. Darren Gough was always in that group – like one of those toys you put in a budgerigar's cage that once pecked collapses, but then springs straight back up. Goughie couldn't give a shit what you said or did, he just wanted to play cricket.

That was a positive thing in Gough but a similar attitude exposed a weakness in Tufnell. He wanted to play cricket but he could not be doing with the peripheral stuff that went with being an international player. Namely fitness. His attitude towards it was an issue over many years and one reported thoroughly. There was no sensationalising going on when it came to these stories either – he categorically hated it and did nothing to hide the fact. My tactic with him was to include rather than exclude him, chivvying him along in his gym and cardiovascular sessions to get him through them. During the 1997–8 tour of the Caribbean, the whole squad were booked on a three-mile run from the Pegasus, the team hotel in Jamaica. 'Philip, you and I will run at the back,' I told him, wanting to be as encouraging as I could. We did get through it and he finished up coughing, wheezing and spluttering, with his hands on his knees. 'How did that go then, Cat?' I asked him. Gasping for air, he looked up at me and said: 'Well if they ever find a f— who can hit it three miles, I will be able to fetch it back.'

Tufnell is a card, a lovely lad, a real Cockney rebel who has seen life differently to the majority of his England predecessors and successors. He plays up to his uniqueness brilliantly; outrageous at times, he also has his dark moments and can withdraw. But the complex personality and public persona can mask what he knows about cricket. You would imagine it difficult to get analytical cricket thoughts out of someone like that but he has definitely got the ability. Without naming names we were once in an England team meeting when he came up with a view on something and somebody quipped something like 'what would Tuffers know about it?' Quick as a flash, Tuffers jumped in and said: 'I'm just f——ing telling you, that's all.' There was not another murmur, and he was dead right to pull this bloke who was taking the piss out of him. He has a sharp mind when it comes to cricket, and he has flaunted his expertise during his work with *Test Match Special*. He has far more to offer than the public might have imagined, given his image within the England team environment. His good impression has not been a surprise to me but it might have shocked people whose perception of him is not necessarily close to reality.

He has always been misunderstood to some extent, never getting full credit simply because he was undoubtedly Jack-the-lad. But actually, when you scratch the surface it is blindingly obvious that he knows the game. That is something that has come across in spades with his broadcasting career. He has got a great voice to go with his lived-in face and muscle-less body. Half the battle on radio is to sound interesting and his knowledge of spin bowling, in particular, holds up against anyone. Cricket also needs characters and Tuffers is a man who has never lost his great capacity for living; everything he has turned his hand to he has done well in. You cannot fail to see that whether it be his reality show appearances, his *Question of Sport* team captain's role or his roaming reporter stuff. He is a naturally funny bloke, and someone people like being with. He is far from up himself, he plays himself down all the time, and is bloody good fun. I am on his wavelength, and although I am not sure I have got up to a fraction of what he's got up to, our personalities are not so different. I feel very affectionate towards him, always look forward to seeing him, and always have a good yarn. Whenever I see him before a day's play he will say: 'You got anything for me? Anything I can tell 'em on my radio stint?' So I try to give him a line or two. He's the kind of guy you always want to help.

I always considered him a loveable rogue rather than a disruptive presence, most significantly so, I guess, when I took over the England job and there were those only too willing to make it known he should not be picked again, given his previous misdemeanours. But, I thoroughly enjoyed dealing with a group of diverse characters, and wanted to make my own judgment on individual players rather than be guided by the oily assessments of others. To me Tufnell was bang on, absolutely no trouble, and someone whose company I enjoyed. But with the benefit of hindsight I think I found him such because by that stage of his career he knew how to never get caught. He might have been up to all sorts – and I am sure he was – but he could always cover his tracks.

The closest he sailed to the wind with me was on the New Zealand tour in 1996–7, when the whiff of scandal which had followed him for much of his England career filled the nostrils in Christchurch. I was having a walk through the pedestrian zone of the city on a day off – it was late morning and I was on my way for a coffee – when who should cross my path but Tuffers. 'Alright boss, how's it going? How's it going?' he said, breaking off from one or two of his colleagues, who were sat with him at one of the open-air cafes. 'Yeah, great thanks, just having a coffee.'

'You ain't seen anything, have you?' he said.'Eh? Er, no.' With that, I accepted his invite to sit down and listened to his account of a night out that had – unbeknown to me as I had slept in – resulted in the local newspaper running a story alleging he had been smoking wacky baccy in a downtown bar. As I did so, a billboard caught my eyeline: 'Phil Tufnell thinks Bardellis' is the best joint in Christchurch.'

Of course, he was desperate to get his side of the story across to counter a public one which was giving one local hang-out maximum publicity. But, out of the corner of my other eye, I could see two of our press pack, Peter Hayter, of the *Mail on Sunday*, and David Norrie, of the *News of the World*, lurking in the vicinity. I decided to box clever and arranged to see Tuffers later on at the hotel. We met up with John Barclay, the tour manager, that evening and Philip began with: 'No, no, I wasn't there. It wasn't me … Well I was there, I was dancing on the tables with my underpants on my head but … oh, I can't remember anything else.' With such overwhelming evidence of his innocence we agreed to dismiss the allegations forthwith, and the furore died as quickly as it had sprung up. John later told the press: 'We've had a thorough investigation and Philip cannot recall being there.' Nobody bothered. Undoubtedly that was because we were winning.

With ball in hand, Cat was an undoubted matchwinner, but his greatest theatre was saved for when we were batting. When those fearsome West Indies greats Courtney Walsh and

Curtly Ambrose were in tandem you have never met a greater coward. He would be watching from the balcony, chuntering about how they would kill him. 'I'll never play them,' he used to say. It was hilarious in some ways because this was not something that developed as the innings progressed – he was shitting himself from ball one. Then, when it was his turn to face the music, he would waddle into the middle like Robocop's stunt man, padding poking out through every one of his garments, and steer one to third slip from somewhere near square leg. 'I did all right, didn't I?' he would ask, for reassurance. 'Blinding, wan't I?' Yeah, yeah absolutely fine. Now go and bowl them out.

The Gaffer

While Tuffers promoted chaos, Alec Stewart was the embodiment of good order. With Alec everything was absolutely flippin' pristine: when it came to his kit or even training gear it was pressed and folded as though it had just come off the shelf. Everything was in order and arranged just so, exactly as Graham Gooch would organise his own things. The Gaffer always looked the part – the trousers would be dapper and the shirt, with collar pointing skyward, made its own statement.

When his dad Micky was coach of England, he networked everybody within the domestic structure. I was umpiring at the time and Micky would always say whenever he bumped into you, 'remember, if you see anything that you feel we should know about, let us know'. To me, that was a good way to find out about potential players and I just happened to see one when I was standing at the Oval one day. With Jack Richards away on international duty, a young keeper-batter opened for Surrey and got a brilliant 97. It encouraged me to pick the phone up. 'I've seen one,' I said. 'Kept really well, scored runs quickly, and goes by the name of Stewart. Plays for Surrey.' With that I hung up.

Alec went on to captain England for the final year of my three as England coach and boy did he get the best out of himself as a player. In short he was a winner, and had a great personality within the team. His leadership was one by example. When he was captain he just told it as it was, stated the obvious about what people needed to do in their own roles, there was nothing dynamic about him. Just like Gooch, he was very matter-of-fact, precise with what he required from his team-mates and was brilliant at managing his own game.

In my opinion, he was never given the credit he deserved as an international cricketer. He was a world-class wicket-keeper-batsman, who dropped nothing, and as a batsman he scored runs and was brave like you wouldn't believe. You will not come across a sportsman more organised in any facet. Alec was fit, he worked hard at everything that he did, watched his diet, and made sure he turned out immaculately. Within the team everybody loved him. Yet I never felt he got the recognition outside the dressing room that his talent deserved. He was world-class in an era when – though there were some very good players around – few were better. But he was undemonstrative and just did the job, rather than shout about it.

His fierce competitive edge was also key to his personality; fit and strong, he would take anybody on. He has been sent off in charity football matches, one particular set of fisticuffs in the centre circle with 1966 World Cup winner Alan Ball, sending Micky into despair. Alec always fancied himself as a footballer but you had to keep your eye on him or he would have you with his underhand tactics. He was a massive piss taker and so, in the pre-match kickabouts now part and parcel of players' warm-up routines, he would suddenly start rolling in agony on the floor as if shot down by a sniper in the stands. He would either be holding his head or grabbing at his calf. With a wicketkeeper you cannot be too careful, so he was forever creating comic panic on matchday mornings.

His dressing room party piece used to be to position himself behind the door and pretend he had been smacked in the mush as someone entered. There would be an extravagant yelp, swiftly followed by apologies and an 'are you alright?' from the assailant. 'Yeah, fine,' he would say, springing upright. In addition to these Laurel and Hardy style comedy capers, he had a very subtle piss-taking wit which came to the fore amongst the fast bowlers. He was one of the primary jousters with big Angus Fraser, who only needed minimal baiting before being ensnared in a row. Gus would bite every time and more often than not it would be the Gaffer who set the trap. On particularly good days, he might get a treble up – a kind of buy one get two thrown in for free – if Andy Caddick and Darren Gough were also around. The Gaffer would start a conversation on an inane subject matter, offer a contentious observation made up on the spot, then walk away, leaving them all steaming. Priceless stuff.

Chapter 9

'There has been a lot of bullshit and negativity this week, but we've kicked ass,' bellowed the towering Texan, who had just delivered one of cricket's stranger impromptu speeches, perched on a table above his assembled guests. As whoops and hollers filled the air of the 'after-show party', there was not much doubt as to exactly whose ass 'Sir' Allen Stanford was talking about. England had been flogged on their first foray into cricket's new commercial world.

We all know what happened next, and Big Al was last seen modelling what looked like one of those Netherlands World Twenty20 kits in a very big house in Houston. But his brief flirtation pre-slammer left an indelible mark on our sport. It may have ended in embarrassment for the English authorities, but it showed the endless possibilities the 20-over model can provide. Yet unfortunately a failure to grasp the nettle whenever the chance has presented itself sums up English cricket in relation to the 20-over format. As its pioneers, we delivered the global game a raft of possibilities but didn't jump on it ourselves.

Sadly, when our national team were thrust into the land of opportunity in the autumn of 2008, they gave a typically British response. English rumps were given one of Chris Gayle's hefty size 13s and should still be sore now. They're not, of course, owing to the revelations regarding Stanford's business past, but to me it is too convenient to hide behind that. Make no mistake, England missed a trick during their week in Antigua. They simply got it wrong from the off.

Just as people had done five and a half years earlier at its inception, Twenty20 was again being misunderstood, this time because of its new and groundbreaking riches. Stanford delivered a contest of a financial magnitude incomparable to any other one-off team event in history, and previously unthinkable in cricket. Yet well in advance of the $20 million showdown, we were talking ourselves out of competing. It is all very well being wise after the event, but I don't think we were very wise before it. Here was a chance to embrace a new era – had Stanford not been bent who knows what might have developed? – but we met it with scepticism.

One thing I have learnt about cricket is that it never stops. Never stops evolving, never stops surprising, never stops enthralling. You have to go with it or it will leave you behind. It is why I embraced Twenty20 from the off while some others with a vested interest in the sport, whether as players, administrators, media men or traditionalist supporters, poo-pooed it as a fad. English folk are generally fearful of change – we don't do the unknown, do we? – and so often get our retaliation in first when confronted with it. Here we were again throwing rabbit punches at a giant cash cow.

When 20-over cricket became a part of the English county fabric in 2003, some eminent writers and broadcasters vowed not to entertain it, let alone allow it to entertain them. My feelings could not have been more contrary. It was something to expand the game I love so dearly, one that has been good to me, and this was my chance to be at the forefront of its new journey. My passion for the new format meant I became the face of Sky's coverage. Yet not even in my wildest dreams — most of which feature a desert island, a pint of Timothy Taylor's Landlord and Lulu — could I have envisaged the position the game had found itself in on this balmy Caribbean night of 1 November 2008. Twenty-two men competing for the right to pocket $1 million cheques for winning a single cricket match.

Yet as soon as English cricket had welcomed this new age of possibilities, there was unrest at the concept, its timing and the image of our national side. How should England celebrate if they won, captain Kevin Pietersen pondered in public before the domestic summer was even out. Should they celebrate at all? News of the credit crunch permeated the air, bankers in the City of London were losing their jobs, and here were fifteen England cricketers being dispatched to have a shot at some life-changing wonga for a mere three hours' work. It had pricked his conscience. Andrew Flintoff, England's other A-list star but as down-to-earth a bloke as you will come across, also questioned the authenticity of the autumn adventure. There was obvious concern within the dressing-room at how an England team with more than 130 years of heritage would be perceived. But it was not their job to worry about that. Sportsmen don't need cluttered heads when they cross the white line, yet the team appeared to be stockpiling any criticism thrown at them. The vibes were negative from the start.

I might have been in a minority in getting behind the venture, but I did so because I genuinely believed it was good for the game. For some bizarre reason we developed a big problem with cricketers coming into line with other sports stars – I wasn't aware of Cristiano Ronaldo offering to hand back his £130,000-a-week salary when Lehman Brothers went belly up, or Lewis Hamilton, the very same weekend, refusing to pass Timo Glock on the final bend in Brazil in a gesture of solidarity with those made redundant in the motor industry that year. A young British fellow went round and round in a motor car at breakneck speed, picking up a shedload of shillings as a result, and everybody thought it marvellous: millions and millions of pounds bestowed upon him for churning petrol fumes into the atmosphere. For generations cricketers have been subservient, so perhaps that is why we gave a subservient performance. Perhaps it is part of the character of English cricket not to ask for more than you need. The players were stand-offish when they should have thrown themselves headlong into the challenge. A briefing by their Lord's bosses, who were keen to portray the match as primarily a philanthropic gesture to West Indies cricket, and not to dwell on the cash aspect of the contest, only added to the confusion when clear thinking was required. The England team were dangled a carrot and not allowed to crave it.

They fell, some would no doubt say to their credit, into line. I've never been like that. If the money was on offer to me, I'd have a right go for it. Sport has traditionally been founded on playing for prizes. You strive for ultimate reward. Yes, there were other aspects of the ultimately doomed five-year Stanford deal which the England and Wales Cricket Board wanted to promote, and with the Chance to Shine scheme having been so successful in allowing youngsters to play the game in Britain's inner cities, the intention of launching a carbon-copy scheme around the Caribbean was commendable. But even at the top money ultimately creates interest. An influx of cash, no matter what people say to the contrary, will improve the game in the long term. While $13 million was ring-fenced for the players and their support staff, a further $7 million was guaranteed to the respective English and West Indian boards, to be spent on cricket at all levels. To me that was a good split. Such sums should effectively filter down through the system. My hope at the time was that the grassroots level would get a substantial slice. We were struggling to buy cricket balls at my beloved Accrington, and I wondered whether Big Al's chest of Benjamin Franklins could account for a few.

For those who considered the financial aspect of all this vulgar: get real. Of course it requires careful management, but the current 20-over revenue streams across the globe should be used to support the top-level game as a whole, not line film stars' bulging wallets. Test cricket, the pinnacle of the sport for more than a century, is under threat in certain parts and administrators need to act quickly to maintain its position. As each 20-over tournament goes by, the longer version of the game is more and more vulnerable. I know an international Test match cricketer who is also an Indian Premier League player, and he told me personally that Test match cricket is secondary to him now. That was after just one season on the subcontinent. How many more players are feeling like that? It makes me wonder. He is in a minority, I am convinced of that, but I am a believer in Twenty20 cricket and Test cricket thriving alongside one another, protecting the sport's past and future simultaneously. One is cricket's soul, the other its modern heartbeat.

The revenue from Twenty20 events should be used to subsidise the more complex drama of Test cricket before too many players make earth-shattering career choices. We have to make playing all forms of the game financially viable to the next generation; it has to be an attractive proposition for aspiring professional players, because those are the guys that will drive the sport forward. How sad to think a young man might enter the sport with the sole ambition of chasing the 20-over pot of gold. Those at the very peak of the sport should be competing and showing their credentials in the most testing environment possible, and that means Test cricket. I remain convinced that modern English players understand where each form of the game stands in the hierarchy. The next generation should want to emulate the feats of Michael Vaughan, Andrew Flintoff and Kevin Pietersen in the 2005 Ashes. That series made stars of those men and engaged a new audience because of their success. Stuart Broad twice snubbed the Indian Premier League to concentrate on his main objective – Ashes cricket.

But if the money is on offer – and they are rupee loopy for 20-over cricket in India – and it fits into their schedule and does not affect preparation for important series, take it. Youngsters associate with success, so let's not be shy about wanting to compete in and win big events. Genuine supporters want their team, and their favourite players, to be as successful as possible. Sitting on the plane home from the Stanford trek, that was the feeling relayed to me by fellow Brits. People who had paid to come and witness cricket history being made spoke of disappointment that our national team had not claimed the bounty – if there is cash on the table we shouldn't be embarrassed about doing our damnedest to grab it. I'll declare my hand here: I'm a gambler. A 50–50 shot at winning £620,000 is a very attractive proposition in my book. I wouldn't have minded a dart at it, I can tell you. Not that my comeback for Accrington at the age of 60 in 2008 was born out of anything other than madness, I can assure you. I have it on good authority. My body told me so.

I managed a meagre 15 off 31 balls in my first game out of retirement. You hardly need to be an expert to conclude that's not Twenty20 form. This game is about pushing the boundaries, hitting plenty of them, challenging the norm and defying it with bat and ball. Without sounding like the Big I Am, I think I know a little bit about it. I've made it my niche, and when I get into something I do so with a passion. When we set out on the unknown road back in 2003, it was then Sky cricket producer Barney Francis who pushed me into it. 'This is you,' he told me. Almost instantly, I felt he was right. I got it straight away. In pop music, if you're introduced to The Fall, you either get them or you don't. I did and feel richer for it. Twenty20 was exactly the same. I got it straight away.

Suddenly we went from matches watched by one man and his dog (as long as *One Man and His Dog* wasn't re-running on UK Gold) to gates being shut at compact county out-grounds two hours before the toss. Prior to the inaugural season's big launch, the thought from the administrators was that the cricket could not stand alone, it had to be part of something bigger, a day out incorporating fun for all the family. We have since learnt that the product itself is enough.

I recall the first live Twenty20 match we screened, between Hampshire and Sussex down at the Rose Bowl in

Southampton, and one of the multitude of gimmicks used in those early days was a fairground which had been set up adjacent to the action. One of my co-commentator Charles Colvile's catchphrases at that time was 'all the fun of the fair'. Quite naturally therefore we spent the pre-match build-up discussing exactly what kind of rides were on offer. 'Of course, the Screamer's here,' Charlie said, with relish, and a mischievous twinkle in his eye. 'Is she, where?' I replied. We had got off on the right foot. Twenty20 is fun. Yes, it is intensely competitive, and playing standards have risen immeasurably, but we had a laugh from the start. It is serious sport, but not to be taken too seriously.

This may sound as if I am downgrading it. But to me it is not cricket, rather a form of entertainment using cricket equipment. I appreciate its place and what it represents. Others are not so generous of spirit. Two of our Sky team, Michael Holding and Ian Botham, steadfastly refuse to cover games. But it is beyond doubt what the crowds like. It's unashamed larking. And I guess that's my bag. In turn, an expectation has developed, both from the production team and from viewers, for me to be outrageous at games. Just to be me, as I am off camera, and have a giggle. The director will be in my ear telling me to 'rev it up', and I know where I fit into the scheme of things. I try to be thorough in my job but I have no inhibitions. It's a format which promotes the comic side of the sport.

One of the games that sticks in my mind was in July 2006 at Taunton where Somerset hosted Warwickshire. It featured my old pal Andrew Caddick, who in my time as coach of England could never do enough for you in the dressing-room. He was good old Andy-Man, like a Harry Enfield character come to life, fixing this, that and the other. This time he was obliging in a different way as his bowling went around the park. Like that old Heineken advert jingle, he was refreshing parts others couldn't reach. His figures of 3-0-51-1 must have been the costliest of his career. And did he lose his rag? Did he ever. He kicked the footholes into adjoining counties, chuntering away in his usual irascible style, and all the while I sat pissing myself. As a commentator, laughing at someone's misfortune would be unacceptable in any other form of cricket, but in 20-over cricket it goes with the territory.

The humour is rather black at times, I guess, because Twenty20 is also a competitive business, which from a technical point of view leaves no hiding place. Every mistake is magnified, and one at the wrong moment can result in defeat. Throughout the Stanford Series week, people anticipated the jackpot being decided on one slip, one no-ball, one dropped catch under pressure. 'Catch it, and it's all yours – drop it, and it's gone,' I'd said rather darkly in Sky's commercial in the build-up to the game. Here was the hand of sporting fate deciding that a single slip would be costly, whatever had gone before. It rather reminded me of Mickey Stewart's edict on fielding. There is no point completing a massive dive to stop the ball on the boundary, Mickey used to say, and then throwing it over the keeper's head. Everything has to be synchronised: you have to ensure the stop is combined with a quick release and accurate throw. Twenty20 skills are about precision, and the overall rise in standards has made for great theatre.

With such narrow margins, the difference between winning and losing has never been smaller, and while the taste of success has been given a few sweeteners, failure comes with its own pangs. Winning Twenty20 titles is sexy; losing them can be ugly. Just ask the Lancashire lads who were forced to reflect on a semi-final exit of the 2005 competition while so-called supporters hammered their fists on the dressing-room windows at Edgbaston bellowing, 'You're a f——ing disgrace!' And they, I am told, were the ones that had taken it well!

As I made my way to Antigua, my prevailing mood was one of good spirits (might have been something to do with the fact that for me it was a relatively short journey following a week's holiday in Barbados). It was not a mood that prevailed long, however, thanks to the usual chaos that marks Liat out from just about any other airline on the planet. Two hours of standing in a queue to be met by one of about 500 operatives on the other side of the counter, who all appeared to have a Masters degree in the art of doing sweet FA. No wonder the computer always says no – so would I, surrounded by that lot. Things are never smooth when you're touring the Caribbean, so it was something of a saving grace that this was our only travel day on that trip. This week was all about one ground, one tournament, one main event.

I soon found it was all about one man as well, and that very fact riled me as the matches got under way. My first impressions of Sir Allen Stanford's Coolidge site were entirely positive. What a stunning little cricket ground he had constructed. So easy on the eye. Simply magnificent. I naturally expected the teams to enjoy playing in such an environment, and anticipated the opening match of the week, between the Stanford Superstars and the Caribbean champions Trinidad & Tobago, to be a real hoot. Unfortunately, it soon became clear that the cricket was secondary.

It was all about the big lad, schmoozing around the boundary. Stanford was a man who made meeting and greeting look like an Olympic sport. Now, up to this point Sir Al's bravado had quite appealed to my laid-back disposition. Seeing him arrive at Lord's by helicopter in midsummer was like seeing Jed Clampett from the Beverly Hillbillies coming over to visit. When I watched him clambering out, waving enthusiastically, even though there was no one to wave at, I had fallen for the showman. I had half expected the England and Wales Cricket Board to give him a child to kiss, the way they do with Premier League footballers, when he trudged across the Lord's nursery ground. But instead of a child confronting him it was another knight of the realm, Sir Beefy, who – despite his own interest being comparable to that of a turkey at Thanksgiving – was made one of his 20:20 for 20 ambassadors.

On home soil, however, Stanford was at ease among his own people, and when it came to the televising of this event, boy did he have some people! Century TV, the production company, were more focused on getting their man on camera – even allocating him his own producer – than concentrating on the product he was bankrolling. His entourage was so big that people were falling over themselves to satisfy his ego. It meant that the international commentators like myself had no idea whether we were coming or going. It also showed me just how good Paul King and Mark Lynch, the guys I am used to working with at Sky, are. With them we know where we are at any given moment. Here we were in a right spin, playing second fiddle not only to Stanford's laps of honour, but also his sidekick Mike Haysman's obsession with inter-viewing as many folk as possible while games were being played. To me, having covered a match or two in my time, the cricket does the talking for itself and you fill in the gaps when necessary. The week had begun with massive teething problems for us broadcasters.

By the second game between England and Middlesex, there was a real storm of negativity brewing over how the cricket was being projected back home. It was Twenty20 but not as we knew it. The conditions – the outfield was getting longer and the pitch slower – were restricting stroke-play and boundary-hitting. Players found it extremely difficult to score and were clearly not enjoying the experience, which made the cricket hard to be enthusiastic about. Meanwhile, on screen, the Mike Haysman Show had moved up another level. Not content with the interviews interrupting the action, he had now taken to interviewing and commentating simultaneously. It didn't take much television know-how to understand that the moment Andrew Flintoff joined Kevin Pietersen at the crease for the final six overs of the England innings was the time to halt a banal chat with the fourth umpire. My email inbox was jamming, and my mobile phone buzzed with texts enquiring 'What is going off?' Our press lads were soon on to the underwhelming nature of the product and, from a personal point of view, for all my pre-tournament positivity, I felt my own credibility as a commentator was going down the pan.

All this Americanised, in-yer-face shit wound me up. It might work in some parts of the world, but not in the parts that play cricket. For the tournament to be seen in the best possible light, he needed some better advice about what foreign audiences might expect. The British public would have been happier if there had been a bit more mystery about him, I am sure. We had a very fine cricketing philanthropist, who is sadly no longer with us, in John Paul Getty. You never saw him, as he kept himself to himself, and sometimes your image is better projected from a detached position. So, in the aftermath of England's low-scoring victory over Middlesex, I opted to speak out at the production meeting called by Tony Still, head of Century TV. I passed on the negative feedback reaching me from back in the UK and found that it stung Haysman quite badly. Stanford was very keen on the walk and talk, he said, and they were of the belief that their style worked. But I wanted to have my say and stood my ground. I am proud of Sky's production of Twenty20, we know what works for us, and we stick to it.

Not that my criticism of the way Twenty20 has been presented is confined to the now defunct Stanford venture. Has anybody managed to sit through an entire Indian Premier League game without becoming nauseous? If I wanted to watch a Bollywood movie, I could hire one from the corner store up the road from where I grew up. Why they think viewers want to see Indian actors smiling in the VIP area between deliveries is completely beyond me. I am sure the cricket would be fine if allowed to stand alone, but it is compromised by this celebrity obsession. So is the commentary, in my opinion, with the homogenised lines plugging sponsors of 'maximums' and strategic time-outs. I am afraid it is all too gimmicky for my taste.

Not that I am against the introduction of new ideas designed to improve the viewing experience. Far from it. For the record, I have never been a great fan of players wearing microphones during matches. I have never been convinced that discussing projected scores or the state of the pitch with players while the innings is in progress adds to the entertainment. However, I was in favour of one of the technology proposals made for the Stanford week, which, coincidentally, was knocked back during the days of brinkmanship which led up to the matches – the wearing of heart monitors during matches. While attention was mainly focused on sponsorship rows, with Trinidad & Tobago threatening to pull out and the Superstars threatening to cover up their Digicel logos, under the radar the England team and their opponents were refusing to have their heart rates scrutinised. Now that to me would be an intriguing viewing aid: who needs to ask questions about how pressure is taking its toll when you can see from an on-screen graphic how players are really feeling inside? Seeing who keeps coolest under pressure would fascinate me.

The early part of the Stanford week led me to think about ways of improving the cricket. The main problem was the pitch; it was simply too slow to produce the kind of 20-over stuff we were used to. A thick outfield was also to blame for restricting the number of boundaries, and scores of 121 and 117 should simply not be competitive. Drop-in pitches would have been a better option, but the tournament had to progress with what it had got. The floodlights were also being made into an issue, but I did not buy that one. The England players claimed that the lights were of poor quality and that this explained the high volume of dropped catches in the opening matches, but in my opinion there was absolutely nothing wrong with them. In fact, the lux value of the lights was much greater than those used in the rest of the cricket world. Paul Collingwood was spot on when he spoke of the need to practise more under them. You always need to get used to individual grounds because of the different heights of the pylons, the angles at which they are pointing and the strength of the light emitted. To me the visibility issue was just another excuse; something else to blame. By the end of the week, people were catching everything.

Some of the 'negativity and bullshit' which Stanford spoke of in the ground's Sticky Wicket bar later that week had been self-inflicted. Some of it had been unjust. I was not overly fond of the image being portrayed at the start, but as the week progressed I observed that Stanford appeared to be a well-meaning man who was struggling to cope with the clash of cultures. My mood was softening, in fact, as others' opinions appeared to harden against him. If you wanted to track it on a graph those two opposing lines converged just about at the point at which Mrs Emily Prior bobbed up and down on the big fella's knee. That incident occurred during the England–Middlesex match but was missed at the time, and it was not until it was replayed on the big screens at the ground during the following night's contest between Middlesex and Trinidad that English indignation poured out. Neither were Pietersen's team happy about Stanford's access-all-areas approach to the ground, including the dressing-rooms, into which he wandered on a couple of occasions before being asked to refrain from doing so.

I confess to getting my jockstrap in a twist too easily in the first few days, and it was the golden oldies in town who high-lighted the spirit we all required. They captured the mood perfectly with their beach cricket competition, the day before the big showdown. Held at the appropriately named Jolly Beach – where the dress code appeared to be a spare tyre around the waist – West Indies and England legends renewed old acquaintances. The crowd enjoyed the razzmatazz: the great Viv Richards still had the unmistakable strut, Curtly Ambrose still cocked his wrist like a serpent's head in delivery, and Richie Richardson looked as if he should still be playing. As for the English contingent, they all retained their wonderful nuances – Allan Lamb puffed out his chest as only he could, Devon Malcolm still missed the pitch occasionally, Phil DeFreitas finally conceded that he had a 'lack of nip', and Darren Gough and Andrew Caddick were still arguing, as they did whenever they shared the new ball. This lot were stars of just one generation earlier, who were light years behind in earning power, and they were having a ball. No resentment, no jealousy, just goodwill. It reminded me that everyone needed to lighten up.

Meanwhile, England were latching on to excuses like half-volleys outside off-stump. 'There is a feeling that it's turning out to be a bit of a garden party, which shouldn't be the case with international cricket,' Sean Morris, the chief executive of the Professional Cricketers' Association, said on behalf of the team following an emergency meeting at the Verandah Hotel. Those who believed the England side had been pawned for a pretty penny were letting it be known: it was a hot topic of discussion in newspapers, radio phone-ins and Internet blogs.

As a result of all the debate, on the morning of the final itself the ECB spin machine kicked into full operation mode, briefing the assembled media of its intention to conduct a full review of England's involvement with Stanford. This was announced just hours before an England team was attempting to create history – a further example of a distraction when, in contrast, the Superstars remained single-minded in their approach. I spoke to their coaches Eldine Baptiste and Roger Harper, and the only goal they had was to win that match. Their squad had spent six weeks preparing at a boot camp, and make no mistake: they were drilled for the purpose. I had never seen a 'West Indies' team so disciplined, and they really stole a march on us. England encountered what was effectively the first-ever professional Twenty20 outfit, a well-oiled machine with each of its parts working in unison.

England were a far from harmonious bunch when they took the field, and the contrast in moods between the teams manifested itself in the result on the pitch. After winning the toss, England were quite frankly never in the game, struggling to hit early boundaries despite the fulfilment of a promise made in midweek by Stanford that the pitch and outfield would be improved drastically for the showpiece occasion. I had been an advocate of throwing Luke Wright and Graeme Swann up the top of the order, but typically the selectors plumped for the conservative option of Ian Bell once more. England managed just two boundaries in the six powerplay overs, both struck by Matt Prior, and they simply failed to cash in. It was a strategically bankrupt performance.

In contrast, Chris Gayle blasted his way out of the blocks and the Superstars played up to their billing. When an England team which posted just 99 lost at a canter, with a massive 44 balls to spare, the relief was palpable. One side had committed to winning it, the other was committed to getting out of there. Pietersen had told his counterpart Chris Gayle at the toss that he didn't need the money. 'Who doesn't want a million?' Gayle later said. 'You got to be crazy!' His response typified the difference in outlook on the week, even though subsequent events proved deflating for the hungry youngsters from the Caribbean.

Pietersen spoke in the post-match interview of the 'nonsense' building up to the 10-wicket defeat, but there was no dwelling on what was or might have been from the young home players as they committed to the cash quest. The talented Andre Fletcher from Grenada, whose unbeaten 90 against Middlesex emphasised an improvement in the surface, had at the age of 20 hit the jackpot. Watching the television interviews afterwards, even I was welling up. 'This will change my life and it will change my mama's and papa's lives too,' said Fletcher. This match meant plenty to the people of the Caribbean, and they turned up in their droves to watch it. You had to be there to fully appreciate the impact it had on the Antiguans, who jumped, danced and jigged to the blowing of conch shells around the ground. Back home, there had also been something of a sea change as some of the same people who had texted criticisms performed a U-turn, having been touched by the atmosphere of the event. Cricketers cherry-picked from around the Caribbean dropped to their knees, tears welling in their eyes, futures changed in an instant. It was emotional stuff. Real-life drama on a sports field.

It saddens me to think that the immense effort of some of those lads proved futile after the finer details of Stanford's financial past unravelled. Because to me the scenes at the end had emphasised what this kind of winner-takes-all concept was all about. Being paid handsomely for having fun. Yes, there were hiccups, but this was supposed to be an exhibition week of cricket, at which the finest players in their regions would be rewarded for toiling at a sport they fell in love with as kids.

Modern Twenty20 is essentially where recreational cricket is played for huge purses, yet we simply did not get enough out of it financially when the opportunity was ripe to do so. Even after the Stanford shenanigans we had a chance to tap into what was becoming a world market – but we were reticent because the core of that market is India, and our domestic structure is based on serving eighteen counties, or eighteen separate businesses, rather than them serving the needs of a central body.

By and large these businesses are made up of members and, unfortunately, although understandably historically, it is their interests that are served rather than those of general cricket supporters. We have crammed our domestic season so full of fixtures, chasing paltry amounts of revenue, that we have blocked off the road to greater wedges of cash. The Indian Premier League and Champions League are going to fit into the calendar year annually, and if that means cutting across the English summer, tough tit to us.

Now Lalit Modi, regarded as either the villain of the piece or the modern-day Kerry Packer, never cared for the tradition of eighteen English counties, and, one could ask, why should he? His events were always going to slot into gaps convenient primarily for India, and then for Australia and South Africa – the other stakeholders – and we should have been more adaptable. Our counties are gobsmacked at the effrontery of encroaching on our domestic programme on one hand and yet want to take a slice of the Champions League pie with the other. It is understandable, with county finances as they are, why two teams getting a shot at £4 million in prize money has caused the conflict of interest. The basic fact is that our outdated county system gets in the way.

My opinion of the county game has never changed. I have always been a massive fan of county cricket; I see it as an institution and I love its tradition. But I am absolutely certain we need to move with the times to accommodate the other massive money-spinning competitions held around the world. These lucrative 20-over tournaments have the potential to underpin a club for a couple of years, and our most successful ones would be readily available in the future if those in the corridors of power were not so myopic. Excuse me for putting the broken record back on, but we need to play fewer games. Doing so would leave more room for manoeuvre when it comes to fixture re-scheduling.

The argument that fewer fixtures would be costly for counties is in my opinion a hollow one. I don't think gate receipts would be significantly down over the course of a season, because with fewer games the spectator would get a better-quality product. Thinning out fixture lists would allow players to be better prepared to perform at a higher level. I have been at major England and Wales Cricket Board meetings, and forums, where directors of cricket or coaches from counties, even the coaching staff of England, have insisted there is far too much domestic cricket to prepare players for meaningful matches.

Any athlete, human or animal (I'm talking about racehorses or greyhounds here) needs to go through a four-part cycle of preparation, practice, performance and rest. Just apply cricket scheduling to a racehorse, for example. A top racehorse would run every single day if you wanted it to but it wouldn't win very often, certainly not after its first couple. It would like a regular run out, no doubt, but it wouldn't be in prime condition. Racehorses are not prepared like that, they are prepared to win. In my view, you need to prepare county cricketers similarly: prepare them as if each match is an event rather than maintain the model I was accustomed to as an emerging player in the 1960s. The most damning word we can possibly use in relation to our domestic cricket is *circuit*. Players pound round and round it until their bodies blow up.

All the coaches are singing from the same hymn sheet – we are not preparing properly for matches. Once the season gets going there is no time to work technically with the players, so once errors creep in, they remain, which means that punters are essentially watching a flawed product. Players are so knackered, even when deemed to be fully fit, that they are going through the motions. Forget this convenient excuse of serving county members for a second and ask whether anybody has questioned why we are prepared to short-change them. Why should they field players operating at well below their optimum capacity?

County cricket should be a great product and, with some daring, it could be. We need to have a serious think, as South Africa did, about starting all over again. Overnight the South African board ditched their provincial competition and reverted to a franchise system – with great success. A reduced number of teams has produced a far better system and they are developing good cricketers. And if you want an alternative to franchises, I can give you one, and one that would not mean traditional teams were scrapped. It is an idea I have put forward to the ECB hierarchy: increase the number of teams, with the end result being a decrease in the number of matches.

No county is lost, no careers are culled (which would keep both county and player representatives happy); you simply introduce Scotland and Ireland into our system. A two-division split is maintained, but instead of playing sixteen rounds home and away, you reduce the County Championship regular season to nine matches. As the optimum number of first-class matches in a summer is around a dozen in my estimation, you could introduce title, promotion and relegation play-offs, meaning the intensity of the competition would be maintained throughout the entire summer.

Reducing the number of matches would open up rest periods, and the international fixtures could be structured around the Championship, so that our top-notch players like Pietersen and Andrew Strauss would have a route back into county cricket. The calendar has become so dense that county fixtures now always run concurrently with Tests, when they should be carded in the build-up. Up until recently Pietersen went through a spell of playing once for Hampshire in the Championship in about four years. With a reduced fixture list, he could play a couple of games every season in preparation for playing for England.

Now if the product was enhanced with players such as Pietersen returning, isn't that a winning situation for any county member? Wouldn't you really look forward to the Lancashire versus Yorkshire contest if it was played just once a season, and both teams had a week's preparation for their shot at it? All through the period from the 1930s to the 1960s, that was a really important fixture in the English cricket calendar – all the way through the ages it has been a tough game. I played for a poor Lancashire team against that crackerjack Yorkshire XI of the Sixties, and the ground was always jam-packed wherever we played. I remember full houses at Bramall Lane, Sheffield, and at Bradford Park Avenue in Roses matches. You couldn't get a seat, and there was a premium on standing room too. Romantically I would like to get back to that, because at the moment it has become just another game. I think it would be great to market that properly and reignite proper Roses cricket. The same with Middlesex versus Surrey and

Worcestershire versus Warwickshire. Re-create that derby rivalry and encourage more people to turn up.

Cutting down to nine games would immediately free up twenty-eight days of the summer, and that would provide flexibility should counties need to rearrange their schedules for Champions League action and also offer the chance to rest weary limbs. You lose count of the number of televised matches in which players are running on empty to get through just another meaningless affair. Such spectacles do not reflect well on anyone. Living in hotels and bolting up and down the country is the way my generation did it, but times have changed.

Some may question why consideration has to be given to the counties at all, particularly when strong first-class cricket is played in South Africa and Australia in empty grounds. Nobody bothers to turn up, because the sole purpose of their domestic teams is to provide cricketers for their international sides. Contrast that to England, where the sole purpose of our cricket board appears to be to provide cricket, and therefore income, for eighteen counties. I can fully appreciate Giles Clarke, as the chairman of the ECB, protecting what he has got because that is his job, it is what he was elected to office for, and you would expect him to do no less. But from somewhere there needs to be an alternative vision, because we may just have to dismantle everything to embrace all the other stuff happening in the cricket world.

By the same token, if Mr Lalit Modi and his fello revolutionaries acknowledged Test cricket's primacy he would get far more kudos and support for his ventures from a generally distrustful British public. It was not until its third season that the IPL began to make any impact over here at all – it is still minimal judging by the lack of people who talk to me about it in comparison to other forms of the game or Premier League football – and I am sure the Indians view our market as important for their baby's growth. My opinion is that we need them and they need us, so it's a shame the powerbrokers did not negotiate more mutually beneficial time slots and availability agreements on the top players from the off. At the moment cricket has got a lot of plates in the air, and we have to make sure we prevent the ones that truly are important to us from smashing.

Chapter 10

Whichever era you are from, there is no doubt in my mind that Test cricket is, was and always will be the pinnacle of our great game. I have certainly not seen anything to alter this opinion despite the fast-paced modernisation of cricket in the 21st century. We have to do all we can to preserve its position, to cherish its idiosyncrasies and move it on with the times.

These lads who play at the highest level now are the custodians of Test match cricket, just as their predecessors were before them. It has always been the case that the players of any given era – from the great Sir Donald Bradman, going through to Peter May, Tom Graveney and Colin Cowdrey, then on to Dennis Lillee, the Chappell brothers, Sir Viv Richards, Steve Waugh and Sachin Tendulkar, take on the role of custodians. All the greats through the decades, all the way up to Andrew Strauss, Kevin Pietersen, Ricky Ponting and M.S. Dhoni as modern-day cricketers, protect its integrity with their on-field performances and general conduct.

From all my regular dealings with contemporary players, I am glad to report that I get the distinct and heart-warming impression that, while they recognise that limited-overs cricket is an absolute necessity, which provides excitement and draws crowds around the globe, they retain the belief that the true examination of ability is provided by Test match cricket. Cut through the glitz and razzmatazz of a 20-over show and what is underneath? There is not much substance. It is fabulous entertainment, but scores and analyses are remembered for about as long as a game lasts. What a contrast then to the true marker of a player's quality – a Test. Each individual is still judged by naked statistics: the volume of runs he scores and the amount of wickets he takes. Forget what scores you've got elsewhere; how have you done in Test cricket? If you are a Test match batsman, how many hundreds have you made? If you're a bowler, how many five-fers have you taken? In series like the Ashes and England against South Africa it is still five days of massive physical and emotional slog, and the response you get from the players is fantastic.

Oh, and has anybody tried buying tickets for an Ashes match recently? Anyone involved in the epic 2005 series and the small screen follow-up of 2009 will always talk Ashes cricket. There is no contest in cricket which comes close to the tradition and rivalry associated with Anglo-Aussie battles. Andrew Flintoff existed for nothing else after three career-extending ankle operations. His body was wrecked but he somehow got himself up for one last Test hurrah, and played his part. With each appearance his physical condition waned – he is such a big unit and speaking technically his front foot comes down sideways, so there was an enormous amount of strain going over his ankles and his knees and down his back

– but he kept on pounding in. Whatever else he has achieved, people will remember Andrew Flintoff for his efforts in two Ashes-winning teams.

If you want evidence of Test cricket's greatness beyond our shores, then it is out there. Just think about a box-office player like Virender Sehwag, of India, who is wonderful on the eye in all forms of the game, and wherever he is playing. Forget all his other career landmarks, though, because this guy managed two triple hundreds in Test matches – before any of his compatriots managed one – and still wants more, as he proved when he slammed 293 at better than a run a ball against Sri Lanka. That tells you exactly how good a batsman he is.

I know that Chris Gayle, the West Indies captain, has muttered that he would not be too sad if Test cricket died, and that Twenty20 is his bag. But he is wrong to think that he will be judged on his performances in the short stuff. He will be judged as a Test match player, and judged to be a fantastic Test match player at that. To be able to play the way he did against Australia in Perth in 2009–10 in a proper time game and celebrate a hundred in just 70 balls, the fifth fastest in Test history, pushing the Aussies so close in a three-match series in the process, far outweighs what he has done elsewhere. Yes, he scored a hundred in a flash in the first World Twenty20, but his Test innings was far superior – because of the intensity, the quality of the opposition and the circumstances it came in. We all like to go in and swing from the hip, and sometimes it's your day, so you can just have a lot of fun. But in a Test situation you have to contend with three slips and a gully, as the new ball zips about, then keep your wits about you as the field drops back. Not that that will have flustered him. He's a pretty cool chap – have you seen the way he dresses, by the way? – and relies on the same laid-back approach whenever he plays. Like Sehwag, he does not rein in his attacking intent, and with his phenomenal eye and power, that means he can be just as destructive in the proper stuff.

Despite conjecture to the contrary, Test cricket, for my money, remains in a safe place. Particularly in England. You only have to sift through Sky Sports' inbox or my Twitter account to understand where I am coming from. The number of people that email or tweet is quite unbelievable. People love to chat about it, to have their two-pennorth on everything from team selection to the state of the pitch, and to them it is deadly serious stuff. You can have a bit of fun with the one-dayers and take the Michael out of somebody in 20-over cricket, but the responses you get about Test cricket are voluminous, passionate and informed.

Some might ask whether Test cricket has lost its intrigue in the modern era. Not a bit of it, on the evidence of the matches I witnessed as the Noughties gave way to the Teenies. A game is never over until the very end, which is a contrast to what often occurs in the limited-overs stuff. You only have to think of the trio of matches that England had no right to draw in the opening twelve months of Andrew Strauss's captaincy, firstly the Ashes Test in Cardiff and then two against South Africa at Centurion and Newlands. By rights they should have lost all three games, but the willpower and in some cases professional bloody-mindedness not to lose got them through.

What a wonderful idiosyncrasy of our great sport that a team can be clinging on, nine wickets down, one ball away from defeat, for a substantial period of time, and finish up feeling like winners! It is the very essence of what makes the game so special. The test in 'Test match' being exactly what it says on the tin. 'Can you fulfil all the criteria of beating us in any given conditions over the next five days?' That's the question. Teams pose it every time they take the field, and England have shown under the leadership of the Strauss–Andy Flower alliance that it can be a very big ask. Determination to avoid defeat can be as important over the course of a series as the killer instinct required for victory. Never was that more apparent to me than when big Angus Fraser showed some stiff upper lip against South Africa at Old Trafford in 1998. That summer we won at Trent Bridge and Headingley to take the five-match series 2–1, the best result during my time as England coach, but without the rearguard action in Manchester we would have been two down, and my view would be quite different.

The noughts on the end of Indian Premier League cheques can prove awfully distracting, I am sure, but when I have talked to England players with years remaining of their twenties, let alone their careers – who have been struggling for form – their focus is on one thing. They are striving to play at the highest level and improve their performances upon the greatest stage. When Alastair Cook had a bad trot in late 2009, his anxiety to work out how to play, how to get back into nick, showed what Test cricket meant to him. You can only surmise the feeling of achievement, against the backdrop of his struggles, when he hit his tenth Test hundred in that crushing victory over South Africa in Durban. When Ian Bell was dropped from the team in the Caribbean in early 2009, his total dedication went into getting back into the Test XI. It wasn't a case of settling for being in the one-day squad or looking to do well in other formats. He was in search of the runs to earn a recall – because that Test status is a crucial measure for all the forms of the game. Your profile at Test level will send you into one-day cricket and into Twenty20 cricket. For English cricketers, it is still what provides you with a platform.

My time on that platform amounted to a little more than eight months, but it was a time I will always cherish. I felt immensely proud when I made my Test match début. I knew that I was playing well for Lancashire, and it was a real feeling of achievement to have got to the stage to which I had aspired since the age of 15 and to be playing for my country. Even from that age it was drummed into you that if you wanted to play international cricket it was hundreds you would be judged on. Not 70s and 80s, because those scores won't force anyone to consider you for the next level, but hundreds. I didn't play much for England, and my entire Test career took place between June 1974 and the end of January 1975, but the fact that I achieved what I set out to do meant something.

There was no greater feeling than in my second appearance, against India at Edgbaston, a match which provided a classic moment that I still love watching television replays of now. It was the moment that I celebrated a double hundred in just my second Test innings. If I had been transported back in a TARDIS I might have done things differently when I got a sneaky inside edge to midwicket for the single to bring up my 200. The modern player celebrates in order to be seen, and they all have their own ways of doing so, whether it be glove-punching, taking the helmet off, looking to the heavens, tapping the bat to every stand in the ground, holding the sponsors' logos to the cameras because it will guarantee a bob or two coming in, bear-hugging your mate at the other end, or whatever. In comparison, my moment was as flat as the pitch we were playing on. If Mike Denness hadn't declared, I would still be in now. India had no bowling and they had given up really when, thanks to the leg-side squirt, I ran down towards the pavilion at Edgbaston. Chuffed to bits, I lifted my bat to some polite applause, nothing more, and one voice boomed out from the handclaps: 'How much f——ing longer?'

Not long, as it happened, as the declaration came with me unbeaten on 214. I knew my team-mates appreciated my efforts in becoming only the fourth man in Test history to spend an entire match on the field – though it wasn't for the reasons one might expect. It was because they were all glued to the telly and the Wimbledon championships, to be exact. John Edrich was due in at number five, but at every break he would say, 'You keep going, I don't want to go out there, I'm watching the tennis.' I naturally followed the instructions of a senior pro. Things certainly moved at a more sedate pace in those days. A world apart from the manic celebrations of the modern game. Michael Slater, bless him, was like a whirling dervish when he got a hundred, careering around the ground, and who can forget Tino Best's first international wicket? He lay on the floor kicking his legs skyward in an overflow of joy. He'd only got one chuffing wicket! But I guess it goes to show that cricket is a lot more instant and emotional now. When Jim Laker took his nineteenth wicket of the match against Australia at Old Trafford in 1956, he just hitched his trousers up, somebody shook hands with him, and he cleared off.

Those were the days when men were men. As it happens, my virility was put into question by a typically ferocious Jeff Thomson in the 1974–5 Ashes series. That winter, when you were in the firing line you took your punishment, you had to, because quite frankly there was no time to get out of the way. We were still playing by the old Australian regulation of eight-ball overs, of course, which meant that a number of times in quick succession the ball would be flying past your nose or throat. No welcoming signal from the umpire that you'd had your share of bumpers for the over in those days. Trouble was, if you got away from Thommo with a single, Dennis Lillee would be lining you up at the other end.

When John Edrich and Dennis Amiss were KO'd at Brisbane, the SOS went out to Colin Cowdrey. He had turned 22 on his first Ashes tour, but that was twenty years previously. Now he was viewed as the man for a crisis, and he roomed with me after joining up with the squad.

Colin was a real ambassador for English cricket, and it was so typical of him to maintain the utmost goodwill and courteousness in the face of heightened Aussie provocation. Various indignities from the opposition's fire-breathing fasties were shrugged off as he unexpectedly resumed his international career. He did so at Perth, on the notoriously quick and bouncy pitch, and, having taken up his customary No. 3 position, soon joined his room-mate out in the heat of battle. Typically, he greeted Thommo with a 'How do you do?' and got the inevitable stare and Exocet directed at his ear lobe in return. The next delivery reared into his rump, but there was not even the hint of a grimace. Between overs he was the essence of jollity, and his mood definitely had its effect on me as we combined in a stand of 55 for the second wicket. He chuckled his way through the barrage of bumpers before we were separated one short of three figures. I also fell one short of a milestone mark – an Ashes 50.

We got the chance to resume our alliance at the start of the second innings (after Brian Luckhurst joined the casualty list) and once again were good for a half-century stand. Shortly after registering it, however, we were separated, not by a mode of dismissal but what in dressing-room parlance is known as a crisis in the Balkans. And it was my crisis. The thing is, I should not even have been there to take my blow because I had already been dismissed, only the Australians clearly hadn't recognised the fact. In Thommo's first over of the innings, as I tried to avoid a short delivery, the ball ran off the face of the bat and was clutched comfortably by wicket-keeper Rod Marsh. Straightforward enough, or so I thought, as I started to tuck my bat under my arm and turn towards the pavilion. I have always been an advocate of walking but, for that to happen, your opponents have got to appeal first. It sank in very quickly that the Aussies had missed the nick when Ian Chappell, rather than get excited, offered a cursory 'well bowled' from slip – so I stayed. Retribution was served, however, when I was unbeaten on 17 in a score of 52 without loss. This Thomson delivery struck me flush in the box, completely changing its shape in the process, and left me doubled up in pain. After assessing the boys in the barracks, I was led from the field and did not take any further part in that day's play.

The next morning, still feeling violated in certain areas, I enquired where in the order captain Mike Denness would now like me to bat. 'Next,' he instructed. So, when great roars filled the air just a couple of minutes into play, I picked up my bat and gloves, one of the overnight duo surely having been dismissed rather than having launched the ball into the baying crowd. Back out in the gladiatorial arena, I might have guessed what Thommo was going to serve up as his first offering, but dealing with his missiles was always easier in theory than in practice, and so I was struck for the second time in as many deliveries, this time in the throat. As I prised myself from the canvas for the compulsory eight count, he welcomed my return to the fight with: 'G'day, ya Pommie b———' Having resumed my effort with the score on 106 for 2, I could take some pride in extending my personal time at the crease to six hours in the match which, given the conditions and quality of opponent, was quite an achievement.

And the Star Prize Is ...

Landmarks in cricket, big or small, are celebrated in a multitude of ways, some bordering on the utterly bizarre. None more so than when Makhaya Ntini played his 100th Test match, the first black South African cricketer to do so. It was such a historic event that the whole week at Centurion was about him, and it was a terrific tribute that preceded the series opener as they let him take the field on his own ahead of his own South Africa team-mates and England. He was accompanied by his young son Thando, and they had a lovely cuddle on the outfield, to a huge ovation. Over the next few days, the match turned into a cracking contest, dominated by the home side, and the ingredients ultimately cooked up a dramatic conclusion. With tension in the air and just one wicket required by South Africa for victory on the final evening, Graeme Smith recognised the romance of the occasion and threw the ball to Ntini for the final over of the match. There was to be no fairytale ending, but it was a fitting gesture and would have gone down in the sporting annals had it panned out as Smith dreamt.

As it was, Ntini had to settle for two wickets in the match, the first of which was keenly anticipated, because Ntini had a tie-up with South Africa's Test match sponsors Castle, and they had promised everyone in the ground a free pint when their man took his first wicket. Now that's my kind of sponsorship! It added a dimension to England's first innings and also caused a few hoots up in our commentary box. Each time he began his approach to the crease, Ntini was being roared on by the parched locals – it can get pretty hot on the High Veldt, you know – and even the Barmy Army's most vocal were prepared to trade a wicket for a refreshing cold lager. So the moment came, and they had not had to wait long. Alastair Cook got a thick edge to a beauty and the ball flew to the dependable A.B. de Villiers at third slip. But the chance went begging, and you should have heard the boos when the crowd missed out on the booze.

Anyway, after all the excitement of England saving the Test, the post-match presentation ceremony provided the chance for one final hurrah for Makhaya. All the advertising clobber was hoisted up and SABC, the local broadcasters, got their logos emblazoned at the back of the stage. Ian Bishop interviewed the two captains, Graeme Smith and Andrew Strauss, and Graeme Swann was called up for his obligatory chat after being nominated as man of the match by Roshan Mahanama. Then came the moment everyone had waited for – the special presentation to Makhaya Ntini on his 100th Test match. You could see this object protruding behind Bishop as he did his thing – 'This has been a hard-fought draw' …

'England got out of jail' – and it began to cause quite a bit of mirth as the scene was being set. 'Please step forward, Makhaya,' Bishop requested. Would you credit it? In the land of diamonds and gold, how were they recognising one of their all-time greats? What were they giving him to commemorate his career achievement? Well, I was left aghast. They gave him a f——ing fridge!

What the heck is someone supposed to do with a ruddy great refrigerator? People hooted with laughter at the image of Ntini lugging this thing on his back as he checked into Johannesburg airport. But just who comes up with such left-field prizes? It reminds me of the one presented to Mark Butcher for being best turned out in the match between England and the Australian Cricket Board's President's XI back in 1998–9. His reward … a trouser press. It might not have been such a bad thing, for Butch always liked to look sharp, but you have to remember that the Lilac Hill match was the traditional tour opener. This match was at the end of October and we weren't going home until February, so he was forced to cart this thing all over Australia for the best part of four months.

At the end of England's first tour of Bangladesh in 2003, a man of the series was named for both sides, and the Bangladeshi selection Mashrafe Mortaza was given by way of recognition a second-hand Hero Honda! This motorbike was covered in shit and all sorts of stuff, but he got on it and rode around the boundary, a big smile daubed across his face, proud as punch. As far as post-match celebrations go, it doesn't get any weirder than that.

Tests for the Future

People talk about a threat to Test match cricket, but I don't see genuine threats, really. To me it is here to stay. Yes, it does puzzle me some years when some teams don't play a lot of it. New Zealand and Pakistan can seemingly go through a year without a single match, and South Africa did not play one between March and December 2009, which seemed to be too big a gap for my money. That doesn't seem to be satisfactory at all. The task that the stakeholders in the game have got is to ensure year on year that there is a balance between one-day internationals, Twenty20 and Test matches. The iconic series have to stay that way.

Yes, we are losing Tests here and there to fit in one-day series, but as long as these series remain they will retain that special edge. There is work to be done to ensure the balance is right between the different forms and that everybody plays their share of Test match cricket. And this is not going to get better overnight. We know that India drive the game and that Twenty20 is now very much a part of the Indian scene, but the organisers of these tournaments have to be made fully aware that Test match cricket has to be played, because it is *the* game, the serious game that has always been played, stretching back to the turn of the 19th century. It is number one. It is traditional and was the seed which germinated into financial fruit. The rest of it gives us money and entertainment, but the players will be judged by what happens in Test match cricket.

If you look at the Barmy Army, a huge organisation founded on fun, they come to Test match cricket. That is where their camaraderie takes place. They enjoy themselves, they dress like extras from *Nightmare on Elm Street*, imbibe all day long, and sing until they're hoarse. But they are aficionados of the sport. You don't see many of them at one-day games. Their bag, their forte is Test match cricket. There are thousands of 'em touring the world with England every winter and that should tell the authorities something. Personally I wouldn't do down any form of the game. I am quite adamant about what Twenty20 means and its role in family entertainment and attracting teenagers. One-day international cricket is a good game – admittedly in need of constant review to tweak those middle overs – which produces some massive scores now because of the quality of the players. But the real passion in England is reserved for the five-day game.

Contrary to what folk might think, the television age is not dictating cricket's progress. Of course, I can only speak from the perspective of Sky, and what we do, but it has always been the authorities, whether it be the England and Wales Cricket Board or the International Cricket Council, who come up with the formula of cricket to be played, i.e. decide on the number of Tests, when they're scheduled, and how many one-day internationals or Twenty20 contests fit into the calendar. Sky then set about scheduling cricket as part of their overall output. Some of us commentators have gone to our bosses, suggesting that we be more proactive, more involved in the fixture landscape. We've said: 'Why don't we ask for this? Why don't we ask for that?' But credit to our bosses, because their response has been unequivocal. They are adamant that they bid for the product that is put on the table, England's international fixtures for example, nothing more. We do not get involved in the format of the tournaments, the number of games, or anything like that. There are many things you might like to see improved, but Sky have always resisted the temptation to have direct influence on the product. To Sky it is all rather straightforward. If it ain't broke, don't fix it.

Where television has to play a part, though, is in decision-making at the highest level. I am massively in favour of the use of technology to aid umpires, and I am sure it is something that will prove successful in the long term. Without doubt, the decision review system is good in principle, but it was always going to take a while to smooth out the flaws. The biggest of these is self-inflicted to some extent. If you are going to advocate the use of technology, then you have got to go the whole hog. The technological aids have to be universal, and it is no good bringing in a review system if you do not have the necessary gadgetry to support it. I sent a couple of emails communicating these points to the relevant people at the ICC following England's series in South Africa during the 2009–10 winter. It was the limited technology available to the officials that caused the disharmony, but the match officials received the flak.

The system will not work unless you have got technology aids such as Hot Spot and an ultra-motion camera. Forget Snickometer, which is specifically a viewer aid that involves lining up pictures with sound; it is the Hot Spot that provides conclusive proof of where impact has been made by the ball. And ultra motion can be almost as effective. Those two things are essential to the whole thing moving forward. As a member of the panel who chose the elite umpires, along with Srinivasaraghavan Venkataraghavan, Ranjan Madugalle and David Richardson, I felt strongly that it was limitations in the local broadcasters' visual and audio extras, not limitations in the umpires' ability to make judgement calls after observing replays, that caused the rumpus. You have to have the best technology available around the world, it has to be universal, and you have to have a good feed, on a clear flat screen. Crucially, Daryl Harper did not have that in South Africa and was pilloried when he acted in good faith.

A major problem is the disparity between different broadcasters' budgets in the global game. Some production teams have invested in the advanced technology, while others cannot because of economic constraints. This is costly equipment, and the failure to get uniform implementation of the new ICC-approved system as soon as it was rubber-stamped was partly because of a dispute about how the use of technology would be funded. TV companies arguably have the right to charge for the use of their equipment, so the best solution would seem to be for the ICC to shell out for it. Otherwise you end up with decisions being a postcode lottery dependent on whether your match is in Chester-le-Street or Chittagong.

In addition to the array of aids, you also need a competent operator in the trucks. Without a top-level, impartial engineer you have created a possible anomaly. I am not saying this has happened, but there could be a suspicion, if your engineer is fanatical about the home team, that he would be selective when operating the replays. I know how easy it would be for him to hide an essential angle. All he would need to say is: 'A more definitive replay is not available.' No further questions would be asked. I remember that when the international authorities brought in the use of TV replays to adjudge line decisions, Sky Sports' Australian producer John Gayleard said: 'If it's Ricky Ponting or Steve Waugh, I won't be giving you the right angle, I can f——ing tell you that.' He was having a bit of fun, of course, but joking aside, it does open up the possibility of foul play.

I do not see any value in applying half a theory. If the technology available is not good enough, not extensive enough or not readily available across all territories, there is no point in attempting to enforce its use. Rather than carry on with limited resources, I would prefer to see the ICC wait until such time as the technology is up to scratch throughout the circuit, and all Test-playing nations and their relevant broadcasters agree on its use. But the raw statistics will undoubtedly lead the ICC to view it another way: even allowing for all the teething problems in South Africa, they will point to the increased number of correct decisions. Factoring in the big clangers, including Graeme Smith escaping a caught behind just 15 runs into a Test hundred at Wanderers – because the sound on the video feed was not up to required capacity – the ICC's research showed that the officials were still right 97 per cent of the time, compared with 91 per cent when umpires are left to make the call on the field of play. So, even allowing for all the problems, they will argue that you are still gaining 6 per cent improvement.

Another source of frustration is the general lack of communication to the spectators, both in the stands and their armchairs, about what is transpiring. They must get confused as to what is going on, and the longer it takes for a decision to be reached, the greater the annoyance. They can see something is being replayed, but the third umpire should, in my opinion, be talking through the decision-making process step by step, as they do in American sports, so that those watching are kept informed.

I would have preferred the players to be out of the loop when it came to decisions being challenged, because I believe their participation leaves umpires feeling more vulnerable than if they chose to review their own calls. Once upon a time the umpire's decision was final, but that isn't the case now. To me, the technology should be endorsing their decisions, or at the very worst advising them to overturn their original judgement because of 'conclusive evidence' seen by their television replay colleague. I've been an umpire, standing 22 yards away when a batsman pushes forward and the ball hits him above the knee roll – it's so hard to be sure if it's hitting or going over the top, and the rule of thumb always used to be that an umpire should give the benefit of the doubt to the batsman. Hawk Eye showing balls clipping the bails has never been helpful in persuading people that this should remain the case, so I was heavily in favour of the decision to factor in a probability ratio, allowing a percentage of leeway to uphold the umpire's call if replays showed the perceived impact to be on the outer edges of the stumps.

When it comes to it, I also think players could do more for themselves. We should remember that this is a sport for gentlemen, and with that in mind batsmen should be more willing to walk. I am sick of seeing players standing there, gambling on a decision that might be overturned, hoping to get away with an injustice, i.e. to cheat their opponent. It's a bit like a golfer moving his ball in the rough – it's just foul play. People are so desperate to do well that they see the circumvention of machines' evidence as acceptable. Perhaps I am old-fashioned, but I would like to see players toddle off if they've nicked it behind, because otherwise their integrity will be questioned by the replays. It is certainly an attitude I would try to drum into any youngster taking up the game. That is how I was taught, and if I'd failed to walk and the captain found out, I wouldn't have been picked for the next game. Some people say they are playing for higher stakes nowadays, but I would totally contest that. Nobody was playing for higher stakes than me and my contemporaries. We were playing to put bread on the table.

I anticipate the referral system being tweaked regularly over the coming years, so that it can be applied as successfully and as smoothly as possible for all concerned. After all, the idea of it is to improve the game – not slow it down unnecessarily. But I want a much tighter control of players in the light of its implementation. Power must be given back to the on-field umpires, because my fear is that reviewing has challenged their authority rather too robustly. It is fairly straightforward when a player wants to review a decision – the third umpire is asked to scour the replay and advise to either uphold or overturn the original call. But what I have a problem with is a player or players questioning what comes out of the review. That should not be allowed to happen.

It might be a natural inclination to want to know why the challenge you have made has not been successful, and you might feel aggrieved, but the guy in the middle should not be harangued. That is something that has got to be tightened up. The umpire has to have more power to dismiss their protestations, so that when the answer comes back, the on-field official simply relays the decision and play continues. As things stand, he has suddenly got players in his face, and that is a change in the game that really riles me. It is not up to him to justify the final outcome. The matter is closed as soon as the

TV umpire has consulted replays with the tools available to him, and this is an issue I think we need to get hold of.

My solution would be very straightforward, and very familiar to followers of other ball sports. I have always advocated yellow and red cards in cricket. In my opinion, it is a very good idea and one which would allow us to get back some of the discipline of the game. I know I am in a minority in pushing for this, and I know most cricket people do not want to replicate soccer, but we need to show that in cricket the umpire is in complete command. It is something I have recommended to the ICC, not in any official capacity but as a genuine lover of the sport with an interest in its future. My concern is that there is so much cricket on TV from around the world these days that a dangerous pattern could quickly emerge in which players are challenging umpires as a matter of course. Now that gives the sport a horrific global image.

The impact of that behaviour is not just felt within the confines of the ground at which it takes place but on television screens all over the world. And I am not the only one concerned at on-field conduct. I have received many tweets from mothers and fathers, and coaches at grassroots levels, who are appalled by it. Because the natural knock-on is that their kids are seeing it happen and are now questioning umpires too. Or if they haven't yet, they soon will. I know that it's happening in the leagues, because I have played club cricket recently and witnessed it at first hand.

There needs to be a stricter control of the players by the umpires. The ability to produce a yellow card would enhance the official's authority and in turn act as a deterrent to players. Receive two in an innings and you're off – out of the game. If your behaviour warrants a straight red card then you are out for three matches, as in football. My reason for pushing for this is not that I want to see cards brandished left, right and centre. Completely the opposite actually – because, in my opinion, they would never be used. With the threat of being forced out of a match hanging over them, players would shut up straight away.

There is evidence that this abhorrent act of challenging an official's judgement is happening even with the Under-11s, and that is just totally wrong. Umpiring should be a fun job, particularly at that level. In the junior game you aren't just standing there, you are partly educating the players. You are helping them along over the course of a game. If they're getting in your ear as they do in junior soccer – I have seen it with my grandson's team – it is eroding your power. I am not comfortable with that. I think that there is a danger of the umpire being persecuted, and that's worrying because we need officials, especially at junior level. The guy whose seven-year-old son is just getting into cricket may be dissuaded from thinking about doing the job. Why should he want to take that crap? We have to sort that out, because without willing officials games do not take place.

When I umpired, my ethos was simple. You had to get on with the players around you. You had to be on the same wavelength and let the game flow. If anything untoward happened in my three years at first-class level, the bottom line was that the team is the responsibility of the captain. I would pull the captain over for a word. 'I am not happy with so-and-so's behaviour. Now either you tell him to straighten himself out or I'll get very interested,' I would tell him. It worked every time. You could see the captain have his word, reasserting his own authority, and the culprit would come across and say sorry. 'That's all right, let's move on,' I would always say.

One world-class international batter, who will remain nameless, created a real scene in a game at Taunton, where I was umpiring with John Harris. John gave this particular batsman out and the decision was met with an initial refusal to walk and a distinct shake of the head. After the day's play, John asked me to stay in our quarters because he was going to pull the bloke in question in for a talking-to. He then went to the captain and asked for the perpetrator to be sent in. This lad was ashen-faced when he entered. 'I'm really sorry,' were the first words he spoke. 'I don't know what I was doing. I would like to apologise.' John accepted it, agreed to put the incident behind us all, but warned him: 'Don't ever do that again.' That was the power an umpire used to exercise in private, not even on the field. We need to get some of that power back, and the lads will definitely enjoy their time on the field more if we do. I like to remind people that there are big, hairy-arsed rugby players who could readily snap that little bloke in green in two should they so wish, but when he is blowing his whistle he is God. That is something that marks rugby out as a sport to be respected.

Whatever happened to 'It's just not cricket'? The essence of cricket should be that it is a tough sport played to the maximum but ultimately a game for gentlemen. For a while now I've had the idea of a system of cautioning players, and I think it would work. It would be good for spectators as well. They don't want to see players stepping out of line. You accept that cricket, although non-contact, is quite a verbal sport. But you cannot condone vindictiveness towards the umpire, because this is the bloke that rules the roost. At least, that is what he did in my playing days, and that was how we were brought up to think, and everybody got on just fine. The erosion of this power cannot be allowed to continue, so let's hand it back and therefore uphold the traditions of the game. A game is ultimately in his hands, but as player power has developed we have let these officials down. Yet I am convinced that the players would enjoy the game more if they just got on with it, without the confrontation with the umpire – with the attitude that you will win some, and you will lose some.

When we were playing we had some really great characters standing on the county circuit – Charlie Elliott, Sid Buller, Dickie Bird, Arthur Jepson, Bill Alley and Cec Pepper, to name but a few. Some of them were real disciplinarians that you dared not step on. Nowadays, with more matches than ever on TV, any ill-discipline is immediately under the microscope due to the presence of approximately thirty cameras around the ground. Any act of petulance is picked up immediately and often bypasses the blokes in charge. Whatever you say or do will be on screen in an instant. There is no hiding place if you overstep the mark.

Now one of the greatest passages of cricket anyone could ever wish to see was between Mike Atherton and Allan Donald at Trent Bridge in 1998. It was simply magnificent, and it involved no scorn being directed at the umpire. It was a full-on duel between the two of them, all triggered by Donald claiming Atherton had nicked one and the batsman standing his ground. Donald really had his dander up, and the spell that he put in and the determination of Atherton made for real theatre.

I would love to umpire again now. I don't know if they still do it, but I would expect to go into the dressing-rooms before the game, just as we always used to, and tell them what I was looking for. 'Let's have a good day,' I'd say. 'Hope all goes well, lads. This is what I will not tolerate, I will tell you now. Bad behaviour is a no-no. I will not have foul language or anything towards me. Come in after the game and I will discuss it as long as you like. But not on the field. Hope you are all happy with that. Enjoy your day. Bye.'

Chapter 11

CROWDED STREETS, LONELY HEARTS, ALARM CLOCKS AND SNAKES

Being on tour in Asia can be a lot of fun but it is quite drastically different from being at home, or wintering in Australia or New Zealand. The streets of the major cities teem with people, most of whom are head over heels in love with our great game. Cricket is their equivalent of our Premier League football and everyone has an opinion on it. It is a game that is played on the roadside while life continues around it – buses chock-full of folk whizz past the batsman's outside edge like searing leg-cutters. In some cases it is their life.

Remember the game of car cricket? It was a game designed to pass the time on long journeys – before your mobile phone consigned it to history – and in which you would score runs every time you passed a pub. One run was credited for every leg contained in the establishment's name. The Fox, for example, would be a four, while the Coach and Horses would be worth eight. There were always arguments about how many you got for the Duke of York's Men, but you would be struggling to avoid the follow-on if your opponent claimed the full 20,000 for it. If the name featured only inanimate objects, each counted as a single, so for the Rose and Crown you got two. If you saw a pub with arms or heads in its title, you were out. It certainly passed the hours in the days before the coming of the motorways.

Well, in India there is a similar game, but instead of pubs you use bikes and motorbikes. Every time you see one with more than one person on it you get the relevant number of runs for the hangers-on. Every time someone rides solo you are out (which means many long innings), while the carrying of objects while riding is the equivalent of a boundary. My best sixes have been a 30-foot ladder and a garden shed. I kid you not.

India can be manic, to say the least, but that in itself presents you with a lot of fun. When you sift through the chaos, you can unearth some truly wonderful comic moments. Indian names crack me up on occasion. Delhi's long-serving chief minister was called Sheila Dikshit. Now I am not sure I would be able to take any of her speeches seriously. Then there is the intriguingly named Dum Phuk restaurant in Bangalore. Not sure you would get away with that one in Cheadle Hulme high street. And their newspapers deliver some corking misspellings and *faux pas*. How about this from the Lonely Hearts column in *The Times of India*: 'Dear doctor, I am 18 years old and have been masturbating for 18 months. I am taking medication for anxiety and finding difficulties. When will I get my form back?' They do a nice take on innocence but, with one of the biggest economies in the world, they also have some rather groundbreaking sales ideas. I was in howls when I saw a shop in Chennai with a sign in the window which read: 'Buy one shoe, get one free.'

In some parts of the cricketing world, communication can be a problem. One year, while staying at the Sheraton in Islamabad, Pakistan, I wanted to get on line. Technology has always moved forward quickly on the subcontinent, more often than not outstripping progress back home, and I had taken my laptop with me, so I could surf the Internet in my hotel room. As was customary in most hotels at the time, you needed to ring down to reception to acquire the username and password to gain Wifi access. Normally that would be no problem. They're cricket mad in these parts, so when the teams and the media circus roll in, the staff usually make a real fuss of you.

'Yes, Mr Lloyd, I am getting username and password. Are you getting good pen and paper?'

'Yes, I've got good pen and paper,' I said.

'Right, username is SHERATON – 0 – 0 – 8. Password, now, you have good pen and paper? Listen very carefully for password on good pen and paper.'

'I've got the good pen and paper, so you go for it,' I added.

'OK. The password is C for Henry, V for William, Wee for Victor, S for Thomas and B for Iqbal.'

'Eh? I think I will bring my computer down there, on reflection, and let you input it all, if you don't mind.'

These tours can bring everyone together. For westerners these places can be interesting, but also demanding – especially somewhere like Bangladesh. As a country it does not have the social attractions of India or even Pakistan. So at times you have to make your own entertainment. While we were in Dhaka during the 2003–4 tour, Paul Allott and I organised a quiz night for everyone on the trip. All the players, all the backroom staff, all the press men turned up in anticipation of a rare social night, and a big crowd piled into the hotel room we had booked for the evening. As we set out the ground rules – the usual thing, teams of four, silly prizes and a bit of a laugh – it became apparent that two of the players were late. And it was Andrew Flintoff and Steve Harmison, of course, aka Tweedle-Dumb and Tweedle-Dumber.

Needless to say there was the usual chorus of moans, groans, oohs, aahs and challenging of the quizmaster as we called out the questions. But the quiz was settled with the tabloid team, as they so often do, scooping the main prize. When it came to the crunch, they were the only ones able to name all of the Nolan sisters. After the prizes had been distributed, just two remained, these huge mosque alarm clocks. Now these things were unbelievably loud – and not just in appearance – as Walt and I had discovered after purchasing them at the local market. When they blurted out their call to prayer wake-up wail, crikey did they hit some decibels! So, appropriately in the circumstances, we made a special presentation to the two lads who were late, and after much chuckling, went off into the night for a cup of coffee.

I suspected nothing when I went to bed an hour or so later, but at 4 o'clock in the morning I received an almighty jolt. I was abruptly awoken by this horrendous noise emanating from somewhere in my room. Disturbingly, I recognised the unearthly din. It transpired that Flintoff and Harmison had gone to reception during my coffee trek pretending to be me – security, what security? – got the key card, and ploughed through my room, pulling all the furniture away and concealing these mosque clocks in obscure places. The first one was wedged behind this humungous telly, not dissimilar to what lads and lasses of Lancashire back in the 1950s might have gathered around at a Saturday matinee showing. As I came out of my deep sleep, I twigged: 'It's that bloody alarm clock!' So I am awake at four in the morning with this flippin' noise that I simply could not stop reverberating off the walls. At first I couldn't work out where it was coming from, but as I came to my senses I was able to pinpoint the source. Unfortunately, there was not a lot I could do about it, with the TV being so heavy, so I just sat and listened to this screeching cacophony, which was unleashed every five minutes.

Then, suddenly, after what seemed an eternity (or three-quarters of an hour more likely) the battery must have gone, because the incessant cacophony stopped. Hallelujah. But for maximum effect, the other one began its stint at five o'clock, positioned somewhere even further back among the room's furniture. I later found out they had not only pulled the telly forward but ripped it out of its housing and shoved the second clock in behind the unit for good measure. It really was a two-man operation to get this furniture away from the wall, and they are two big, strapping lads, so what chance had I got? All attempts to retrieve the clock were futile, so I was up for two hours praying, appropriately enough, for it to stop. The next morning my pair of tormentors came down for breakfast and, playing to the same crowd that had ribbed them the night before, sniggered in unison: 'You get your early morning call, then?'

However, the best prankster I ever came across was yonks ago, back in my playing days – an Australian called Mick Malone, who joined us as Lancashire's overseas player in 1979.

He played for Western Australia, and had already been capped for Australia. He came with a reputation as a good cricketer, but when overseas players arrive you also want to know about them as people, and everyone tries to size the new boy up. What sort of lad is he? What's his character like? Are his family coming over? That kind of thing.

He was personable enough from the very start, making a real impression with his jovial attitude, and it was during his initial conversations that he dripped what was to become his career gag into the team's consciousness. 'We keep reptiles at home,' he said, casually. 'Our pet snake is over with us but it's being kept in quarantine in Manchester for a month.' The dressing-room was aghast. 'What, you keep snakes?' He went on to explain that there was just one in particular that was special to his family, and for that reason they had decided to bring it over.

Every now and again, as he was getting to know the lads, he would refer to the anticipated release of this snake. 'Just a fortnight to go now' or 'Be picking the big fella up next Tuesday' and so forth. Finally, on the eve of his big day, he declared: 'I'll be a bit late tomorrow, lads, I am picking the big fella up.' Well, when tomorrow came around we were all a bit apprehensive, in anticipation of him bringing his prized asset into the sanctity of our changing-room.

I had been designated as Mick's room-mate for away trips, and naturally enough he and I got on like a house on fire. Our relationship meant I was also the first one to meet this reptilian edition to our squad. As I held my breath in antici- pation of a deadly python, Mick produced this rubber monstrosity, which was ridiculously life-like. It could curl, go into a ball and then suddenly expand as if aroused by your presence. Now it was a case of waiting for the right moment to introduce it to the rest of the lads.

At the time we had a lad called Bob Ratcliffe playing for us, a seamer from Accrington who was quite highly strung. Mick happened to be ruled out of a game that week by an elbow injury, and that meant he was on twelfth-man duty. So when Bob called for his sweater to be taken out to the middle, Mick was only too willing to run out with it, and slipped this snake down one of the arms. Having answered his colleague's request with all haste, Mick was legging it back towards the Old Trafford pavilion, when all of a sudden this sweater was hurled to the turf.

Bob was jumping up and down, dancing all over the afore-mentioned garment. Ready for his big moment, Mick dashed back to the middle à la Crocodile Dundee and grabbed hold of hissing Sid as if was it alive and frisky. 'I don't know how he got in there,' Mick declared. 'I never fetched it. Honest.' We remained out on the field, a concoction of giggles and horror, while back in the dressing-room Mick somehow managed to acquire the keys to Bob's locker. He expertly inserted the snake on to the top shelf, so that it rested against the door, ready to spring out, and administer another scare, as soon as Bob opened it.

Later that season, when Dickie Bird was in town, Mick went off to the chefs at Old Trafford and got them in on his act. ''Ere, this famous fella's gonna be here, let's make him something special for his lunch,' Mick told them, handing over the snake to be concealed on one of those grand plates covered by a silver dome, which you see in the plushest eateries.

Dickie was sitting there in his full official's clobber and cap when the waiter arrived with the plate, bowed graciously and declared, 'Compliments of the chef.' He explained how chef was one of his biggest fans and how it was his pleasure to have made him something special. Meanwhile everybody in our team had been telling Dickie the same story. 'That Mick Malone, the chap bowling from your end, is crackers. He's an absolute madman. He keeps a snake, you know?' Well, you can imagine what Dickie's response was. "E's gorra wha'?' he grimaced.

So, having been primed that our reptile friend was around the place, he was presented with this silver service offering. 'Eee, that's nice, eee. Luvverly.' Of course, the second the dome came off the thing moved, it literally sprang into life, and so did Dickie. Straight out of the dining-room, and back into the middle. 'Snake! There's a snake! Snake!' Dickie chuntered, arms akimbo as if directing traffic at Manchester airport.

IN THE BLOOD

Chapter 12

GET 'EM IN!

It is fair to say that the majority of my time is spent in debating chambers. Well, chambers of two varieties to be precise. The Sky Sports commentary box, where I can sit back in a privileged seat and pronounce on world cricketing affairs, and the traditional pub, in which I can wade in on matters of even greater importance, such as Walthamstow losing its dog track, how Luton pipped Hull to become the crappest town in Britain, and Jordan's staying power.

When I am in the UK my *Good Pub Guide* goes everywhere with me in a search for wooden or flag floors, decent pumped ale and a good atmosphere. British pubs have a charm all of their own. You can go in, sit down, mind your own business, or say 'How do?' to a total stranger and start nattering.

Both my work environment and my favourite leisure environment cherish opinion, and it's fair to say I am never short of one. No wonder I feel so at home with microphone or pint in hand. Actually, come to think of it, my opinion isn't cherished at home at all. Unless, of course, it happens to match that of Diana. You know where I'm coming from, don't you, lads?

Funnily enough, those nice gentlemen of the England and Wales Cricket Board and the International Cricket Council have made sure that Mrs Lloyd is one of my rarer dinner companions throughout the year. The saturation of fixture calendars, both domestic and international, means there is not as much leisure time at home as there once was, but following cricket around the globe has its benefits, and has enabled me to make some good pals both inside and outside the game.

In the diminishing downtime between seasons and tours, you can find me in one of my favourite local pubs, indulging in real ale and putting the world to rights. Although talk occasionally reverts to cricket, this is my escapism, a time to indulge in a parallel universe: one full of characters, and I mean characters, who offer me a different perspective from the non-stop merry-go-round that cricket has become.

Whenever I am at home, I am a big fan of 'early doors' down at the Admiral Rodney, my local village pub. There is something so appealing about the evening sup. It is one of the funny quirks of life how regimented 'early doors' can be. Unlike cricket there are no laws of the game to be upheld by its participants, but it has a pretty stringent sense of order nonetheless, with people having their own spots around the bar. Gordon's stool, Bernard's chair, Albert's window are only supposed to be occupied by Gordon, Bernard and Albert. 'I see Tom is sat in the window. Albert must be away,' croaks the landlord, as if keeping a register. 'Ah, Albert's here now … Tom, Albert's here.'

'All right, Albert?' enquires Tom. 'Been keeping it warm for you.'

He immediately vacates the seat, as is expected in this twilight zone between the lunchtime and night crowds. It's tradition. And when someone snuffs it they get a plaque on *their* seat with a suitable inscription: 'In memory of Arthur Sykes. Get 'em in!'

Your positioning is not a random event, it is almost a matter of class as to which half of the pub you occupy. When I moved to the Cheshire village of Prestbury, I was asked on my first visit to the aforementioned boozer where I stood. On the right or on the left? 'On the right,' I innocently replied. Fortunately it was the correct answer. The thespians, sages and retired gentry are on the right, with the young bucks, the working lads, on the left. Young at heart, as I've gained confidence, I've actually tried to be something of a Lib Dem and hover somewhere in the middle. Like Nick Clegg's lot, though, I get totally befuddled at times and don't know which way to turn.

As a non-smoker I generally stay indoors – summer evenings are not what they used to be now that you have to dive back inside for a breath of fresh air. Accommodating those that like a fag with their beer has been a challenge for landlords since the new legislation was brought in during the summer of 2007, and like most pubs, the Admiral now boasts a temporary shelter outside for the gaspers. Jonty, one of my long-standing drinking pals, put one of these up at my other favourite watering hole, The Hesketh, and upon its completion the landlord, Captain Chaos, requested all those using it to hang on to the sides. You see, Jonty's erections don't tend to last very long.

The Admiral Rodney does not have fruit machines, a pool table or music, just good old-fashioned conversation, which, in my opinion, is how a good pub should be. The bar staff actually face you when you walk in and say things like 'Good evening, sir. Is it the usual?' I like that … it's the local. Not like the chain pub in the next village which I have frequented just the once. It was one visit too many and I wish I had never bothered.

I stood for a full quarter of an hour, as if invisible, staring at the backs of two lasses who were engrossed in a conversation about 'Julie'. As I recall, it went something like: 'Julie, right, she saw him again, right, and he was with his wife, right, and Julie said that he said, right, that it wasn't a wedding ring, right, and that he won it at a game of cards in Blackpool.' For brevity's sake, I have condensed the details, but you get the gist of this *ménage à trois*. Anyway, just as I was losing the will to live, Billie-Jo (at least that is what was emblazoned on her pimped-up name tag) swivelled around and barked, 'Yeah?'

I seized my opportunity to order: 'Pint of Badger, please.'

'S'off,' BJ rapped.

'I'll try the Canon then.'

'S'off, too,' she said.

'What cask beers have you then, please?' was my meek and thirsty comeback.

'Lager,' she snapped in agitation.

'But lager isn't a … I'll have a pint of lager, thanks.'

At this point she took on the pose of a contortionist, half facing me and half facing the till, with a hand outstretched behind her back like a true daughter of Norfolk. 'Be two ninety-five,' she said. At no time during the transaction did we make eye contact and the noise from the jukebox made it hard to earwig the most sordid details of Julie's tangled love life thereafter. Call me an old stick, call me a grumpy sod, but for me the local is a place where renditions of 'C'mon Eileen' should never be heard. Unplug the speakers and disarm the bandit.

It's the traditional aspect of pubs that I love. What I want is good bar stools and good ale: the ideal tools for chewing the fat, recapping your day or enjoying a healthy argument. Wherever I am, I like to sample the local brews – never drink anything else. For me, it's Brain's in Cardiff, Shepherd Neame in Kent, Fuller's in London. Whenever I am in the capital, I make a pilgrimage to Soho to the Coach and Horses, where the actor Peter O'Toole used to hang out, as they have excellent hand-pumped beers. Just around the corner, the French House is another favourite haunt. It is steeped in history – Charles de Gaulle drank there with other servicemen who'd escaped France when the Nazis invaded – and as it is technically a French enclave I like to stick to my principles and drink Breton cider. Because of its West End location you'll never fail to spot a familiar actor having a tot. On one of my visits I could not shake a fit of the chuckles because Mark Williams, the fella who played one of the camp tailors in *The Fast Show*, was at the bar. 'Suits you, sir. Suits you.'

It is also where I met my southern drinking pal Struan, one of the more interesting companions I have come across on my travels. Like many of the clientele, he is an actor. Myself and a couple of the Sky production crew often join him on a ramble during London matches, normally with the French House as a starting point. It's real Struan territory, is that, right in the heart of Theatreland. And he has drunk in that pub since the 1960s. You will often bump into famous faces off the telly in that neck of the woods, and our Struan has been in a fair few productions himself. On the stage, he has toured

Europe in productions of *Julius Caesar* and *Waiting for Godot*. On the screen, he played Eric Liddell's mentor Sandy McGrath in *Chariots of Fire*. He also featured in *Stardust* with Michelle Pfeiffer and Sienna Miller, lucky swine. And he's the voice for Mr Muzzle in the *Wallace and Gromit* animated adventures. But none of the characters he has played over the years can match him *au naturel*. They don't come close.

Struan is a very dear friend, and someone who has got bundles of stories filed away in his memory archives. He's rather like Rowley Burkin QC, another of those great *Fast Show* caricatures. You know the chap, that retired barrister whose hundreds of rambling tales inevitably end up the same way with the immortal line: 'I was very, very drunk.' Struan usually finishes with something similar after our jaunts around Soho, but the lines delivered along the way are priceless. He has been here, there and everywhere. And he loves his cricket. He's a real enthusiast, who has twirled out his leg-spin and succeeded against the best of them. As we trudge along from pub to pub, he will happily re-enact the googly that drew the highest praise from West Indies great Richie Richardson, or the delivery which fatally floored Mike Denness, bowled around his legs.

In his most enthusiastic moments, in fact, there are few of the world's great batsmen he could not dismiss, and he has played with and against some fine cricketers as a regular player with the Lord's Taverners and MCC. And on nights out he is just unadulterated fun to be around. He can be like a walking encyclopaedia at times. Every street, every pub has its own history. And he knows every last detail of it. 'That was Karl Marx's house, you know? That's where Francis lived. Yep, Francis Bacon lived there,' he will say. Every face that passes him on the strolls between boozers triggers a memory, usually revolving around cricket. He'll pass someone and say: 'He reminds me of a bloke I dismissed to put me on a hat-trick twenty years ago.' Then off he goes: 'Missed the chance, of course, as I had to dash off to answer the cries of a woman hanging from the window of a burning building down the road.' Good old Struan, getting his priorities right.

On one rip-roaring midsummer session, which of course included the compulsory curry, he took three of us to his private members club, Gerry's, frequented by his fellow actors, as a treat. 'Don't worry, I'll get you in, lads,' he said. 'Leave it to me.' We were impressed when, after he rang down via the buzzer, we were admitted with minimal fuss. Less so when, upon negotiating the steps down to the bar, we trebled the numbers present, including staff. We were a bit early, to be fair, and only intended it as a refuge for our last snorter of the evening. As it happened he only really had time for a couple anyway, because he was due in Chelsea by 11 p.m. for another engagement. He was playing Bob Geldof at snooker.

Characters are essential to any good pub experience, and my late mate CJ was another one. Boy, did he get a thirst on at times, one that was often quenched during a meander into Tallstoryland. Once there, habitually just before a full gallon was on board, he would set up camp for the night. If he was a native American chief he'd have been called Talkin' Bollocks. But he never failed to entertain.

One particular occasion in The Hesketh comes to mind. Apparently his undercover work for the Government had dried up and he was back in the trolley park at the super-market. He was, of course, bound by the Official Secrets Act but did from time to time confide in a chosen few (of which I was privileged to be one) the grave dangers his line of business inevitably placed him in. These confidential exchanges usually took place in the privacy of the tap room.

'During the Cold War I was on active service behind the Iron Curtain, working for MFI,' he garbled.

'MI5, I think you mean, CJ,' I interjected, helping him along.

'Yes, that's what I said. My code name was Chuffy and the operational cell consisted of me, Wheezy Dobson and Lumpy Dagg. I was working out of Milan.'

'It must have been a big curtain, CJ ... sorry, Chuffy,' I said.

'Yes, but my Latin looks meant that I blended in perfectly with the locals.'

'Ah, got you,' I mused. 'The local Italian Russians.'

'Precisely,' he replied. 'Lumpy and Wheezy were on the ground in Moscow flushing out Miloc Khozinov, who was the Mister Big of the Russian media, on a similar level to Eddie Shah in his Wapping days. The unions were all-powerful and it was our brief to destabilise the print industry and pave the way for a more western, democratic view. My role was to filter into Moscow disguised as an Italian aristocrat who was looking to buy a football club.'

'Rather like a Roman Abramovich in reverse then?' I pondered.

'Precisely,' replied CJ, as he tottered towards the gents and I replenished the glasses.

On his return he appeared to have lost his thread: 'Yes, the oil rigs were my biggest challenge. Piper Alpha and the Dagenham Girls Pipers presented great problems to the country. Gas was there, yes, as I told James Callaghan all those years ago, but the question was always "How do we get it out?" That was the challenge. As an advanced deep-sea diving instructor I was perfectly placed to head up the project and the Government seconded me from espionage to British Gas.'

'And you have stayed with the Gas Board ever since?'

'Yes, that's my cover now, you see. The trolley park by night and on the meters by day. I don't miss a thing.'

'Do you keep in touch with Lumpy and Wheezy?' I enquired.

'Who?' said CJ, as he was ladled into the taxi for his journey home.

One of my favourite pubs, and probably my favourite on the cricket circuit, is the Circus Tavern in Manchester. George the Greek, the landlord, is a beauty. Without warning he will either lock you in or lock you out. It doesn't matter how you're behaving, just how he feels at any given time. There are two rooms, split like the city itself into red and blue, one for Manchester United fans, the other for Manchester City. Old photographs of teams of yesteryear adorn the walls, but what the place lacks in terms of décor it makes up for in atmosphere. Business go-getters sit alongside those with nowhere to go. If you're feeling peckish, out come crisps and cheese to your table, while if George is feeling particularly generous of spirit he will pop next door to the KFC and dump Colonel Sanders's finest on the bar. I have pretty simple tastes and this place suits me. You get a good crew of sports-loving folk wanting a natter in the Circus. And it is where opposition counties traditionally drank during my Lancashire playing days.

After all, life as a professional cricketer is a thirsty job, trust me on this one. Or, if you want a second opinion, then just ask legendary Australian No. 3 batsman David Boon, who was alleged to have downed sixty-five cans of the amber tackle on one flight from Melbourne to Heathrow in his pomp, which to this day remains one of the sport's most cherished records. Many have tried, some have come close, but Boony is still numero uno. It is a sign of the times that long-term Aussie captain Ricky Ponting gave up the booze in the late 1990s in order to dedicate himself to performing at his best for as long as physically possible.

On my travels across cricket's liquid empire, the same rules apply as on home soil when it comes to choice of establishment in which to sup, but sadly real ale is unavailable except in isolated pockets of New Zealand. The universal tipple is lager, which has to be served very chilled. Australia has Toohey's, Castlemaine XXXX, Foster's and VB Bitter. I am not being paid by them (although it could easily be arranged, if any of you PR types have made it this far) but it's VB for me Down Under. There is a little cracker down in Tasmania, by the name of James Boag's, not widely available nationwide, and probably for good reason. Rumour has it that this little beauty accounts for why all the blokes down there, Boon included, look like extras from ZZ Top. One teeming hirsute brigade. No wonder they never leave Hobart.

The Caribbean rocks to Carib in Trinidad, Bank's in Barbados and Red Stripe in Jamaica. All these brews tend to make you dance a lot, stay up all night and sleep all day. South Africa is all Castle, or as the locals call it K-A-A-R-S-E-L-L (adopt your best Tony Greig impersonation at this point). Your typical South African has strong Castle ties, it is what makes him look like a farm outhouse. Castle must be taken with food, preferably a full cow with its horns shorn off and its arse wiped, then cremated on a braai. It is a beer with side effects and should carry a health warning. If taken in any substantial quantity – say forty-eight per evening, for argument's sake – it has been known for a consumer to take on a purple hue, grow an enormous head and shout a lot. His sexual prowess and longevity will also diminish to under three seconds.

English Cricket's Best Watering Holes ... Official!

London

The Princess of Wales, Primrose Hill. Been frequenting this one for years with Mike Selvey, erstwhile England fast bowler and long-time *Guardian* cricket correspondent. Beware, no standing outside, due to some fussy council ruling. But you can open the windows!

The Coach and Horses, Soho. This is a pilgrimage for me. The famous play *Jeffrey Bernard is Unwell* is based around this pub.

The French House, Soho. Steeped in history. Charles de Gaulle drank here with fellow French servicemen during the Occupation of France.

Manchester

Circus Tavern, city centre. Always first on my to-do list when there's a match at Old Trafford. One night I dragged a dozen commentators in there.

The Beech, Chorlton. Left-wing, with lino-covered floors, and rough as a badger's derrière in appearance, but never seen trouble and there's always a good atmosphere. Not one of Maggie Thatcher's haunts, I would wager.

Nottingham

Ye Olde Trip to Jerusalem. Built in the walls of Nottingham Castle, but unlike Robin Hood it won't rob you blind. Apparently it's the oldest pub in Britain, stretching back to the 12th century. When a Test is on you get a mix of proper drinkers and the la-di-das in straw boaters and ties.

The Lincolnshire Poacher, Mansfield Road. A dozen real ales on tap on any given Tuesday. Landlord looks the part in his apron and serves up decent sandwiches to boot.

Leeds

The Scarborough Hotel. Opposite the city's train station and where Leeds United fans gather on match days. Always rocking with cricket supporters in the summer and always six deep at the bar.

Whitelocks. A Dickensian-looking tavern tucked away down an alleyway in the city centre, packed early evening with a post-work crowd.

Birmingham

The Old Contemptibles. Used to be a dingy old place, but there has been a real effort to spruce it up.

The Prince of Wales. Doesn't look promising from the outside, as everything around it has been demolished and it is up against the dual carriageways. But this listed building is a beacon for real ale.

Southampton

The Wykeham Arms, Winchester. An absolute find, this one. Inkwells for tables are a feature of this stunning-looking pub. Perfect stop-off for the Rose Bowl.

Chester-Le-Street

Half Moon Inn, Durham. Opposite the County Hotel, set on different levels with a lengthy bar. Locals always up for a good chinwag.

Cardiff

The Cardiff Cottage. I've always found Brain's to be a good drop and it hasn't got far to travel.

Chapter 13

IAN RUSH? WHO'S HE? EXACTLY!

Cricket has been my life, and my living, but football has always held a special place in my heart – and my long-term love has been for Accrington Stanley. In my formative years my dad took me to the old Peel Park ground every week. As a young thruster I had the honour of wearing the famous red shirt following expulsion from the league, and I still belt out the club song, 'On Stanley On', to this day. Like most love affairs there have been some hard times, they have not always been there for me (they weren't there for anyone for a while), and I have not always been there for them (sometimes Sydney has been closer to me than Stanley). But we've mucked through.

We have been together since as long as I can remember. Peel Park was just two streets up from 134 Water Lane, the house in which I was raised, and it was like a second home. In fact, most of our neighbourhood treated it as such. It was one of the first grounds to have floodlights in Division Three (North) and folk leaving matches on a Saturday evening would stream past our front room. I would be back in position after watching the match, looking out the window, waiting for the players to come past, because that was the way they had to go to reach their digs. There were some huge houses up in Avenue Parade, and that's where they stayed. My aunt Edith used to be the housekeeper.

On match days as a kid I'd go armed with a house brick – nothing naughty here, your honour, I just couldn't see over the wall behind the goal without standing on it – and the moment I passed through the turnstiles was always magical. My dad would plonk me on top of the wall occasionally, and sit me in front of it on others, getting me that bit closer to the action. Can you imagine what health and safety would have to say about that these days? Walter Galbraith, the manager, produced a predominantly Scottish team – every time he needed a new player he seemed to go on a scouting raid north of the border – with forwards Les Cocker and George Stewart as the focal point. Stewart was a great header of the ball, while Cocker was the cult hero, who took full advantage of barging still being very much on the agenda. His party piece was to poleaxe the opposition keeper. What Englishman Cocker, who went on to coach under Sir Alf Ramsey in the 1966 World Cup and was rightfully awarded a winner's medal posthumously in 2009, lacked in subtlety as a player, however, Stewart made up for in goals, scoring 136 times in the league between 1954 and 1958.

The football club was a cornerstone of a tight-knit community. I attended Peel Park School, as did my father before me, and my children and grandchildren subsequently. There was clearly something alluring about the town at that time, because everyone got behind the team and the community spirit was reciprocated in the fact that most of the players from that era stayed on in Accrington after they retired. Heroes of mine as a kid, Terry Tighe and Bert Scott went on to be window cleaners, Joe Devlin repaired Hoovers and Jimmy Harrower took on the Castle pub. Tommy McQueen – whose son Gordon was schooled in Accrington before he went on to greater things with Leeds, Manchester United and Scotland – used to be Stanley's goalkeeper. Great men all.

It was an absolute tragedy when we dropped out of the Football League in 1962, owing about £60,000. The finance might have been lacking, but a strong will to fight on was not, and my father-in-law-to-be Wilfrid Wallwork fronted the original Save Our Stanley campaign. When we began again in the Lancashire Combination, though, all our good players had long gone, so it was a matter of starting from scratch. As I was one of the better footballers in the town – I was offered schoolboy terms at Burnley and had spent the previous year playing for their B team – that meant pulling on the cherished red shirt at the tender age of 16. My ultimate sporting icon also played in red. The red of Manchester United. To me, Duncan Edwards was just the most perfect footballer and the one I tried to model myself on. I was distraught – I can remember crying for ages – when he was killed in the Munich air disaster.

My playing stint with Stanley lasted not much more than two years and my memories as the club's No. 11 are hardly romantic. In fact, the single thing I recall is this bloke nearly decapitating me in an away game at Prescot Cables. My customary position was inside-left, but on this occasion I happened to be filling in as centre-forward, and I was through on goal when he hacked me down from behind. The pitch was bone hard and, crikey, did I bang my head as I crunched into it. Eventually gaining my breath, I hauled myself up, knees scraped and nose bust. In those days you could tackle from behind, you could tackle knee-high and you used to get some fearful kickings. Well, I did, anyway, because I was so slight. I went from pillar to post and back again.

I was, theoretically at least, rewarded for my toils as a semi-professional, and the payscale meant you got the equivalent of 50p or a quid, but usually it was neither. Wages were picked up after a match, but the secretary used to lock himself in his room – we knew the sod was in there but he never made a sound. That was all part of the fun, I guess. My hometown adventure ended a couple of years later when I got transferred to Rossendale for an 'undisclosed sum'. In plain English: nowt. By rights, given my commitment to Lancashire, I should never have been playing football once April came around, yet I loved my time in the Combination and would like to report that I made a name for myself. Quite literally. To avert unnecessary attention from my county employers, I would play under the pseudonym David Ramsbottom. I have always been the same – anything for a game – and would still have a 'do' now if my body would allow it. The serious stuff actually came to a halt with my final club Great Harwood when I hit my mid-20s, mindful of doing myself and thus my developing cricket career harm.

Whenever I got the opportunity, however, I always loved to get in on charity games or social kickabouts. One of my last was a real hoot between the English and Australian media on the 2002–3 tour, a match which proved there never can be a friendly between the two Ashes rivals in any sport, or at any level. Word got out in the build-up that the Aussies were taking this media match mega-seriously, with rumours abounding that a couple of ex-Socceroo ringers had been called up, so our ringmaster Machine Gun Mike Walters, then cricket correspondent of the *Daily Mirror*, began his own recruitment drive. Phil Neale, a fine lower-division footballer with Lincoln in his younger days, and press officer Andrew Walpole were drafted in from the England touring squad's backroom staff, to bolster our ranks, Phil to marshal the defence, and Andy the Octopus, once a youth-team keeper at Norwich, to stop the ball going into our net. As MGM Walters laid claim to being a former goalie with Paris St Germain's 13th XI, he alternated with Walpole between the sticks, starting on the field and overseeing the final stages from the bench.

As it turned out, it was a good job we sought reinforce-ments, because the Aussies had taken inglorious action and raided Perth Glory, upon whose ground we were playing. But we were battle-hardened and keen. I formed a dynamic midfield combination with the other David Lloyd, then of the *Evening Standard*. Or not so dynamic as it turned out. Now Toff has something of a reputation as a bloke who can run all day, but on this occasion he went in the fetlock a minute after I had limped off. Even before the small smattering of a crowd had warmed up with a rendition of 'There's only one David Lloyd', the two of us were off. What a pair of 'nanas.

Ruled out of the action and desperate to retain an influence on the contest, I attempted to have some managerial input as the game progressed. There were plenty of others on the touchline to keep us Lloyds company, while the redoubtable Myles Hodgson, whose own organisational skills as a news agency stalwart were unquestioned, was kitted up in readi-ness for the cause. Having worried about getting an XI together when the fixture was arranged, we had been over-whelmed by the final availability. Now Hodg is not the most athletic specimen in the world, but he does embody the all-for-one-and-one-for-all spirit you need in a sporting battle Down Under. So, as the seconds ticked over in the second half, and with legs tiring, I persuaded player-manager MGM (a dead ringer for the dog in those Churchill Insurance TV adverts) to protect what we had. Our hosts, two goals down, were coming back into the game and only some fine saves from Walpole, and no-nonsense defending by *Sun* correspondent John Etheridge and Neale at the back, was keeping our goal unbreached.

'Send on Hodg and flood the midfield,' I urged. 'Get the big lad off up front. Fraser looks like he could do with a blow.' Now big Angus always fancied himself as a centre-forward, and had indeed bagged one of our goals, so you can imagine his response to this tactical change of shape. 'You x£$&ing what?' (Insert anything here and you will not be far wrong.) His reaction to being dragged off was an absolute classic. I'd had first-hand experience of the Gus chunter and stare upon removal from attacks, around the global cricket empire, but nothing to compare to this. It was priceless. Talk about wounded pride. Thank God we held on. Not for victory's sake – no matter how sweet it is to beat the old enemy – nor the fact that it was the sole English win on the tour in the opening couple of months, but for the mileage in the story ever since.

Throughout the years, wherever on the planet cricket has taken me, whichever role I have fulfilled, I have kept up with Stanley's results. All us football fans go through it, don't we? How've we done? In the days before the Internet, the weekly phone call would inevitably include a score check. Whenever I go to commentate in India, Harsha Bhogle also makes a point of asking me on air: 'How's that football team of yours doing?' It's the sport which unites the world. Much more so now than in decades gone by.

But greater appreciation for it does not necessarily mean greater application in it. Watching some of the international cricket teams limber up ahead of match days is like watching a herd of rhinos take on ballet. In the final Test between England and South Africa at the Wanderers in 2009–10, I went to get Graeme Smith's autograph on what transpired to be the final morning. His team, as usual, had been playing football. Some of their management actually believed that if half of them couldn't play football as a warm-up they would quit international cricket. But boy are they bad. As I approached Smith across the outfield I said: 'In the ICC rankings you are just above Kenya in pre-match kickabouts.' I happened to have a letter in my hand and I told him it was the results of the Inzamam-ul-Haq memorial soccer boot gold award.

He had a chuckle and asked if I would be so good as to join the South African team huddle. Here they were on the verge of winning a Test match to level the series when Graeme welcomed me in and announced to his men that I had some observations for them. I told them I had played football all my life and had got to semi-professional standard. And in my opinion, they were, without doubt, the single worst set of players I had ever seen together. For some reason, they were in guffaws of laughter at this point. I wasn't joking, lads. And then the final ignominy as I opened the envelope. 'Congratulations … Morne Morkel. You are the very worst player I have ever seen.'

As it happens, Accrington have unearthed some real talents in the modern era, thanks to the tireless efforts and keen eye of manager John Coleman, who returned league status to the town with his third championship-winning season at the Crown Ground in 2006. Coleman, a former schoolteacher, is a Scouser but has become Accrington through and through, and wears his heart on his touchline. The team he put together against the backdrop of financial crisis in the 2009–10 season was phenomenal. I make the most of seeing them when I can, and one of the games I got to before England's tour of South Africa was a Johnstone's Paints Trophy encounter against Shrewsbury. Michael Symes looks like a hell of a centre-forward and was one of the more experienced members of a side whose average age was 22. They played some good stuff that night, and won to boot, which was extra special because I had made a night of it with my old mate Andy Lloyd. Towser is a Shrews fan and it was good to get one over on him.

It's hardly glamorous, but supporting Stanley suits me. There are no airs and graces around the club, just an atmosphere of one-for-all-and-all-for-one. I book in for my pie and Bovril with the best of 'em. So when the club faced winding up for a second time in the autumn of 2009, it was a worrying time. Cometh the hour, cometh the man. I publicised our plight through Twitter and my TV appearances, but it was another local lad, Ilyas Khan, that came to the rescue. Ilyas, son of an Accrington bus driver, made good in the financial markets of Hong Kong and London, and he became Stanley's non-executive chairman after a crucial eleventh-hour intervention in the modern SOS. It was his cash that helped settle an unpaid tax bill of £308,000 and gave us an extended chance.

To me it's vital that the community has a football team, and we don't get behind them enough. It's a constant struggle to get more than 1,300 folks to go. OK, we are no great shakes in the greater scheme of English football, but this young team deserves our support and a lot of people have worked hard to get the club back to where it is. I am constantly ridiculed by my fellow Sky commentators, but I think we are a great story, and one that needs to be appreciated by more local folk. It would be nice if the kind of attendance which greeted arguably our biggest game in history, the 3,712 for the visit of Premier League Fulham in January 2010, the club's first FA Cup fourth-round tie in fifty-one years, would turn up every week. Everybody was up in arms that it was £20 a ticket, but we need the money to exist. Bigger gates would certainly help in the perpetual struggle to break even.

Although it ended in a 3–1 defeat, that game against Fulham was special. They played a major part in our day. It was a real family affair and my eldest lad Graham and my grandson Joe were all kitted out in commemorative bobble hats and scarves. There was a real sense of occasion about it. So it was a disappointment that Fulham swerved the use of our facilities, modest as they admittedly are. Come on, lads, play the game, you simply have to muck in when it comes to the FA Cup. The arrival of top-flight players for the first time made our little town buzz, but snubbing the use of the changing-rooms was a little disrespectful. There was absolutely no need to get kitted up before arrival, and the fact they chose to change en route, and then clear off straight after the final whistle, put a bit of a dampener on it for me. I know where Fulham is and it's flash, but they came somewhere that ain't flash.

The only time I have ever known a cricket team do that was on England's 1996–7 tour of Zimbabwe – and that was thrust upon us. For some reason all the rubbish from the opposition dressing-room was tipped into our room every morning, and we had no running water, so we had to shower and change at the hotel.

At least Fulham's fans took it all in the right spirit, though, standing open to the elements in front of the gypsy camp. I know because most of them tweeted me throughout the ninety minutes. Our lads gave it a real ding-dong, and when we got to one each I thought, 'We're in here, hitting downhill second half' – only for the sending-off of Darren Kempson to knock the stuffing out of us.

It failed to blunt my half-time appetite, though, and minutes later I was tucking into a Clayton Park potato pie with crust (accompanied by red cabbage and pickles) which seems to have ousted Holland's on my old stomping ground as the pie of choice. No mean feat, that, because Holland's is a multinational company. Unfortunately, the theme of the little guys winning was not extended when the match resumed. Whereas watching Premier League matches can be like witnessing a game of chess, our young lads harried and hustled for openings and matched Fulham for fitness, only fading at the very end. They did us proud and showed why they deserved greater attention in the local area. On the way to the ground, the billboard headlines said it all to me: not Stanley's first FA Cup fourth-round tie since 1959, but Fred the dog getting hit with an ASBO. An equally rare event, I grant you, but surely for once we were worthy of top billing.

Chapter 14

HIT FOR SIX BY A PENSIONER!

Accrington has been my cricket club all my life. Like Peel Park, it had been a second home to me long before I began playing senior cricket as a 13-year-old, left-arm spin hopeful in the third XI. The ground itself was not a vision of loveliness, far from it; functional rather than fetching. But the familiarity of the place had its effect. I even look back with great fondness on my negotiation of the terror track – not the one in the middle of the square but the Thorneyholme Road entrance, which was covered in potholes and a bicycle accident waiting to happen. For that was a journey I would navigate on a daily basis in school holidays. I was simply there all the time, and the people at the club became like a family. I was opening the batting for the first team at 15 – in July 1962 to be precise – against some seriously hostile fast bowling and in an environment which provided the perfect preparation for the county career which followed. My gratitude to those who set me on my way at the club, deeply entrenched by the time I signed on at Lancashire, has never left me. So when the club hit the financial rocks over the winter of 2007–8, I got in on the act to steer Accrington into calmer waters.

It was a grave situation, make no mistake, with the club absolutely skint and in need of the mother of all rallying calls. An extraordinary general meeting was hastily organised and the problems of the club – a combination of a woeful financial position and poor management – were revealed for the first time to those outside the inner sanctum of the committee. Quite simply, from a financial perspective, the club had bitten off more than it could chew. It had slipped into a routine of spending far more than it actually had, shelling out money for Indian professional Nishit Shetty in spite of the club coffers being bare. The club was in the doldrums, big time, and the drastic problems needed to be spelt out. In a nutshell, the situation was that without immediate action Accrington CC would go under. As things stood, we couldn't afford to pay the bills.

In such times everybody has to muck in, and thankfully that was what happened. A number of individuals pledged to get the finances right. Several made donations – at a club like ours you are not talking hundreds of thousands, but it was a hefty enough deficit we had to overcome – and Ilyas Khan, the benefactor at Accrington Stanley, bailed us out with a five-figure intervention. Once the debt was addressed, the rest of us did what we could to get the cash flow of the club back in order with some social events. Now fundraisers have a two-fold benefit: both money and impetus find their respective routes back into your club. I took on the responsibility for the resuscitation as campaign figure-head – my job was to do everything I could to preserve an institution established in 1846 and one of only fourteen clubs in the Lancashire League.

And it was not only Accrington that was to be revived. In a bid to enhance the profile of our bid further, it was decided that Lloyd, D., now in his seventh decade, would get himself as fit as possible with a view to playing a number of matches.

Everybody at the club was happy to go along with it, not least me, but I still had to do what I had done as a 15-year-old on the verge of my first XI League début, and show them that I could play. It had been a while since I had pulled the flannels on, a full twenty seasons to be exact, and my last match for Accrington, against Rishton in the 1980s, had ended with me snapping an Achilles tendon while batting. Memory suggests that was the reason I called it a day at the age of 42, but then again the knee operation which followed probably played its part. Nevertheless, I have kept myself in decent shape over the years while on tour with England, both as coach and more recently as commentator. So I was prepared for the full-on regime I embarked on in New Zealand in early 2008.

Now it was all very well me agreeing to cross the white line once more, but there would be no point in me being the garden gnome. At a serious level of cricket, as in any sport, you cannot send out a team effectively consisting of ten men. Neither did I want to be in as a token selection. I had to be able to contribute; there was an onus on me to get in proper shape. So while I was in New Zealand I threw myself into a really tough programme of physical activity. There was general cardiovascular gym work, running sessions and big weights sessions, with two workouts a day the norm. You could not choose a better place to set yourself such targets than New Zealand, with its outdoors lifestyle and the general attitude to health that prevails. There were no excuses and I didn't make any. Then, when I got home, I went to club practice and batted pretty well. I knew that I would be OK playing straight from memory. But the sense of being on trial was enhanced by the selectors turning up, standing behind the nets and peering through them at me. I thought: 'I don't flipping need this, really.' But I played all right and they said: 'You're in.'

Due to the wet weather in the summer of 2008, a couple of matches early on were lost, which inevitably delayed my return. I realised exactly how much I was up for this crackpot idea when I considered this a genuine shame. As it happened, the first match in which I batted was in a game against Haslingden. My previous knock had taken place when Kylie Minogue was near the top of the charts with 'The Loco-Motion'. Now I walked out to a real commotion. To set the scene, Dasher, one of the Lancashire League's real characters and a bloody good cricketer, was on a hat-trick. Now Dasher – or Steve Dearden as he is known Mondays to Fridays – always had some wheels as a fast bowler and most of them were still intact, I had noticed from the sidelines, despite the fact that like the rest of us he was now getting on a bit. Having played against him on numerous occasions over the years, I was fully aware that he was very capable of cleaning me up. The fact that he was placing fielders all around the bat as I strode in suggested that it hadn't escaped him either.

During my previous stint in the league I always had some-thing to say, but before the game I told our Graham, one of the two victims whose dismissals set up this scenario, that I was simply not getting involved if anything kicked off. 'I know I'm going to get loads here, but I am not going to bite,' I told him, confidently. Well, blow me. Talk about sledging, this Haslingden lot would have given that Jamaican bobsleigh team a do. And all the chirp was about me. As I approached the crease, there was all sorts flying about, and so I resolved to wait until they'd finished before taking guard. Credit to them, I would have been waiting longer than it takes Nasser Hussain to get to the bar, had I not changed my mind and got on with it. I had already walked away once when, upon taking guard for a second time, right on cue, they started up again. So I walked up the pitch to do a bit of gardening. Whilst tapping I thought, 'I'll get ready when you lot shut up.' Anyway, John Pemberton, at short leg, a lad with both youth and excess timber on his side, was particularly mouthy. His last salvo as we got down for a third time was: 'Come on, lads, he was no f——ing good twenty-five years ago, he'll be no f——ing good now.' Sod it, I thought. We had reached tipping point, so I walked a pace towards him and said: 'You obviously know who I am, but I've no f——ing idea who you are.'

With silence guaranteed while he thought about my retort, it was time to get on with things and so I set myself in readiness for Dasher. His run-up is on the long side and I decided as he set off that, no matter where the ball was pitching, I was going to play forward. With his close catchers in place, I knew he would be aiming for the stumps, maximising the modes of dismissal open to him. I opted to bat out of my crease – remembering to nod at the square-leg umpire so he knew where I was standing – in anticipation of something coming down which was full and on target. As he delivered, I accomplished all I set out to do – apart, that is, from hitting the ball. The lunge forward resulted in me being thudded on the pad. The sense of anti-climax was enhanced by an umpire's bellow of no-ball.

Having clambered over the immediate hurdle, I stuck around for a while, before eventually falling for 15, sweeping.

Typical. With the Sky Sports cameras there to make a little feature of my return, I was now set up for further piss-taking when I got back to work. 'Yeah, got 15 and nicked off to an away-swinger' would have been just fine as a self-assessment. But out sweeping! Aargh! When I was coaching, a player getting out sweeping – whether it was Hussain, Atherton or any of 'em – was my pet hate. It drove me to distraction. 'Chuffing sweeping again,' I used to chunter. 'Hit it down the ground. Hit it that way. None of this sweeping business.' So you can imagine the reaction to my dismissal when the lads saw it replayed. Now that the boot was on the other foot, they clambered into me. In my defence, flimsy as it was, I just hit it too well, and straight to deep square leg.

If I had just managed a few more we might have won, but as it happened we lost by a dozen runs. During the final stages of our failed chase, I went to sit with my family on the boundary. My daughter Sarah, my grandkids and my son Ben were all in tow. Incidentally it was the presence of Ben, then in his mid-20s and built like a brick shithouse, that allowed me to have the final say in the sledging wars and avert a diplomatic incident to boot.

'How'd it go, then?' Ben asked.

'All right, in fact I really enjoyed it,' I said.

'Did anyone say anything?' he continued.

As it happened, right in front of us, fielding with his back to us, was Chief Chirp, the lad from short leg.

'Actually, now you come to mention it, there was one lad, I can't see him at the minute,' I said, pointing feverishly at my combative opponent. 'A real fat lad, he was. A lard arse. He had a bit to say at short leg. They've moved him from there now and I am not sure where they've found to hide him in the field. Difficult, I would have thought, given that he's such a unit.' He must have been seething!

I only batted a couple of times that season due to the appalling weather and my weekend television commitments with Sky. Anyway, the following year, the spicy contest was against Todmorden, the club with an identity crisis. Never know if they're in Yorkshire or Lancashire, them lot – which probably explains something. I was quite taken aback by the persistence of their banter:

'Here he is: John Arlott.'

'Hush, everyone, show some respect, Richie Benaud's here.'

'No one told me Christopher Martin-Jenkins was playing.'

'Come on, skip, let me have a bowl at Brian Johnston.'

They kept going on and on, with wicketkeeper Danny Brown leading the chorus.

'You've got a lot to say, pal,' I told him, not long after I had arrived in the middle.

'His head's gone, lads. Head's gone,' he advised the rest of his team-mates. So the stage was set for a verbal battle royal.

'There's nobody else can hear this, it's just me and you from now on,' I muttered. 'I'm 60-odd, so no one's expecting much of me. But just between the two of us, are you any good?' During the next over, while I was at the non-striker's end, he dropped a catch. So, upon its conclusion, I took the opportunity to carry on our conversation, accompanying him on the change of ends. 'Really good stop that,' I said. 'You've just saved your lot four runs. You've done really well. Just out of interest, is your normal wicketkeeper not available today?' Needless to say, he was getting a bit uppity.

Anyway, I had been in for quite a while when their captain James Morgan brought himself on. It was damp and the pitch was made for seamers, but he opted for his own off-spin by way of a change, perhaps because he thought the ball would grip, or perhaps because he smelt a cheap wicket. But, given the match situation – I was in extremely early for a No. 7 and three figures seemed to be somewhere in a neighbouring county – his decision made my eyes light up. As a left-hander, it opened up the short leg-side boundary for me. 'If there is one place I can hit him, it's there,' I thought, lining him up over long-on. I was just waiting for him to give one a bit more air, confident of launching it over the rope, as it was not a big hit. When it presented itself, I seized my chance. As the ball sailed skyward, I turned to my mate Brown behind me. 'You're not saying so much now, are you?' I observed. 'Just so you can warn your mate, I'm going to do it again this over.' I was true to my word. I was having a ball. Morgan joined in the theatre, hands on hips, giving it the full teapot. 'Ask him what it's like to be hit for two sixes by a pensioner,' I advised the mouth and gloves.

I was eventually out for a top score of 28 in a total of 113 for 9; absolutely thrilled to bits with my performance. It had not been easy to bat, and our bowlers put the conditions into perspective when they got them seven wickets down with 34 still required for victory. It was very much game on when in walked Browny. As he approached, our lads were shouting over to me: 'Your mate's here.' So, as he went past me, I enquired: 'Are you injured, pal? You don't normally bat this low down, surely? With your performance behind the stumps, I didn't think you were fully fit.' To his credit, his response was first-class. He played brilliantly and steered Todmorden home by two wickets. There was some more banter in the bar afterwards, washed down with a couple of pints, the way it should be. Everybody agreed what a good day it had been.

Who Writes These Scripts?

As things panned out, the final game of my Accrington comeback, and as it transpired, of my entire career – OFFICIAL – had a fairytale ending. It was the last round of the 2009 Lancashire League season and, as I had no commentary commitments that weekend, I rang our captain Dave 'Dibber' Ormerod (I'm sure you've all played with your own Dibbers up and down the country, those blokes who trundle up with their dibbly-dobbly bowling and land it on a length to great effect) and told him I was available. There is always someone off playing football when September comes around, or else whoozit has got a great last-minute holiday deal. So, as we weren't in a position to win the title – or so we thought – he told me I was in. Part of the keenness on my part was that we were playing against Lowerhouse away. Now Lowerhouse is a suburb of Burnley – they wouldn't tell you that, but that's what it is – and folk would not normally be rushing there. But I was keen to play because it's the club of a good old mate of mine, Stan Heaton, a policeman, whose tireless work keeps them going – as well as being club chairman, he runs all their youth teams, and has ensured they now have fantastic all-weather practice facilities alongside their ground.

They got a decent score, of 170-odd, and I thought a win was probably beyond us. The match had a real end-of-season feel about it, and with us not playing for anything, we set off in pursuit in a fairly relaxed manner. But unbeknown to us, Haslingden, whose domination of the league all summer had left them requiring one win from the last four matches to claim the title, were imploding once more. In late afternoon we began to get score updates from their match – they were getting absolutely spannered. We had been merrily going about things in the knowledge that they couldn't lose. But having got a start, and with one or two of our lads putting some runs on the board, we discovered a little over the halfway point in our chase that Haslingden had lost. For us, the equation was now simple: win and a second successive league title was ours. Four games previously it was unthinkable because Haslingden are the best team by a distance. No one could give me an explanation as to why they suddenly forgot how to win. It was comparable to Manchester United or Chelsea coming up against the four bottom teams and losing every single match. And they weren't just losing, they weren't picking up bonus points either. So here we were, having won our previous three completed matches to close the gap, with a 62-year-old due at No. 7. With music playing in the dressing-room at tea, and everyone sipping their brews, we were relaxed about the target ahead. But as our requirement diminished, Dibber began to fidget with the order.

'Don't you go in, I am sending such-a-body in,' Dibber muttered when the fifth wicket went down.

'But I'll smack this bloke,' I countered. 'This off-spinner is right in my sights. I'll give it some welly.'

'No, I'm sending James in.' So in went James Hayhurst and my chance to get into the action had been delayed. Sitting padded up alongside me was Paul Carroll, our 47-year-old opener, who had barely got a run all season and was paying with a stint in the lower half of the card. Infuriatingly, I felt I was about to fall off the card altogether as another one went down. 'I'm sending the Carroller in now,' Dibber declared.

'For flip's sake, Dibber, what number am I?' I implored.

'You go number nine,' was his decisive response.

Chuntering about the order was irrelevant soon afterwards, however, as I made my way to the middle to join the chunky Caroller, a man who, despite alleged proficiency with the bat, had averaged 8 all year. Suddenly our club's Lancashire League title aspirations were in the hands of a duo with a combined age of 109. But hey, a pair of old gits in one man's eyes are experienced pros in another's. Up against such an authoritative number, a requirement of 9 looks puny – but when the pressure is on, any amount needed for victory can prove tricky. My eighth-wicket partner settled us both down, though, when he hit the aforementioned offie straight into the car park. 'Jesus, where's that one come from?' I quizzed him as we shuffled towards a mid-pitch conflab. 'Straight out the screws that,' came the matter-of-fact response. A single left me on strike in the penultimate over. And my eyes lit up when I received a nice little shortie outside off-stump. Watching it straight on to the bat, I hit it for four and we'd won the league. All the lads came running on – probably as shocked as excited. Haslingden later claimed we had not won the league, they'd lost it. They were right in one respect, but we had won four in a row, and their thoughts, not as relevant as the final league table, were not going to bother us.

We were absolutely thrilled. Accrington, as a team, were always on a very even keel during my two seasons back. Everyone was always taking the mickey out of everyone else. There were no flashpoints. Calmness prevailed at all times.

And we have some handy guys. Dibber, or Dibhendra Singh as his nickname mutated, can land them on a sixpence and has 1,000 career wickets to show for that skill. On the batting side, our Graham scores the majority of our runs and never gets fazed by anything. He takes everything in his stride, chuckles a lot and continues to find humour in my failings. If ever I tripped up in the field it would be 'Come on, Bumble, do your best.' And we have a couple of up-and-coming lads, Stuart Crabtree and Graham Sneddon, grandson of a professional footballer with Stanley, who can both play a bit, and do so with a smile on their faces. Our wicketkeeper-batter Matt Wilson has the best set of dreadlocks I have ever seen on a white bloke. We've got some good cricketers but some really good lads, and a happy team can count for a lot. A few opposition clubs can get very volatile if they are not winning: somebody is leaving, so-and-so is packing up, John's fell out with Jim. But our lot are a terrific set. A set, as I later contemplated, that no longer needed me either. With some good young 'uns coming through, it was the time to step aside once more.

Same Game, Different Ballpark

My association with Accrington had begun fifty seasons earlier when Peter Westwell, then goalkeeper with Cedar Swifts, the local football team run by my dad, introduced me to the club and paid my junior annual subs. Traditional Lancashire League rules dictated that you had to live within five miles as the crow flies of the club you played for. Where I lived in Accrington made me eligible for nine out of the fourteen clubs. The rules have been relaxed ever so slightly since then, but the same principle applies. You couldn't, for example, just go out and lure someone from Wakefield to come and play, you have to be within five miles of your home ground or have been born in the district. It was such an easy concept to understand in the 1950s, because it was in the days before motorways, when each individual pocket of housing was a subsidiary of a little mill area. The district of Hyndburn takes in Accrington, Oswaldtwistle, Enfield and Rishton, all four providing clubs to the Lancashire League. There are then two Ribblesdale League clubs, which is maybe one grade lower in standard, namely Baxenden, where Ian Austin played, and Oswaldtwistle Immanuel, a lovely cricket ground. It is representative of the other small enclaves in Lancashire. There are plenty of clubs – in my view, too many.

These worthy clubs were founded when the world was a different place and before, as I touched upon, the presence of major road networks. The sense of space was quite different back then and you didn't venture very far, whereas now you can be quite a distance away when you're ten minutes down the road. Now that everything is sprawled and just one mass, people move on and away. Other things in life have spread out, but the number of clubs has not, and that has diluted their worth. Yet people remain parochial and cling on to them like priceless antiques. They all want their little club, concerned with its history rather than what it offers in the present day, when the sensible thing would be to amalgamate, to make one or two powerful clubs in the area. Unfortunately, it will never happen. With that number of people we could have one or two stonking teams in this area, with feeder teams underneath. It would be in keeping with the England and Wales Cricket Board's thinking on Premier Leagues.

In my own mind, to get better cricket in England that is the way to do it, and the ECB recognised this fact during the late 1990s. But they were swimming against the tide in their challenging of traditionalism. In my argument, I use Accrington as a model because it's a familiar one. There are far too many clubs, it's far too parochial, but I concede that it will never change because you are up against people who will scrap furiously for their own patch in the face of overwhelming evidence for change. I know what it is like nowadays to get teams out on the field – quite simply it's a nightmare. It's a totally different situation we face now from what we did in the 1940s and 50s. Identity was very important to folk back then, but without trying to belittle other people's views, it doesn't hold as much water in a 21st-century world which is effectively a lot smaller. The solution would be for two or three clubs to amalgamate and combine their funds. Imagine the stack of cash you could pile up if a ground or two was sold off for redevelopment. It would generate the level of finance sufficient to produce top-notch facilities for the best youngsters in the district. Unfortunately, however, the English way is to provide sport for people in little communities. It is totally different in Australia, where if you ain't any good you ain't playing. We play recreational cricket. They don't.

I know this is far from new, but if we could completely dismantle it and start again, which means fewer clubs – like the terrible phase we are going through just now with pubs, where lots are shutting down and only the lean ones and the good ones are able to survive – it would be better for the sport. If we could reduce the number of clubs it would give the best of the young 'uns coming into the game a fabulous opportunity to make it to the very top very quickly. Because with all the raw materials at their disposal, only the strongest would survive. As they came through the system, they would be used to competing for places and able to do so in the best possible environment. But the social aspect of our game and traditional rivalries, which are everything to some, will not allow the necessary progress in certain parts of the country.

Elsewhere, there are more professional structures in place. The Surrey Championship is excellent; and the Northern League, which runs from Liverpool up the west coast, is also good. They have top-notch facilities, good pitches and a bob or two. A couple of excellent examples of modernisation within our club cricket system. But that process just isn't going to happen in my area. Not in my lifetime, anyway. Having seen cricket worldwide I can say, 'This is what we should be doing,' but I won't get the light of day on my own doorstep. The Lancashire League have a committee and I am surprised (because of my affinity with the league, and my attempts to give it some profile in any way that I can, whether it be on TV or in other media streams) that they haven't said to me, 'Come and meet us, tell us what you think about our module.' I could help them no end, but it will never happen because these people are long in the tooth and would never want a radical word. Perhaps it's because they know exactly what I would tell them that they keep me at arm's length. They should be asking: 'David, what do you see? And how can we improve our product?' But there is a reticence towards change in our country, and they reflect it.

The current, antiquated system definitely stops the best players getting through to Lancashire quickly, and it restricts the ambition of the best players. In my module, these lads would have a fast-track to their county club, and Lancashire would also be dead keen because they would know the best players could be unearthed at these particular clubs. Emerging players would be fit, strong and benefiting from the money paid out for top facilities and coaching. Any county would be interested in overseeing a system like that. And the system would project forward to the England teams. That was what was envisaged when the ECB tried to get their Premier Leagues system working. My only criticism of that was that the first promises we had, and I was involved at the time, included a lot of money. That has not transpired – yes, there was a bit of money, but not mega-money. If we could plough it into affiliating teams to produce a better overall standard I am convinced we would produce far superior cricketers. In that scenario, it would be difficult for young overseas cricketers to infiltrate county cricket. We would have a far better quality of contemporaries for them to compete against.

At county level there has always been a general frustration, stretching all the way back to when I played, that the league structure within the county boundaries is not that bothered about Lancashire County Cricket Club. There has never seemed to be a great affinity. I know there is the Lancashire Board now, which looks after the amateur game and is based at Old Trafford, and it's true that I am speaking from outside, but when I was a player, a captain and a coach at Lancashire it was that way. There was a real distance between League clubs, League players and the county club itself. So few players came through in my time that the two who did are famous and exceptional. Mike Watkinson and Jack Simmons proved it could be done, but to spot these cricketers you need a good visionary. Watkinson was a fantastic county stalwart and deserved to go on and play for England. He was also a clever bloke – a quantity surveyor by trade – so he had quite a grounding when he came into the professional game. He knew what hard work was all about. As did Jack, who was a draughtsman, or an architect in modern parlance, for the county council. He was playing league cricket as a professional and didn't join until he was closer to 30 than 20. You don't get that now: the player who breaks into county cricket at a riper age.

For the chaps at Accrington, the priority every year is to survive the following twelve months. This is a club that won successive titles in my two years back in action. My cricket vision is quite different from that. What I want to know is how can I improve the facilities? How can I improve the nets and the pitches? How can I get more kids to come here? Because if I do that I might find that one lad who plays for England. We have found a few already in myself, Graeme Fowler and our Graham. Another home-grown product, Bob Ratcliffe, went on to be capped by Lancashire. But how do we now get cricketers to play here and move them up the chain towards international level? Facilities and expertise are at the forefront of my mind, whereas the committee's thoughts are far more primitive. I have a professional vision, which I admit has been shaped by the positions I have been fortunate enough to occupy in the sport; and they have an amateur reality, formed just as naturally by their own experiences.

In one way I know where they are coming from. As a lad, the cricket club was everything to me. It provided the social aspect in my life. I would go there throughout my school holidays and just play. There would be four or five of us and we would just go down and net. On a weekend if I hadn't got a game I would watch. Wes Hall, the great West Indies fast bowler, is the first professional that I can remember seeing – this huge black man, such a nice fella, it was mesmerising to watch him charge in from the sightscreen. There was an overwhelming affection for him from everyone at the club. The other great players from Accrington have stuck in my mind throughout my career. The old chaps that are long gone now: Les Carter, Tommy Cunliffe, Frank Rushton, Derek Rushton, Derek Mark, Jack Collier – a wicketkeeper who genuinely *did* shove two steaks in his gloves when he was keeping to Wes. Eddie Robinson was a wonderful leg-spinner, who would walk into any county team these days, but whose progress at Old Trafford was blocked by the presence of Tommy Greenhough, Bob Barber and Sonny Ramadhin. Russ Cuddihy, another former footballer with Stanley, was still coaching in the area fifty years later. These were my heroes. Growing up, you idolised the Lancashire League players. Australia's Bobby Simpson came. When I was getting good I opened the batting with Eddie Barlow. There were some terrific times. Great days. Coming into the first team in the 1950s and 60s as a young player definitely moulded you as a person. The cricket club used to be the centre of the community, and therefore it had that effect on so many people. Sadly, it influences fewer now, but influences them nevertheless.

Chapter 15

HITTING SIXTIES

When I turned 60 in March 2007, I began to turn my thoughts to what I still wanted to do in life. My personal to-do list visited some things in my past – I wanted to prove to myself I could still compete at a decent level in cricket, and I intend to fish more – but also featured some new pursuits. For example, I eventually want to settle down and live by the sea, and I want to own a boat of some sort. My friend, the Reverend Malcolm Lorimer, the historian at Lancashire County Cricket Club, sold his yellow battalion of *Wisden Almanacks* and bought a canal narrow boat with the proceeds.

My immediate urge, however, was to hit the open road on a motorbike. I had never ridden one previously, as my dad always said I couldn't have one during my youth. After much swatting up – at least regular thumbing of bike magazines on aeroplanes – I plumped for a Honda Varadero 125. So I was ready for the Compulsory Bike Training and Theory Test, which examines your proficiency with the machine and readiness for the road. The first half of the CBT is under supervision in an enclosed area, and you then head out into the wild (Macclesfield in my case) to assess how you handle yourself in traffic. Getting through that, and the computerised Highway Code and motorbike awareness tests, set me on the way to my ultimate goal, which was to take the direct access test and be eligible to ride any bike.

I was helped along the way by Andrew Flintoff, who is a big Harley Davidson man. I was not initially keen on a Harley but could be persuaded, I reckon, if it meant jumping in with his crew. I would bring up the rear, no doubt, because I am an incredibly timid biker. I fully respect the power of these machines, and my own fallibility when on the back of one, and the best bikers, so they say, are neither the fastest nor most aggressive. There's one dude mightily glad to have stumbled over that fact, I can tell you. I was always wary of Harleys, because although they're a great pose bike, they tend to go at their own pace and don't go around corners readily. My own preference is for a BMW R1200 RT. I don't want to be a Valentino Rossi, nose sniffing tarmac – it's the Dennis Hopper position à la *Easy Rider* for me. So, the BMW would do me fine out in the country, I reckon.

Arranging tests and choosing your dream machine is the easy part, believe me. For I have to confess that I found the testing extremely taxing. Being on a bike is all about your hands and your feet. It is all about co-ordination, and although my lifetime as a sportsman suggests I should be, I am not good at it. Undoubtedly, some people will be very good from the off – they clamber on and away they go. But I am careful in the extreme, and the one thing I damn well could not do on my initial tests was the U-turn. In fact, on one attempt I careered off into a grass verge, and my mastering of the exercise took so long that my day-long test doubled in length overnight. Even after passing, I still got myself into pickles pulling Ueys. The key is to look where you are going, not straight ahead, and forgetting to enact this cost me my balance while practising outside my garage in early 2009. In the process of being unseated, I tried to dodge out of the way of the falling bike and tore a hamstring as a result. These days lads like Steven Gerrard can get back from hamstring injuries in a flash, but at my age it takes a month – the length of time my bike was parked up and my bruised leg remained black.

Chapter 16

OOH, WHAT A DING-DONG DU

In the words of Bob Seger and the Silver Bullet Band, 'I think I'm going to Kathmandu!' Well, I did go, as it happens, during March 2010, and what an experience it was, taking in all of the charms Nepal has to offer and getting up close and personal with their biggest hill. Now this kind of jaunt isn't usually me. In my free time you'd be much more likely to find me organising 18 holes or kicking back to some DVDs or music, so put it down to an increased sense of adventure.

Being on tour in Bangladesh presented the opportunity, offered by a company called FSI, whose main specialist field is security and close protection. You know, the run-of-the-mill stuff like embassies, presidents and prime ministers. At Sky, we have always been keen on giving our viewers a flavour of the culture in the countries in which England are competing, but this was something else, and they decided to send me with a camera in tow to film a feature over four days. So, upon completion of the one-day series in the Desh, it was a case of getting on a one-hour flight to the Du, setting off from the

Gong to go via the Ka (Chittagong and Dhaka for the uninitiated). Our operation was run by a group of former Gurkhas
and British military personnel, chaps who you might comfortably term as handy. When they say it's Tuesday, forget settling
down with the weekend papers, it's Tuesday. And our trip
was planned with military precision.

Bryan Henderson, one of the senior producers at Sky, accompanied me to film some diary pieces on the trip, which included
a flight in a light aircraft along the Himalaya Range, over a
number of 8,000-metre peaks before we got to the big lad,
Everest. Our experience was shared with a group of Chinese
tourists intent on taking the perfect picture, which meant not
allowing anything or anyone standing in their way, including
Hendo and me. There were some hilarious scenes as they clambered over us, shoved elbows into our midriffs and sprawled
on to our laps. Now my Chinese isn't great – it probably extends
about as far as 'Herro, isn't this rubbery' – but they kept bowing
and smiling, so we just let them be. We all had a great time.

The perks of my day job certainly get me into some interesting positions, and none more so than on that very flight,
when some silver-tongue talking got me the seat next to the
boss. Now, from the cockpit, I had an unbelievable view of
the mountain, which took on a completely different dimension seen head-on. It's a grand old sight, that's for sure. Truly
magnificent in all its morning glory. Unfortunately the early
flight was over far too quickly and we were back at the
summit hotel inside an hour, before most people's thoughts
had turned to breakfast – but what an adventure. One that I
would recommend to anyone.

It was the highlight of my trip, although I also delved into
cultural issues, with Rita, our tour guide, whisking us around

the ancient temples of Kathmandu. Now, this kind of expedition is not normally my bag, but I listened to the ideals of Buddhism and Hinduism with an open mind. People's devotion to daily worship at their community temple was fascinating: apparently, the lady of the house rises first, visits the temple and prays for the whole family whilst the rest of them go about the daily chores.

But the one story from Rita that really caught my imagination was the one about the Living Goddess. She has to be a virgin girl, the embodiment of beauty, with perfect eyes and skin. In fact, there are more than thirty criteria that have to be met by this infant, who is chosen at about two years of age. Getting through the process makes the *Britain's Got Talent* auditions look a whizz. Two of the assignments would put the heebie geebies up you. The first sees the elders putting scary face masks on to try to frighten the child. Now, if she cries, she is not considered. But if she passes the first test of nerve, she is then left in the dark, in solitary confinement. Again, if there is a whimper from her, the elders reject her claims and the search is directed elsewhere.

Passing the selection criteria results in the newly proclaimed Goddess being taken from the bosom of her family and sent to live at the temple. From this time on she will not leave – being schooled, fed and watered there – although her family are allowed to come and visit, giving thanks for her existence, with the rest of the worshippers. Sometimes she is visible at the courtyard window, and glimpses of her trigger prayers. Finally, on reaching puberty, she rejoins her family to begin a normal life and the whole process begins again for another cherubic tot. The very definition of a child prodigy.

During the filming of *Bumble's Tour Diary*, we came across two holy men in Durbar Square, an international heritage site housing ancient buildings and temples. Now we thought this too good an opportunity to miss: two holy men, resplendent in orange robes and with faces painted in vivid colours. So Hendo got the camera out and, after negotiations with our Nepalese agent Rita, the two budding actors settled for a 300-rupee appearance fee (all of about three quid) for their part in our adventure. Placing myself between them, I tried to picture myself as an Alan Whicker or a Michael Palin. Some renowned explorer.

In my most erudite, nondescript, British broadcasting voice, I began: 'Durbar Square, Kathmandu, and here I am sat between two holy men …' Like a parrot on my left shoulder, one of the chaps piped up with 'Holy men.' Now that knocked me out of my stride, I must admit, but in order to compose myself, I turned to him and said, 'Yes, Holy men.' Right on cue, the other one joins in: 'Holy men.' Perhaps he didn't want to be outdone by his mate, so to equal things up I turned to number two and said, 'Yes, Holy men.' Parity did not last for long, however, as the first was soon back in to make it 2–1. This was turning into a real ding-dong-do of a contest. For the next minute we were like a barber shop trio. 'Holy men … HO-LY MEN … H-O-L-Y M-E-N.' They just burst into song. Now I know I can lose it or go off on one occasionally, but this was just about the funniest thing I have done to camera. Rather than get uppity in my Whicker moment, I decided to run with them, and the only downside was that Hendo's filming of the incident was spoilt by some serious camera shake while he guffawed.

What awaited us next morning was nowhere near as funny but splendidly rewarding – a two-day trek through the Manaslu region of the Himalayas. We drove to Kakani to start and were scheduled to walk to Shivapuri and stay overnight at a lodge. What an experience that was. Walking for four hours was quite a demanding slog, but the scenery was majestic. Nepal has nine of the ten biggest mountains on the planet either partly or completely within its borders. Manaslu dominated the horizon, but our adventure also provided views of Ganesh Himal, Gurje Bhanjyang and Zugul Himal. Our guide was a chap called Geljun Sherpa, who kept us on our guard by warning us to keep our eyes peeled for tigers and red pandas. If, in doing so, he was trying to put the wind up us, it worked.

Our Geljun had conquered Everest on three occasions and bore the facial scars from accidents he has had on that intimidating ascent. Listening to his tales of triumph was fascinating, and he proved great company. By the time we got to our overnight destination, Shivapuri, I was ready for a brew. The lodge was like a staging post, and the individual billets where we shacked up for the night were of the most basic variety – corrugated roofs sheltered us, electricity was available for just a limited period, and running water, no more than a trickle, was solar-powered. But all this simply added to the sense of adventure provided by the intrepid trek. The bunk was the hardest, most uncomfortable thing I have ever slept on, but I wouldn't have swapped it for silk sheets because it was part of such a wonderful experience. A real spirit had developed among the group and, as we gathered around a fire in the main section of the lodge earlier in the evening, a bottle of Nepalese red wine was uncorked. We all toasted the jaunt with this local tipple which, according to the label, was 11.5 per cent. How Messrs Pringle and Gower would have described its other vital constituents, I can't guess. They would be hard pressed to be complimentary about its bouquet or body. 'Trips along the tongue, with subtle hints of Hussain's flip-flop, leaving a lasting aroma of an Arab's armpit,' or something to that effect.

Its well-concealed class ensured that it wasn't taken in any great volume, thus preventing any disruption to our early morning plans next day. A stunning sunrise over the Himalaya range was the precursor to a sharp breakfast and a return to the Du. Our second-day tramp had been going for a good couple of hours, and we were seemingly somewere near the back of beyond, when we were passed by an elderly man with two enormous drums of kerosene dangling on either end of a huge stick, which was somehow resting on the back of his neck. Forget this extraordinary balancing act. Where had he come from? And where was he heading? There appeared to be no sign of civilisation anywhere around us.

That particular impression was disproved seconds later by the rumble of large engines. Even so, we presumed they were some miles off in the distance, their noise echoing through the mountain range. But no, not a bit of it. These roars, I was soon to discover, belonged to two buses which came chugging, screaming and belching around the bend in front of us. Now let me put this into context. Not only are we talking hairpin here in relation to this bend but it was not alone; there were many, and the track, which wound this way and that, was terribly rutted with craters. Every hundred metres or so, it would double back on itself, exposing the sheer vertical drop on one side. One mistake by the driver and the whole chara-banc and its hundred passengers would be no more. As the vehicles spewed out their diesel, teeming with people, as many hanging off the sides and perched on the roof as sat in more customary fashion, I was petrified. The buses rocked from side to side as the drivers negotiated the crevices and potholes, leaving me pinned against a tree, fearing disaster. The same thoughts clearly did not enter the minds of the happy passengers, who smiled, bowed and waved in response to the traditional 'namaste' greetings from our party.

The theme of peace extended to the mood at the Summit Hotel, our residence in the Du, high up overlooking the city. A very tranquil place, it has a terrace where you can sit, read a book, take tea or just look down at the hurly-burly below. Lots of different nationalities were gathered there in one establishment. Now it is usually the English that lower the tone in these situations, but on this occasion it was a middle-aged Belgian woman called Monique. Our first meeting with her was when, sitting two stools away at the bar, she haughtily informed us in her Hercule Poirot broken English that, just in case we were wondering, she was not looking for group sex. What on earth are you supposed to say in response to that?

She had no doubt been on the whiffy tackle, so readily available in one of Asia's sprawling, heavily-polluted, traffic-packed cities. Here, car horns honk, buses squeal, tuk-tuks chug on their merry way and every day there is a competition to see how many folk you can fit on a single motorbike. While in Kathmandu, I decided to take a trip to Freak Street – trip being the operative word. That was where all the beautiful people hung out in the 1960s, where converted hippies, life's drop-outs, karma seekers and promoters of free love all converged. Even now that times have changed, I still half-expected to hear the Beatles blaring out of some den: 'All you need is love … da da da da da …'

We could have spent longer there as it happened, as our flight back to the Desh was delayed by fifteen hours. We were on an airline called GMG (I think it stands for Going … Maybe Gone) and unfortunately they only have two planes. One of them was grounded and waiting for a part to arrive from Germany – and they seemed to have no clue as to the whereabouts of the other. Not sure how you can lose something that size – 'It's got a big beak, huge metal wings and weighs a few tons, pal.' Eventually they located it in Kuala Lumpur, which appeared to be a mystery to them and wasn't a lot of use to us. It meant we desperately had to try and find a different flight out of there. Let's just say that all the karma built up dissipated very quickly and flight rage took over.

Thankfully, cricket saved the day. We went to a local hotel to plot a course of action and to our surprise the manager recognised me. Thanks to his contacts we were able to fly out with United Airways instead, although we failed to make our Chittagong-bound connection at Dhaka, as a result of which our jaunt turned out in the end to be one of six days rather than four. Oh, and I had another valuable life lesson in the following days. I learnt what dengue fever feels like. Rearrange the following letters for the answer: I-E-H-T-S.

Chapter 17

I'M DREAMING OF A HOT CHRISTMAS

Christmas spent away from home has been a normal occurrence for me, ever since my playing days. Every couple of years we are in either South Africa or Australia, celebrating in stinking hot heat. You get used to that, but it's still a little weird to hear your first Christmas carol with sunshine blazing in Perth or while walking through the air-conditioned Sandton City shopping centre in Johannesburg. It hits you around 23 November as some poor Santa dives out of his suit and goes for a swim in his own sweat.

By the way, piped music and saxophonists – Satan is working overtime here – should never be used to re-create traditional carols. The saxophonist is nearly always Kenny G. I reckon he's cloned somewhere in Central America as autumn approaches. He produces music to jump off cliffs by, in my opinion, does our Kenny. I have to declare I am not a great lover of the festive season, though it's great for the kids, and it's so special to see them opening their pressies and listening to the stories of how Father Christmas got down the chimney after landing the reindeers on the roof. That is always worth being around for.

Being with Kenny in Joburg, however, does mean I avoid that annual ceremony when the long-lost relatives show up again. You know the ones. Them that you haven't seen since … erm … last Christmas. There is the in-law, usually twice removed, who turns up half-pissed and then quickly goes the full trip after a burst at the drinks cabinet, before later declaring: 'It's so nice to have a drink at Christmas time with family and friends. If you can't have a drink at Christmas, when can you have a drink?' Looking at the size of their purple hooter, any time seems to be the obvious answer.

Then there is the bloke who you have never clapped eyes on before but assures you that he is a relative of Maureen, second cousin of Doris, who used to be married to Arthur before he ran off with the girl he met in Thailand. Name badges would help. Santa ought to get a job lot for his sack. We could all be labelled, the way people are at those seminars, hosted at budget hotels with conference centres attached, filling in our own names with felt pens. Personally, I would give myself a grand title, something like Commander Farquar Farquarson [Retd.] and wander round my own house regaling these total strangers with tales of derring-do on the streets of Monaco when I was in charge of the principality's army.

One bloke (unidentified to this date) always turns up and takes the biscuit … or, more accurately, takes the prawns. I have watched this tight git since the turn of the century and his main aim at Yuletide is to eat all the crustaceans present before anyone else has even spotted the buffet table. He is the same bloke whose kids don't like dogs, and so we have to keep ours locked away for the duration. My house! My dogs! Ask *them* what Christmas is like. Give them bonfire night, any time. I can see little Tags, my enthusiastic fox terrier, looking up at me as I shut her in the garage. 'That bloke with the snotty kids around again?' her eyes ask.

Christmas is a family affair. It just so happens that my day job provides me with a surrogate one. While everyone is freezing their nuts off in the UK, we are becoming more and more dysfunctional in 35-degree heat. We have to take it in turns to go into the shade to cool off! Meanwhile, sympathetic emails flood in, if you happen to whinge about the sweltering conditions while on air, including such choice phrases as 'you bastard!' or 'why don't you piss off!' Charming. And it can all get a little bit rowdy as the wine flows. One year in New Zealand, I found myself at a table with former England all-rounder Derek Pringle, of the *Daily Telegraph*, and his grace David Gower. They were singing the praises of a particularly expensive bottle of Sauvignon Blanc. Pring reckoned it tasted a little 'slatey'. I had to ask the question: 'How many slates have you eaten?' They both told me to pipe down before going on to agree that the next bottle was 'a little gritty'. I chipped in again with 'Partial to a bit of grit, are you?' Something about a 'northern prick' followed, but I cannot believe they were talking about the taste of the wine.

In the run-up to one Christmas, in South Africa, our path crossed that of rapper Busta Rhymes. I have never seen so many large men wearing earpieces located in one place. It was pretty obvious straight away that they weren't there for the ICC's third umpire convention. But Busta proved about as popular as the Indian Cricket League and opted not to play at the local convention centre owing to lack of interest. He appeared on stage at Port Elizabeth's newly-built convention centre to announce he was moving his show from the arena to the 500-capacity La Dee Da's club. Busta is American but his dad, it turns out, is from Trinidad and was a player in his day. 'I like da cricket, man,' Busta said. My curiosity stirred, I went on to Cricinfo in search of evidence, but there was no trace of a Mr Rhymes! Kanye West was also in our hotel in Australia one year, as was Paris Hilton, although not at the same time, I might add. I said hello to Miss Hilton but she clearly didn't recognise me.

That reminded me of the time right at the end of my playing career when Dexy's Midnight Runners were on in Southampton. I was with a couple of the lads, Bernard Reidy and Chris Scott, and we bumped into Kevin Rowland. You could recognise him a mile off by the way he dressed. 'All right Kev?' I said. He looked at me as if to say: 'Who the hell's this?' Unperturbed, I continued: 'Hope it goes well tonight, have a good gig, nice to see you again, mate.'

As we got out of the lift and meandered off, my two team-mates turned in unison: 'Do you know him?'

'Of course I do,' I said. Never clapped eyes on him before or since, of course.

Another time, on an internal flight to Adelaide, Bob Willis was completely oblivious of the fact that he was sitting next to George Benson. We kept passing notes to him emblazoned with GIMME THE NIGHT, but he didn't have a clue what we were on about.

Chapter 18

SUCK-IT-AND-SEE MOTORING

Time is precious away from cricket, and whenever I get a stretch I have domestic matters to attend to. So one of my trips home was dedicated to purchasing a new motor. My old car had just limped through its MOT and, in my mind, the time had arrived for change. There was one certain criterion for any potential replacement, however, namely that it had to be an estate, to provide ample room for Bertie and Tags. That always narrowed down the field and I became accustomed to choice being pretty slim over the years. On this occasion, however, I admit that my head was turned when, within minutes of arrival at the car showroom, the young shaver of a salesman got me into a 2008 model Audi fully equipped with Satellite Navigation System. He explained all the finer points of getting from A to B via this modern phenomenon, and as I had once found myself in Evesham on my way to Leicester from the north-west, I thought this was just the ticket. The only problem, as I pointed out to my temporary new best friend, as he was retrieving his earring, which had somehow lodged itself in the headrest, was that the Satellite Navigation System was positioned in the exact same place that I keep my Simpkins tropical fruit travel sweets. Now this was a problem.

Let's consider the naked facts of this matter: Satellite Navigation Systems are a fairly new gizmo, whereas Simpkins have been going since 1921. 'Tried and tested, are Simpkins,' I said to the budding Lewis Hamilton as he embarked on torque, gear ratios and 0 to 62.5 in three seconds.

I slept on it for a couple of days before deciding that I would stay loyal to Simpkins. Sometimes loyalty is more important than progress. They got me through the Brecon Beacons when I lost my way to Cardiff and lasted the full trip when, heading to Edinburgh, I found myself in Hull. In view of all this, I invested in a new atlas, which was available for £1.99 with a purchase of £50 or more of fuel at a BP station. Seemed like a good deal to me – and to Bertie, who always went through atlases at a fair rate of knots. In order to sate his appetite for destruction, Mrs Hardcastle, his instructor at the obedience school, once devised a strategic plan and advised me to purchase ten in a bid to wean him off them. 'That's a lot of petrol,' I explained to Mrs H. Luckily, my good friend Iqbal at the local garage saved the day by allowing me to have them on account at the special offer price as long as I got him Wasim Akram's autograph. It's not *what* you know, you know ...

Chapter 19

EVERY SLUMDOG HAS ITS DAY

Spending a day out at the cinema is not something I can lay claim to have done many times in my life, and it was only when I was asked to do a review for a cracking Manchester magazine called *Chimp* – this plug should boost sales by a dozen – that I put my mind to how long it had been. No sniggering, I am talking about the flicks. There must have been a fifty-year interim (discounting the time I stumbled into a seedy joint and sat next to a bloke who was doing something quite doubtful under his mac.) A full fifty years. Those were the days. Cinemas all over Accrington. I remember the Odeon, the Princess, the Empire, the Palace and the Kings Hall, otherwise known as the Bug Hut. Incidentally, the Kings was later turned into a snooker club, where Alex 'Hurricane' Higgins used to hustle.

Westerns were very much in vogue in those days. On screen, that is. But I was about to experience a different kind of wild west for this movie adventure. Namely Manchester's Trafford Centre. *Slumdog Millionaire* was showing at the

Odeon there, and although the Centre is normally very much off-limits for me – because I can't stand the place (too many folk … too many wandering gangs … too many shops … selling too much crap at ridiculously inflated prices) – it meant I could offer Mrs L an evening out straight from finishing work at Old Trafford. I decided to do the decent thing and took her for an Italian jobby first up and even stretched to purchasing a bag of Maltesers for the fillum. I have to say that I was pleasantly surprised that it only cost £17.50 for the two of us, and that in *premier* seats to boot. In fact I slipped up there, because I could have paid for standard and then vaulted into the prems when the lights went off, at a saving of four quid.

As it was the Odeon, I thought we would have kicked off with the good old Odeon Saturday Club song, as we used to back in Accrington. Many of you may remember it. One, two, three, four:

We come along, on Saturday morning
greeting everybody with a smile.
We come along, on saturday morning
knowing that it's worthwhile.
As members of the Odeon Club we all intend to be
good citizens when we grow up
and champions of the free.
We come along, on saturday morning
greeting everybody with a smile, smile, smile
greeting everybody with a smile.

I used to go with Johnny Anderson, who dropped the 'h' and the 'y' in his name before becoming lead singer of Yes. Johnny would sometimes even play with his band, the Warriors, at the interval. But there were to be no singalongs in the 21st-century experience. There wasn't even a fella cracking the gong. There bloody well should have been. There was certainly enough time for it. A full twenty minutes went by before *Slumdog* kicked off. This was very bad, Mr Odeon. If you say the film starts at a certain time, that's when it should start.

If you're the individual that hasn't seen it, the film in question is a take-off of Chris Tarrant's *Who Wants to Be a Millionaire*, set in India. But I guess you knew that. Jamal, the main man, gets in the chair somehow, and reels off answers to all the questions, each of which is somehow an echo of his desperate past, growing up in the slums of Mumbai. Actually, desperate is a word that does not do justice to the suffering of street kids out there. People who have never been to India, Pakistan, Bangladesh and other heavily populated Asian countries have no concept of what life, if you can call it life, is like. No home. No family. No education. No friends. No money. No fun. Just hopeless existence.

Slumdog offered some good glimpses of downtown Mumbai, a city I know well from numerous cricket tours, but the day-to-day chaos was missing. Buses weighed down at the back, train stations teeming with thousands of people, others hanging off trains as they depart, filth and squalor everywhere you look. In fact, the three-wheel tuk-tuks in the film all looked in good condition. Usually, they are 'ride at your peril' get-abouts, and damn good fun because of it.

But I am a sucker for a happy ending, and in *Slumdog* our hero gets the rupees and the girl and they all live happily ever after. Yes, all the baddies get their comeuppance. And I can vouch for the fact that India does have its gangster side. Trust me on this one, there is plenty of it about; an enormous amount of corruption, extortion and torture. Life is cheap. Somehow and for some reason, in real life these guys find their way into cricket.

There is one fleeting reference to cricket in *Slumdog*, and thankfully, because it takes in some of the great players, it was the one question I got right: 'Who has scored the most first-class centuries in the history of the game? A: Tendulkar, B: Slater, C: Ponting or D: Hobbs.' Jack Hobbs is the answer, as I am sure you knew. I even told the total stranger next to me how many. '199, luv,' I grinned. She gave me a filthy look.

As Jamal gets nearer to the jackpot, all of India stands still. That is the way it is over there. They love a hero. A hero who defies the odds and clambers up from the bottom rung. All the cricketers are gods out there, absolute superstars. Unless you have been to India, you will have no concept of exactly what it is like to be a cricketing giant. Forget David Beckham, Michael Jordan and Tiger Woods. Imagine what it would be like to have to go out in disguise. Actually, Tiger probably has for other reasons. But someone like Sachin Tendulkar has no privacy whatsoever. Everywhere he goes he is mobbed. And the film captured that adulation perfectly. I enjoyed the experience of going to the flicks, and I enjoyed *Slumdog* immensely. My better half said it showed India in a poor light. I explained that she had seen nothing that gets near the reality. Out there society is clinically separated into the haves and the have-nots. And the have-nots have nowt. Zero. Zilch. I wish we could all help more.

Chapter 20

BIRDIES, EAGLES AND MALLARDS

One of the pleasures of being away every winter – aside from sidestepping snowdrifts and avoiding icicles on your imponderables – is the chance to play on some fantastic golf courses. And because of the privileged position our travelling cricket community finds itself in, what with sports teams and television networking and other contacts across various industries, we are often accommodated when others would not be. I am always appreciative of that fact. Occasionally, though, even we have to pay, which is, of course, a source of irritation to Nasser Hussain.

For cricketers, golf is a regular activity, probably because it is a game suited to sunshine (something we follow twelve months a year) and at least a couple of days a week you will find yourself with a morning or afternoon spare. As a broadcaster, I like to prepare for a match the day before with some research, milling around the ground and dropping into the press conferences to suss out how the captains are feeling and pick up on any news threads from the media corps. But I always have some spare time between Tests or one-day matches when I'm on tour. And so the sticks are usually in tow.

I only began playing around the time I went into television full-time, starting with a handicap of sixteen. I got it down rapidly, and that led to me setting myself a target of five. I got to within two of my ambition but then hit a wall and slipped back to eight. If I am honest I have not even been playing to that for the last couple of years. I am just not consistent enough. I hold a membership at Bramall Park, near where I live, but play more often away from home these days. Some golfers prefer it that way, I believe. I just love playing whenever I get a chance.

With my game, if I'm right, my driving is the strong part of my game, but I'm not right often enough. I can hit it long but I'm always tinkering, and that's my biggest problem – I'm always trying to manufacture something instead of just playing. The professional advice I have received has not been good. While we were in South Africa, I happened to be out with Michael Vaughan for dinner, and who should be in our party but Darren Clarke, the Irish Ryder Cup player, who is looked after by Vaughan's management company. As the talk turned to golf, Vaughan piped up with: 'You've got a new thought about your swing, haven't you, Bumble?'

'Aye, I have. I have got the Henrik Stensons. When I address the ball I rock on to my back foot,' I said. So Darren politely asked for a practical demonstration there and then.

'Forget *Stensons*, that's mallards, mate. Mallards,' he summarised.

'What do you mean, mallards?' I frowned.

'You'll be hitting mallards in duck ponds with that stance! You've no chance.'

But us old 'uns don't do so bad when it comes to taking on contemporary cricketers over eighteen holes. Myself and Mike Selvey, two fellas who qualify for bus passes (well, we are in our 60s, any road) have been known to beat Vaughan and Collingwood. I would never fancy a pairing when one of them turns up with a man bag, as Vaughan does. Made by Louis Vuitton, or the bloke who sat next to him in art class, and shipped out from Dubai at a tenner a time by a mate of ours called Freelance Fred. A really nice sideline while he was side-lined was that. Many a time I have trousered some cash against either Vaughan or Collingwood, and sometimes the pair of them in tandem, and had some really good banter in the process.

For some international cricketers, golf can become a bit of an obsession; for others it is just the perfect way to switch off from the day job. Collingwood is usually on the organising committee during England tours and he has plenty of other keen competitors in the ranks. James Anderson can play a bit and Ian Bell is very eye-catching, hitting the ball with lovely balance in every stroke, rather like his batting. But the dark horse of the 'tour' is always England captain Andrew Strauss. A golf bandit if ever you met one. Handicap of ten, he reckons, and goes around in par. And it's nothing new to find players dashing off for a round or two while away on inter-national duty. Geoff Boycott was dropped from the England side on the tour of India in 1982 after being discovered on the golf course. Nothing wrong with that, you might say, but he was supposed to be fielding at the time and had told them he was too ill.

On tours of Australia we even take part in our own golf version of the Ashes, Ryder Cup-style over three days. We

meet up with a load of old friends in Adelaide, winemakers
and ex-players making a rum combination, and get stuck in.
It is really good fun, although the seriousness with which
some take their golf means you are never far from an almighty
strop. Nasser is unlikely to be part of any future Ashes golf
invites as, at the time of writing, he has retired after an incident at the Durban Country Club. Let's just say he can be as
volatile on a golf course as he was on a cricket field. Beefy
plays off eight but thinks he is somewhere nearer three. Like
that chap who had an indefinite break from the sport (I think
he's won a title or two), he is decked from head to toe in Nike.
He might look the part, but out of all of our commentary mob
it is Paul Allott who is our Tiger – he has a really deft touch
game for a big lad and is a fabulous putter. Of the others,
David Gower would not be seen anywhere near a golf course,
unless it backed on to a vineyard. He would argue there were
a million and one other things to do over a period of four
hours. Nick Knight is hopeless. I was saddled with him on a
tour of South Africa and, just as I was about to make a crucial
putt, he chose to ring Jonathan Trott to talk cricket. Very off-
putting. I guess I should be used to such lack of golf etiquette
because Vaughan, a decent and keen player, is the most vocif-
erous of sledgers. He gets on to you about your attire, your
grip, your stance, as if he is standing at mid-off. Another
former England captain, Michael Atherton, is a lovely golfer
and would be comfortable on a single-figure handicap but for
his dicky back. That hampered his cricket career, of course,
and it's funny how people's styles replicate how they were in
their main sport. Shane Warne has tremendous enthusiasm
and energy, just as he did on a cricket field, but is a good few
notches down from his number one cricket ranking when he

gets a golf club in his hand. Ricky Ponting oozes class and Jeff Thomson is like a bull at a gate. There was never much subtlety to Thommo: used to bowl as fast as he could, now tries to hit it as far as he can. In contrast, Rodney Marsh is very studious, and a very talented player.

Over the years I have had the pleasure of playing on some wonderful courses, and some I would usually be ineligible for or where I'd be taking out a second mortgage for a tee-off time. I have been lucky enough to play the Green Monkey, which is part of Sandy Lane in Barbados, a course you can only get on by invitation from the Irish businessmen John Magnier, Dermot Desmond, J.P. McManus and Des Smyth. It was actually Andrew Flintoff who offered me the chance to go and have a round there. It was absolutely gorgeous. A similarly lavish retreat is the River Club in Johannesburg, a privately owned course at which no money ever changes hands. It is owned by sixty people and is available only to their friends and families. At the end of the year, the costs incurred are tallied and split sixty ways. There are no tee times, no membership fees, no complaints. I have been on a couple of times, thanks to Michael Vaughan's in, and not seen another soul.

Every time we go out to South Africa, we head off to Sun City for a round or two. On the 2009–10 tour, however, we headed for the course at the Lost City resort, two and a half hours by road from Johannesburg. Appropriately, Hussain was driving. That was one sure-fire way for us to get into character. When we eventually found the place, we played as guests of the Jockeys' Association. All the great and the good were there – Mick Kinnane, Frankie Dettori, Richard Hughes and Seb Sanders among the international field. Sir Ian Botham was also in tow, which was a welcome relief for all of us. Now he is very keen on his charity work, is our Beefy, but listening to him that week doing television interviews you could have been mistaken into thinking he had solved South Africa's AIDS crisis rather than signed up as an ambassador.

Each group is designated a caddie before heading out, and it's always worth trying to strike up a bond with your man because a little local knowledge can go a long way. 'How's the course playing? How are you doing today? Oh, and what's your name, sir?' Now there are a few belting names doing the rounds in South Africa, but our chappie on this occasion topped the lot. 'Pleased to meet you, I'm Superstar,' he said. That, of course, made things tricky as we already had one among our number who would readily answer to the name. But there was to be no superstar performance as I came in tenth, winning a towel for my efforts. Not bad, you might think, but Hussain got a dozen golf balls for finishing eight places further back. Now surely that's a better prize for a golfer abroad? What would I want a towel for? To plonk on the rest of them in my hotel room?

It's the kind of item I usually try to pass the other way when I am having a round in South Africa. Whenever I go to Cape Town I always play at a place called West Lake and always have the same caddie if he is on duty. Now Dennis is a beauty – he only needs a white tooth and he'd have a complete snooker set. I always raided the bathroom for shampoos and conditioners for him to pass on to his missus, and wrapped up buns and croissants in serviettes from the breakfast room for him to scoff at the halfway house on the course.

Dennis was a creature of habit, something I established the first time I ever engaged him as my bag man. At the midway point, where you tuck into boerewors and biltong, it is customary to get one in for your chap, and so I said to him: 'Do you like a drink, Dennis?'

'Sweet white wine, bossee, sweet white wine.'

As it happened we were down to play a few rounds that week, and next day I promised to bring a drink with me as a treat for him. So I filled him a plastic water bottle with malt whisky and presented it to him before we went out.

'Sweet white wine, bossee, sweet white wine.'

'No, it's not sweet white wine,' I explained. 'This is malt whisky.'

'Sweet white wine? Bossee?'

'No, you're not listening,' I said, going on to explain that you put this much in the bottom of a glass, gesturing an inch or two with my fingers, and then top it up with about as much water again. 'It's a lovely drink,' I explained to him. 'A twenty-year-old malt. One to be savoured. You just need a little drop in the bottom of your glass.'

'Yes, bossee, sweet white wine.'

Anyway, we played the round, and I gave him his tip, while making plans to return next day. As we were leaving the complex in the car minutes later, however, the chances of us seeing Dennis next day diminished rapidly. He was standing by the gate, chin skyward, necking the whole thing in one. Letting off a huge gasp, he started dancing uncontrollably, spun around three times and collapsed in the grass. The following day I enquired after him, anticipating absence. 'He not very well,' his mate Earnest said, earnestly.

Some golfers in South Africa don't need a nip or twenty to be off it, however. There was one chap who came up to me at Sun City and said: 'I know your voice, you're the commentator.'

'That's right,' I said.

'The cricket man.'

'Yes, that's me.'

He said: 'I'll tell you my favourite commentator. It's the chap from *Test Match Special*.'

'Oh, right, which one?'

'Henry Johnston,' he said. 'The one with the beard.'

Not a bad effort that. He had managed to combine dear old Brian, Bloers and Bill Frindall in one!

When we were in Zimbabwe in 1996–7 – on the tour I am not supposed to talk about and because of which if ever I returned I had to do so under cover of darkness – I was party to one of golf's great stories. It was told at the bar of the Royal Harare Golf Club and at a time before I became public enemy number one. The next time I was in the vicinity, a few years later, I got a shuddering sense of my unpopularity. Despite my public slating of the Zimbabweans on my visit as England coach, I was befriended by this ox of a bloke who opened the bowling for them, called Eddo Brandes. Some of you will remember him: the chicken farmer who did us, and did us big time, in the 1992 World Cup. Then again with five wickets to seal a 3–0 one-day series success on the 1996–7 trip.

Back in Harare for a one-day tour in 2000, now in my commentary capacity, I bumped into Eddo, who was now retired, and agreed to help him collect money for a charity he was supporting. I scooted around the press box and got everyone to chip in, so I ended up with a huge bagful of money. Then came a bit of a schoolboy error as I agreed to hand over the loot in the bar at the Sports Club, where the imbibers had been at it solidly since 8.30 a.m. They had been giving it plenty, so you could imagine their feelings at seeing me invade their space, let alone three of me walking straight at them. Although this was a couple of years after the Zimbabwe episode, and despite the pickling of their grey matter in both the short and long term, it was a significant enough occurrence in their minds to disprove the theory that time is a great healer.

'Here's that f——ing ...' they bellowed as they shuffled towards me.

'Before you lot start,' I said, pointing to the bloke behind them, 'I'm with him.' Brandes gave me a quick character reference and we were all fine. But you can imagine what these geezers were like, and what they wanted to do to my limbs.

This small enclave of Harare is where the country's most elite sport takes place. The golf course is adjacent to the cricket ground. There are various things that have to happen at the complex every single evening – the cricket has to finish at six o'clock because if you're on that street in late evening you will get shot. As it is home to Robert Mugabe's house, the road is closed off to vehicles and the spectators have to be away before night falls. It is a procedure which happened at that time on a daily basis, almost like clockwork, and I have no reason to suspect it has not continued since. He had some really strange habits, did our Bob. I noticed a couple of times when we played at Harare that a helicopter would set off from his pad and would return within ten minutes. Splendid way to collect your pint of milk, paper and twenty Bensons. He would be sorted for the day, the lad. Shame about the other 12 million folk who struggled to survive on a hand-to-mouth existence and a diet of torture.

Anyway, back in 1996 I was standing at this bar in Harare, waiting for whoever, and just along from me was Nick Price, who at the time was the number one golfer in the world, and held the prestigious position for a great number of weeks. Indisputably, he was the best on the planet. And there he was gabbing with a bunch of blokes in *his* golf club, the place where the global maestro learnt his game and still played on a regular basis. He was holding court at the bar, starting to tell a tale against himself. I clocked him straight away, knew exactly who he was. But, as I was not in his company, I inched along the length of the bar. Before long I was in. People must have been thinking: 'Who the hell's this?' But with a bit of 'Hello, how you doing?' I kept my place among the throng. I was now in on the story.

The episode he was describing took place at that very club, it turned out, one at which you must have a caddie assigned to you when you go out for a round. This arrangement is non-negotiable, there is just no saying no, whether you are number one or hacking for fun. Fully aware of the rules and regulations, Price told the caddie master that he would be going out with his entourage as there was a lot of technical stuff they wanted to address. He was accompanied by his coach, his physio and his doctor – basically the clan that looked after his career. He told the caddie master: the lad can carry the bag, no problem, but I don't want him telling me about wind directions or strength of putt, anything like that, because I'll be fine. Just tell him to keep quiet because we're working.

They got off with no problem and had been through twelve holes when Price ran into some self-inflicted strife. He had pulled his tee shot on the thirteenth way left and was deep into bushes, shrubs and trees. The real thick stuff. After hunting around for a while, Price eventually goes and stands next to this ball to assess the predicament. He visualises what he needs to do. He is about 190 yards from the pin; there are over-hanging branches, so he's got to hit it under there with something like a four-iron; he has to play it off his front foot; he has to close the face slightly, so that it goes low before it goes high; he has a left to right wind to contend with; there's a bunker in front of the green and he is on the narrow side, the wrong side for holding the ball up; behind that is out of bounds. So, with 180 yards to carry the bunker, you can imagine his feeling when he plays the perfect golf shot. The club comes down, makes great contact, the ball nicks a little twig in flight, drifts on the breeze and just kicks over the sand, checks on the green and, unbelievably, comes back to within about three and a half feet of the pin. Price turns to his expressionless caddie, who is standing there with the bag, and says: 'I've got to tell you, that's one great golf shot.' Breaking his two-hour silence, the lad replies: 'You'd have been better off if you'd played your ball. It's over here.' It's one of my favourite stories. As Price commented with a chuckle, no matter how well you are playing, no matter how confident you feel, there is always something so simple capable of tripping you up. Never get too far ahead of yourself.

The Bumble-approved World Golf Courses:

Sunningdale, UK: An absolute privilege to have played the great course, and to finish and sit on that veranda is like landing in heaven.

Kinloch, near Taupo, New Zealand: A linksy Jack Nicklaus-designed course.

Royal Westmoreland, Barbados: Simply fabulous, has to be right up there with the best.

Green Monkey, Barbados: Even more exclusive than Westmoreland, I doubt I will get another chance there.

River Club, South Africa: What an arrangement. No queuing here, walk straight into golfing heaven.

Pearl Valley, Paarl, South Africa: Geoffrey Boycott lives just up the road but that fails to put me off.

Royal Adelaide, Australia: Take your pick in Australia, there are loads, but this is my favourite.

The Els Club, Dubai: Ernie's own design, makes you feel like you're playing golf in the desert.

Valderrama, Spain: Not on the cricket circuit, but I head there regularly for charity events and never tire of it.

Chapter 21

THE MILLION THAT GOT AWAY

If I was filthy rich, then I would go salmon fishing every single week I possibly could. There is something so therapeutic about the pastime; it is true escapism. Everybody takes the piss, saying it's a waste of time, but to me it's a perfect way to unwind, and switch off from text messages and traffic jams. Oh, and this may sound odd, but in my book fishing is not about catching fish – an anomaly which perhaps explains why my career statistics with a rod are so low. For my money, catching them is something extra which, if added to the overall package, is all well and good. But this, for me, is salmon fishing: scenery, river, flow, seeking, spotting, identifying, baiting. It's a massive collection of ifs and buts. What are they after? Where are they? Top of the water? Midstream?

There is definitely a feeling of respect for your opponent whenever you are on the river. Of that there is no question. I could never shoot anything, I could not even drown maggots or worms. That just ain't me, so fly fishing is my version of hunting. It follows the same principles, after all, and is something I have been into since I was about 30. To add to the sense of ceremony, I had a spell of tying my own flies, something which my limited time no longer allows. But whether you tie your own or not, from the moment you take your fly in hand, even before attaching it, the expectancy begins.

World cricket schedules have cut across my free time, and one of the excursions they have curtailed, unfortunately, is the annual September fishing trip to Scotland with some of my oldest and closest pals. For me that yearly jaunt was a great release valve at the end of every domestic cricket season. The water in question is some way past Aberdeen, at a place called Forbes Castle. We stayed frugally in some little cottages, concentrated on the pursuits of the day and blocked out all other commitments. Michael Atherton, John Barclay and Andrew Wingfield-Digby, all of whom held positions during my England coaching stint, were all core members of the group, with two of Athers's team-mates from his Cambridge University days, Richard 'Pumper' Pyman and 'Doc' Mark Alban, adding to the number. We would go up for as long a beat as we fancied and just chill out.

I went for six or seven years on the trot but only ever caught one fish. But as I say, it is all the anticipation of catching rather than the act itself that makes me love fishing. Good job, I guess. And it's not as if I am jinxed specifically up in Aberdeenshire, or anything like that. On the couple of occasions I have been invited to another unbelievably special place, the River Tweed at Kelso, by David Hodgkiss, the treasurer at Lancashire, I have also been barren. Others in my company have caught stuff – they are better fishermen, they must be, and I accept that. But it does not lessen the enjoyment in trying for me. Of course, conditions have to be with you for you to even have a chance. You have to hit the water right. If the water is murky, inky, mucky, you're catching nothing. If there's no rainfall in the Highlands, water doesn't flow through the river, so the fish won't move. You have to catch it absolutely right.

Just as with trout, which I fish for more regularly and with greater success, fishing for salmon is all about dinking in and knowing where a fish is. It is not like a sixth sense, it is more of a practical skill. You just know what to look for. Overhanging branches and flies hovering around are a telltale sign that there will be a fish in the vicinity. Then, every now and again you will see a tail glint – there's a fish in your presence, staying exactly where it is, almost goading you – so now the gauntlet has been thrown down. It is one heck of a challenge, and to catch a salmon is one of the best things you could ever do. A wonderful feeling. My only success at the time of writing (and there has been little evidence to suggest I will have doubled my tally in the meantime) took me forty-five minutes to reel in. When the task was complete I just lay on the bank to enjoy my triumph. I have never been a smoker, but I always carried a cigar around with me in my bag in anticipation of my first catch. If ever I caught one, I would light up, I thought. And when it came to it that was exactly what I did, and it was perfect.

Trout are a better class of, and more regular, opponent for me, during the course of a year. I used to hold an annual membership on the Derwent and Wye rivers in Derbyshire, and head for a fantastic stretch of water previously owned by Jasper Olivier. Before you ask, yes, he is of the same family. Soon after he sold up, one of his successor's first initiatives was to extend the season, thus allowing me greater opportunity to get into action. It meant I could be on the water more often, and it's only a forty-five-minute journey from my doorstep, which is kicking distance, really. So I would get on my motorbike once a fortnight on average and go down for an hour and a half on an evening, stopping for a pint at the Bull's Head at Ashford in the Water, a truly fabulous pub situated in a village as pretty as you could ever wish to see. My only disappointment on these trips would be the absence of the late Bertie, my faithful old pal, who, in days gone by, would sit alongside me on the bank, even when a fish was thrashing away something rotten, without a hint of a murmur. Not so Tags, who has proved a disaster. At the slightest commotion, she just jumps straight in, scattering the fish in the process. Fishing for trout is all stealth. It is getting out of the shadows and trail of the sun. It is kneeling down, quiet as can be, biding your time. It's playing the long game. Unfortunately, Tags is more cut out for the crash, bang, wallop of Twenty20.

Chapter 22

I never properly got into music until I was in my seventh decade. Over the years, I would keep it at arm's length and treat it as I am sure plenty of others do up and down the country. You go through that process of buying a CD and shoving it in the car because you need something to take your mind off those tedious motorway journeys. You listen to the thing four times straight through and then either scratch it attempting to eject it with one hand while driving, or consign it to its case and history.

Then, one day, my boss Paul King started blathering on about Manchester bands and my ears pricked up. I had heard of most of the names he was reeling off, but I couldn't have named any of their tracks off the top of my head. Nevertheless, my curiosity was stirred. Next day he handed me a CD and told me I would either like it or detest it. There would be no middle ground, he told me with confidence. Because, as I was soon to discover, there is no middle ground with The Fall. It's just love or loathe. They polarise opinion like you would not believe.

When it comes to this lot I am totally hooked, but Diana will not allow me to play them in the house, so I only listen when I am driving or away with work. I think their stuff is quite funny – although I am not sure it is supposed to be – and musically it's sensational. That's before you even ponder the antics of Mark E. Smith. This bloke is outrageous. A complete enigma. I like the rawness, the protest in the voice and the delivery of the lyrics. It is all 'up yours' – gloriously anti-establishment. For him to put the words to music in the style that he has is incredible. I am not sure he can sing at all. But for me nobody has recorded anything comparable – I just get everything about them.

Well, I say them, but MES really *is* The Fall. He is the mainstay of a band that has passed its half-century in band members over thirty years. Get to know his character and you might understand why. MES does not play your typical pop star. He deals in offence as both a giver and a taker. An oddball whose lyrics are on the ball. When I read his book *Renegade*, I could not put it down. Cover to cover inside two days. He has outlandish opinions, and I would dread to meet him because it would probably blow me apart. I know he would be extremely abusive and I am not sure how I would deal with that. He is an urban bigot, whose distrust of outsiders reveals itself in the fact that he believes people from Stockport walk around with deerstalkers on their heads. I couldn't bring myself to tell him my postcode. He would tell you that he is from Salford, not Manchester, which in his esti- mation is a planet away. He also reckons breakfast television is now false because there are no ashtrays and the presenters are not wheezing and spluttering. These are his deep and meaningful thoughts.

If ever I put on The Fall, or those wordsmith geniuses Half Man Half Biscuit, around my fellow Sky commentators, I'm greeted by a chorus of 'Turn that s—— off!' They are complete heathens, of course. When it comes to music, Nasser is like one of those bad motorway drivers, hogging the middle of the road (Elton John territory), Atherton is tone deaf, so I doubt he even has a radio in his car, and Beefy has been known to attend Kylie Minogue concerts. Enough said. But I can hardly claim a perch on the high ground of taste here. I have always been into rock-and-roll artists such as Chuck Berry or Little Richard, but then I have also allowed my guard to drop and slumped into the trap of 'easy listening' artists like Lionel Richie, or similarly tedious stuff that wouldn't even merit getting the bargepole out nowadays.

Overlooking such indiscretions, however, I have always been attracted to the rebel in musical terms – people who are not afraid to speak out. Some might see an analogy here with the way I acted in my Zimbabwe moment, and I would not disagree. I felt a raging sense of injustice, I wanted my say on it, and that was a rebellious streak in me that I later regretted. I was new to English cricket and I don't think they'd had anyone before that just blurted it out like that. But I have to admit, given the chance to rewind, I would probably do things exactly the same – bollocks to it. Even though I know it would not be the best move, I have never been one to bite my tongue. I fire it out, then deal with it.

When it comes to the rebel-rousers, I have always listened to Johnny Cash, and I have always been a massive Rolling Stones fan. I love the rawness of artists like the Stones, and that comes across in their live shows. What a showman Mick Jagger is. It is an event to watch them. They give it some real gusto. I want to hear 'Satisfaction' – the original by Buddy Guy is totally different but equally knockout – at high-decibel level. I like music that makes big, bold statements.

I can't stand twee music and boy bands. I am sure they are very good, but that shit just doesn't do anything for me. However, I cannot help having a great admiration for Cliff Richard. I think he has been absolutely fantastic. He doesn't fit my rebellious artist profile at all, but if I could choose one bloke to invite to a dinner party it would be him. Just look how successful he has been as the chameleon of pop. He evolved from that teen angst persona, up against Elvis Presley, and turned right round into a clean-living bloke who churned out quality music for his loyal audience over forty or fifty years. You have got to admire that.

I wouldn't necessarily listen to his music, and the same would go for someone like Eric Clapton. Yeah, I can appreciate his stuff, because he is obviously a genius slow hand when it comes to the guitar, but he just doesn't do it for me. It's the same with Premier League football – I can watch it all day, but give me the up-and-at-'em of Accrington Stanley, that's what really gets me going. When it comes to music, post-punk is my bag, and my love of The Fall has led me to the other seminal bands of the north-west, The Smiths and Joy Division. None of this kind of stuff is likely to feature on Sky's cricket opening credits any time soon, although I did try to have an influence by putting forward Slade's *Cum On Feel the Noize* as the theme tune to Twenty20 cricket in 2010. That should see me right for a pint or two when I bump into my fellow Prestbury resident Noddy Holder in the local.

I am ultra-disciplined and extremely serious about my work with Sky, and would never dream of stepping out of line. If I am told: 'You will wear this, you will turn up at X, and be there at such and such a time' – then yes, sir, take it as done. But downtime is my time and I don't really do conformity. Every now and again, unshaven and dressed in jeans and an old T-shirt – my favourite one says 'Piss Off, I've Got Enough Mates' – I will head into Manchester for a marathon booze-up. I occasionally get blitzed, and I don't care who sees me, because I will have had a tremendous time with some great mates. You don't get another chance, as they say, so I give it a do every now and again, usually setting off with Diana's words – 'Oh no, you're not going down there again, for goodness sake' – ringing in my ears.

I am a laddish bloke who loves laddish things – football, fishing, music, bikes and beer. My other passion is for comedy, and that means puerile humour at times. Half Man Half Biscuit set me off with lyrics such as 'I'm Sitting on Lord Hereford's Knob'. What a thing to sing. Of course, we all know Lord Hereford's Knob is a hill in Wales, but the *double entendre* brings out the sniggering schoolboy in us all. Well, it certainly does in me. Subtle humour or blatant vulgarity, you decide, but the Biscuit can never be accused of taking life too seriously. Surely there cannot be many better song titles than '99 Per Cent of Gargoyles Look Like Bob Todd'. By my calculations that means one in 100 is an Iain Dowie clone.

Laughter drives me, and every night before I go to bed I watch an episode of *Fawlty Towers*, *The Fast Show* or *Early Doors*. I can recite virtually every line of every episode of the latter. That show has me howling, just as *Fawlty* does, whether it's the first or the fifty-first time I have seen it. My missus can be next to me and not even cracking a smile while I am in tears. One of my Manchester drinking pals, James

Quinn, plays one of the coppers, and it was the show that gave Hollywood star James McEvoy his big break. It also, along with *Bellamy's People*, makes my world go round.

I have been into comedians from way back. My all-time favourite was Jimmy James, whose great trick was to never once look at the audience. Never. And he always had his stooge Eli Woods in tow. Their sketch with Roy Castle, playing a simpleton who has travelled the world and collected wild animals in a box, is pure genius. That sketch was all about their delivery. I loved all the old Music Hall era stuff. Nat Jackley, Jimmy Edwards, the silent movies of Buster Keaton, then Tommy Cooper, Morecambe and Wise, the two Ronnies, through to Harry Enfield, Ricky Gervais and Lee Mack. I just love comics and I am addicted to TV re-runs on Dave and Gold.

The other thing that sets me off on one is listening to Hampton Cummings, aka Star Turn. For the uninitiated, if you haven't heard his comeback gig, the international party night at the Whitley Bay Social Club in 1998, you don't know what you're missing. I suggest you get your hands on a copy of the album *Maybe Definitely the Best Turn Album in the World ... Ever Ever*. As MC Albert Charlton says on the introduction, he's possibly the greatest singer the world has ever known. If not, he is certainly the best ex-merchant seaman to do the club scene, so let's dim the lights for a bit of atmosphere, and get into the mood with his signature tune, 'Are You Affiliated?'

Hit the North

(Crowd: *screams*)

My mind is like a fruit machine
Spinning round.
There are two plums on the bandit
Lend me a pound.
JACKPOT, JACKPOT

When I try to join the club of life
they always shut the door.
The little man wants my members card
and the plums come round once more.

(Crowd: *Whooooooo!*)

Chorus

Are you affiliated?
Let me in, let me in.
Are you affil-e-a-ted?
Let me in, let me in.

I'm always early
but there's someone in my seat.
(Heckler: *'They're only here for the bingo'*)
I'm sweating on a number
but I'm out here in the street.
'House called, house called.'

The walls only hear my cry
I'm living under stress.
(Heckler: 'Give it some melody, man')
The only way to get in this place
is I must adjust my dress.

Are you affiliated?
Let me in, let me in.
Are you affil-e-a-ted?
Let me in, let me in.

* * *

(Albert: rapping)
Son yer not affiliated, you cannot come in!
'Ah knaa, ah knaa.'
Son yer not affiliated, you cannot come in!
'Ah knaa, ah knaa.'

* * *

Ah-let me in, let me in, let me in, let me iiiiinnnn
Are you affiliated?
Let me in, let me in
Are you affil-e-a-ted?
Let me in, let me in.

Hit the North

(The Rhythm Bandits backing singers)
He's not affiliated
Throw him out, throw him out.
(Star Turn: *Oh let me een, oh let me iiiinnnnn*)
He's not affiliated
Throw him out, throw him out.
(Star Turn: *Oh let me een, oh let me iiiinnnnn*)
He's not affiliated
Throw him out, throw him out.
(Star Turn: *Oh let me een, oh let me iiiinnnnn*)
He's not affiliated.

Star Turn: *I love you all*

Then, after the special act imported for the highbrows, the Three Turns, deteriorate rapidly (probably something to do with a three-hour session at the bar), Star Turn is back to rescue the day, showing his versatility as a crooner, and singing the English translation of 'Nessun Dorma':

I couldn't sleep a wink last night
my neighbours drink too much
and start to fight,
and the dogs outside keep barking
and cars keep parking over my lawn.

I couldn't sleep a wink last night
my neighbours drink too much
and start to fight,

all through the night,
the roof was leaking,
the back door squeaking
right until dawn.

Till the dahahahahahwn
Till the dahahahahahwn.

As Albert quite rightly points out, if you think he's good at this stage, just wait until he's had a few pints! You've no doubt got 'Pump Up the Bitter', one of the classic singles of the 1990s, in your music collection, but it cannot be complete without *Maybe Definitely*. As the Star Turn motto goes: Who dares, sings.

Chapter 23

BUMBLE FOR PRIME MINISTER

They say sport and politics don't mix, and I always believed it to be true until recently when I was contacted by the administrators of a burgeoning Facebook group called 'David "Bumble" Lloyd for Prime Minister'. I've had the top job before, of course, but only in the cricketing sense. Perhaps the thought of power had gone to my head, or perhaps it was the fact that there were 2,300 people mad enough to support my claims to overtake Seb Coe on the final bend in the political stakes handicap chase, but my mind naturally turned towards crucial issues like forming a cabinet. From their actions over the years, politicians have suggested anyone can have a go, you don't have to be competent.

So Mark E. Smith for chancellor, I say, and the manifesto would be simple: print more money. The Parliament must be shifted to the Circus Tavern, Portland Street, to allow George to take up his position as speaker of the house. I'd plump for another of my favourite Mancunian characters Phil the Suit as minister for the arts. He would deck everyone out in 'Jaguar' whistles (no one has had the heart to tell him it's Jaeger for twenty years or more) and never be more than two sizes out. In political terms that's a hell of an accuracy record. For the inauguration party, I would invite Graeme Swann's band Dr Comfort and the Lurid Revelations to play Old Trafford, so that England's finest off-spinner and wannabe rock star could follow in the footsteps of the Gallagher brothers, his long-term heroes. The Number 10 role was never among my career goals, but I do have experience of holding a job which every other bugger thinks he can do better, so it might be a home from home. And I couldn't do much worse.

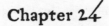

Chapter 24

'To the regiment ...
I wish I was there'

— Joe and Duffy, *Early Doors*

You undoubtedly know me as Bumble, certainly everyone in cricket does, but it is not a name you will hear when I am down the pub with my mates, or the JSS Regiment as we refer to ourselves. To them I am the Commander or, informally, Lloyd. You get a lot of that surname stuff in my neck of the woods. 'How's Clarke? Is Smith popping in for a couple?' That sort of thing.

Our regiment is a merry band of men who talk about anything and everything. Well, anything and everything apart from cricket, to be precise. We come from a fleet of different occupations and various backgrounds but are united by the love of a session in our regular boozer. Headed by Group

Captain Clarke, our number also includes Colonel Faulkner, who always seems to be on manoeuvres around Nottingham with a little firm called IBM, Major 'Shadow' Davidson, Rear Ad-Moral Jonty Ramsden-Smyth, aka Chin Laden due to his facial features, and Private Macca of Bulgaria (and his failed Bulgarian property empire). Unfortunately, General C.J. Smith has departed. But we continue to drink to his health; it's the way he would have wanted it.

Macca, as you might have sussed, invested in these two properties in Bulgaria, looking to make a quick buck. So he put them up for rental, thinking Boris was his uncle. However, after two years without so much as a bean, and sick of being told by the agency that they had not managed to attract any tenants, he went over for a look unannounced. To his shock, and our amusement, he found joyous families dwelling in his rather-less-than-humble abodes. Well, they were happy until they realised they were no longer going to be glorified squatters. In discussions over the rent, it came to pass that the tenants were concerned that the places, although fully decked out, were not furnished to their satisfaction. But would you believe it, as luck would have it, in his hour of need, Macca met a bloke from the town who specialised in furniture. He had around £10,000 eased out of his wallet and, needless to say, never saw this delightfully friendly chap again. But don't feel too sorry for him, he's in recruitment and doing OK for himself. In fact, his best piece of recruiting was of a personal nature – the girl he dates is half his age and turns up in tabloids wearing barbed wire and not much else.

The Brigadier

Those were the days when our mess was at the Church Inn, which has since turned into one of those fancy gastro pubs, where the only standing room is outside. We have since shifted to another pub in Cheadle Hulme, the Hesketh Tavern, where there is plenty of room and a cracking atmosphere. The commotion usually centres around the Brigadier, a man who cannot have a trip down the pub without incurring injury. He's the kind of bloke who needs to keep crutches in his shed in anticipation of his next prang. The street in which he lives has been renamed Brigadier Memorial Drive because every time he gets out of a cab on return from a sup he trips up and hits his head on the pavement. Every other time I see him he has a new lump on his bonce where he has fallen out the car. Yet no matter how much he goes through, it's inexplicable to him why he can't stand up after a dozen pints of Stella. He's even been known to topple before getting into his chariot home. His wife Marilyn was furious one week when, having driven to pick him up, she found him crawling around the car park on his hands and knees. As he slouched alongside her, he was told in no uncertain terms that his place on the lads' trip to Benidorm was in the balance.

He's got previous abroad as well. Namely on a golf trip to Portugal when, upon arrival at the hotel, he dropped off his suitcase and announced he was off for a swim. Now the Brigadier is full on – everything he does is at 100 miles an hour – and having not really been abroad much before he was perhaps making up for lost time. So, he gets his shorts on – if you want to build up a picture, he's the thinnest bloke in the world and runs like John Cleese in Basil Fawlty mode – and hurtles towards the pool, throwing himself into a full-length dive as he reaches the water. Only problem was, there wasn't any. He smashed his head on the bottom and spent the entire trip with this huge crepe bandage wrapped around the wound.

Boy, has he got into some scrapes in his time. One Saturday, the Brigadier was under orders from his good lady to purchase a new set of bath taps. So he set off at 10.30 a.m. from Ramillies Avenue, the road where we used to live, to drop Marilyn off at work on his way to purchase them. He had only got as far as the T junction, however, when who should happen to be walking by, newspaper tucked under the arm, but CJ. Winding down the window, the Brigadier acknowledges his pal: 'All right, CJ?' Imagine Boycey addressing Del Boy and you are about there. 'Just off to the golf club for a livener as it happens,' CJ replies. 'Bit of breakfast, and I'll see where the day takes me.'

'Good idea,' said Brig, hopping out with good haste. 'I'll come with you. Nothing much on.' So Marilyn, planner of Operation Bath Taps, was forced to switch into the driver's seat and take the car on to work, in the expectation that the necessary purchase would be made at her husband's leisure later in the day. Fourteen pints of Stella later, however, when they decided to go down to Cheadle Hulme village and check out what was happening at the Junction, shopping could not have been further from his mind. In fact, he was struggling to keep his current purchases in hand. As soon as he wandered in, he dropped his pint. 'Terribly sorry, sir, let me pour you another,' said a friendly barman. There was no doubt as to whose fault it had been, however, when the next buttery glass slipped through the fingers and exploded on the floor, so an executive decision to leave was taken. Destination Rooster's chicken takeaway.

Having purchased a deluxe meal, the Brigadier decided to look for some tranquillity and toddled off to trough in the little public park opposite. Unfortunately, the bench he had eyed up was so tempting that, before tucking in, he dozed off to sleep. Unperturbed by his snoring, however, a squirrel decided that the Brig's nosh was fair game and began nibbling. Coming round but still in a drowsy state, the Brigadier felt a gentle tugging at his hand and, as a reflex, lashed out. Suddenly, he was in a ruck with a rodent and about to come off second best. The squirrel's gouging of his fingers and palm spurted blood everywhere. Heaven knows what they thought when he turned up at the casualty unit of Stepping Hill Hospital in Stockport. Heaven knows what Lady Carr thought at midnight when her husband, laid out on a hospital bed, arm strapped up and sobering up fast, rang her to say: 'You'll never guess where I am, and what has happened to me, my dear … I've been attacked by a squirrel.'

'Never mind that,' she blasted. 'Have you got the bath taps?'

Marilyn often fell foul of the Brigadier's secret missions, drawn up at short notice to avoid domestic chores. I lost count of the number of times – after we moved to a house in Hazel Road, which was perfectly positioned between his own and the Church Inn – we would receive an almighty banging on our front door. A noise like the world was about to end. 'Come on,' he would breathlessly wheeze, as I opened up. 'She thinks I'm cutting the grass. We can nip up and have a couple. I've left the mower running, it will fool her for about half an hour.' If we didn't lock the door, he would burst right in. The way things were set up was that five townhouses were set back against another set of five, and the Brig's mate Guy lived directly behind us, so he just got to walking straight through our house as a short cut. Like it was a public walkway. 'Just going to Guy's,' he would announce on his way through the kitchen, as Diana and I sat watching the telly.

One year I came back from a tour to spend Christmas and New Year at home. As usual on one of our sessions, the Brigadier took on board his customary soak – at that time of year almost certainly John Smith's Smooth, the drop after which our regiment is named – and departed in his usual manner. His arrival back at Chez Carr was greeted with friendly waves out of the front window from his grandchildren. Cue inexplicable customary stumble. To minimise embarrassment he was shuffled into the garage with the minimum of fuss by Marilyn.

'I had a lovely night with Nigel and Graham,' he reminisced next time he was allowed out to play. 'Good company, that pair. I was engrossed in conversation with them for about six hours.'

'Just a sec, who the heck are Nigel and Graham? Not heard you talk about them before … And what were they doing in your …?' In that state of inebriation, garden gnomes are probably the only species able to understand him.

He often finds himself in compromising positions as a result of his escapades. Marilyn used to work a shift system as canteen manageress at our local Sainsbury's, and mowing the lawn was one of his regular tasks when she was on a Saturday shift. She would be at home for four, so the Brig used to have a precision operation pre-planned. He would be up to the pub for midday with a ploy to get back home for half past three and whizz the mower around quick sharp. This one particular Saturday all went exactly to plan, the grass freshly cut and the lawnmower gleaming in the sun as the lady of the manor returned. But no sign of the cutter. After a couple of hours, she started ringing around the troops.

'Have you seen Geoffrey?'

'Saw him briefly earlier when he popped in the pub, but he didn't stay long as he was intent on cutting the grass.'

'Yes, the mower's running but he's just not there ... I'll try suchabody.'

Everyone had given the same story, and then, while making the umpteenth call, she happened to peer out of the kitchen window at this buzzing machinery and a Wellington boot sticking out from behind the shed at a strange angle gave the game away. He had fallen asleep on the compost heap.

When we first moved to Ramillies Avenue, not long after I met him, I happened to mention to the Brigadier, who lived about eight doors down, my shock at discovering a large greenhouse underneath the unkempt growth in our garden. I had invested in an industrial-sized strimmer, strapped it on my back and, goggled up, gone to work on these eight-foot-high brambles. As I hacked through them, I kept hitting this hard surface. It was only after some serious strimming that I realised what it was. This was a full-size greenhouse and I wanted to be rid of it. 'I would love to see the back of it and put a summerhouse on that base it's on,' I told him. 'There's only one way to get rid of that,' he insisted. 'Set fire to it.' Eh? 'I'll sort that out, don't worry yourself. No problem.'

I didn't think anything of it at the time. Thought it was a lot of hot air. Then, at 10.30 one night, as the Brigadier stood banging at my front door with a can of petrol in his hand, Marilyn alongside him, I knew he was serious. I was hanging out our bedroom window in my pyjamas as he boldly declared: 'We've come to sort out that problem. We'll get it done.' So he trudged off and PERKKKURGHHH the petrol was set alight. The whole thing went up like you wouldn't believe. Within minutes, shouts of 'FIRE, FIRE!' from the neighbours filled the air, along with the thick black smoke. 'It's all right. There's no problem at all, I am just dropping the greenhouse, I am in total command,' bellowed the Brig, as he fell in the fire. Hair and eyebrows singed, hands burnt on the cinders, he instructed his accomplice: 'Marilyn. Bandages, bandages, Marilyn. Bandages.' He was like a turkey cock when he came back the following morning. Of course, the thing hadn't melted and I looked equally stupid to all my new neighbours. 'Who's this flippin' idiot that's moved in?' said the glance of every eye at me for the next few weeks. We had only been in two months or so. Our garden was smouldering away and there was all this blackened glass, like glazed toffee. But it failed to curb the Brigadier's enthusiasm. 'Pretty good job that,' said Red Adair, as he surveyed the wreckage.

Nothing ever quite goes to plan for the Brig. One year he was very excited about seeing *Oklahoma!* at the Manchester Opera House. 'Come and spend the night with Lesley Garrett,' said the *Manchester Evening News*. This was exactly the kind of invitation to get the Brig excited, so you could imagine his disappointment when he turned up to discover poor Lesley was ill and a substitute was standing in. He sat through the first half, but the feeling of let-down had not waned, so he decided to ask for his money back. Trying to placate the aggrieved customer, the girl on reception asked:

'Was there anything about the show that you enjoyed?' 'Yes,' he replied. 'The Opal Fruits from the kiosk.'

In addition to the regiment we have would-be members, territorials if you like. Minty is so dubbed because of his remarkable likeness to the *EastEnders* character, while 34 Regular has an obsession with his weight and, as his nickname might suggest, squeezing into his jeans. He's a 36 waist if ever I saw one, but a man should always have a goal in life, I suppose. The landscape for 34 Regular is unerringly familiar: the inside of the pub. He's been trying to cut down his boozing to five nights a week for as long as I can remember. And if he is on an early shift at work, he lets it be known in advance that he can only stay out until 11. Minty has an astute tactical acumen which usually involves persuading his other half he will be back home shortly, if she wants to toddle off early.

Then there is the Dazzler, a sporting protégé whose achievements include a schoolboy spell with Everton, two maximum scores of 300 at tenpin bowling, a national junior squash title, a place in England's water polo team, a nine-dart finish (although memories of his checkout are blurry) and a victory over a grandmaster at chess (his opponent's name equally elusive). As you can imagine, this guy can turn his hand to anything with great success. He trained as a roofer in Liverpool, then made the obvious change to head up the corporate sales team for Rank Xerox before being headhunted to set up an international marketing agency. He is currently in charge of B & D repairs (Bodge it and Do one, we reckon) and appears at 3.30pm daily at the Hesketh covered in plaster. Archie, his P-reg Fiat van, is one of the posher vehicles in Edgeley, where he resides. His household security consists of two revolvers and a sawn-off shotgun – necessary deterrents when you are pulling in six grand a week. These are known facts that have been relayed to numerous people and anything else you may hear about our Daz are fabrications of the truth and may not be relied upon.

Occasionally we will venture on to foreign terrain, and one such trip to Manchester escalated like you would not believe. The Brigadier was in between Post Offices – he's been through a few in his time – and Group Captain Clarke fancied an afternoon, so we made an expedition to the Circus Tavern. The plan was to start there and branch out as the day drew on. To cut a long story short, we didn't leave. David Knowles, a charity-worker pal of mine and fellow Fall fan, joined us. Ed Blaney from the band and James Quinn, whose brilliance in *Early Doors* I am in awe of, completed our crew. We later fled the scene in a very shabby state, taking a taxi back to the Hesketh where, somehow, I managed to chomp my way through two dinners in the space of an hour. I had the first, forgot about it, and then convinced myself I had yet to tuck in. It had been one of the great days.

Blaney had brought in a carrier bag with four pieces of flooring from the Hacienda earlier that afternoon, complete with authentication certificates, to be auctioned off for the Victim Support, Manchester. Hallowed flooring tramped over by the feet of members of Joy Division, New Order, Stone Roses and Happy Mondays. One of the chunks had an additional piece of memorabilia attached, covered as it was with a substance formerly known as chewing gum. Rumour had it the chuddy in question belonged to Bez. Imagine the toxic levels if they ever analysed it.

The regiment are a group I have knocked about with since the mid-1990s, when I was still coach at Lancashire, and they are a great set. This lot allow me to get away from the day job and seldom talk cricket. And that suits me down to the ground. In fact, the one time my mates and my day job met head-on could have ended in disaster. As it was, it created a real hoot. Rewind to the Test match against South Africa at Old Trafford in 1998, when I was in charge of England.

'Can you get us some tickets?' they asked.

'I'll see what I can do, yeah. Just leave it with me. How many are you after?'

There are always complimentary tickets that are not taken up by players and the backroom staff, so I would have been confident of rounding up half a dozen, but they were after fourteen, as it was someone's stag do. That was quite an ask, but with my connections at the club and the inevitable spares in our dressing-room I managed to accommodate them all.

Having gone to the trouble of getting the block of seats, I knew exactly where they were going to be housed in the ground, and decided to have a gander at them during the morning session from the dressing-room balcony. I knew they would stick out like a sore thumb, and I was not to be disappointed. Sure enough, with the binoculars out, I was soon on to them. Noticing they had my attention, they stood up en masse to wave. The fourteen, however, had become fifteen. There, bouncing around in the middle of them, legs akimbo, was a tall blonde. A real doll.

A doll of the blow-up variety, to be precise, and an upmarket one at that, with matching cuffs and collar. The business. They were enjoying themselves, bobbing her up and down on their knees as the day progressed and the beer flowed. Unfortunately, however, their larks got rowdier and rowdier until they were deemed sufficiently rowdy for the female accomplice to be confiscated by the stewards as punishment. Now this wouldn't have been a problem, but for the fact that this young lady was pricey and had to go back to the shop she was hired from – otherwise my mates would lose their hefty deposit.

One of the lads rang across to relay their predicament and ask for help. So, here I was, overseeing a crucial Test match, chatting to those around me about how to combat the pace threat of Allan Donald, Lance Klusener and Shaun Pollock, with a new and unexpected challenge now on my plate. Luckily I know one or two people at the ground and after a couple of calls between overs – 'I'm not sure how to put this but I am on the look-out for a … ahem, blow-up doll …' – I managed to pin this lass down (excuse the expression) to the club's offices.

Now that is where my wife Diana works as cricket administrator. Normally, of course, you wouldn't be engaging your good lady in a conversation about such a subject. 'Listen,' I explained, 'those silly sods have brought in a blow-up d—'

'Oh, it belongs to them, does it? It's just been delivered to us here,' she said. 'The stewards have just popped her in.'

I explained the need for its return to a loving home, and Diana went about deflating and concealing, with the planned handover arranged for that evening.

In those days, Tetley's Bitter were the England team sponsor and requested the company of all the team and media in their hospitality area for a drink at the close of play each day. 'All right, Bumble?' said Jonathan Agnew, as he shuffled over for a chat. 'I'm all right, Aggers, but my mates have had a bit of a close call,' I said shiftily, explaining the smuggling back of Rubber Rita. Diana had already joined me by this stage but was mingling elsewhere in the room and we had yet to complete the operation, which meant the female in question was hidden from view, in a bag in the corner of the room.

Armed with this knowledge, and always keen for mischief, Aggers scooted across and yanked the doll out in front of everybody. 'What do we have here then?' he beamed. Now Diana is so straight-laced that she was mortified with embarrassment, petrified about what people might think. I am sure the Sunday tabloids could have had a field day – England coaches and blow-up dolls are pretty decent ingredients for a scandal – but the young lady was chaperoned home and the only warnings over future conduct were directed by me at my sozzled pals.

CJ

There have been some scrapes for the regiment over the years, and the majority of them used to feature the much-missed CJ. You could not make him up. He was the kind of bloke who courted calamity everywhere he went, and the kind of bloke who had been everywhere and done everything. At least he said he had. One year I had gone off to Anglesey for a cricket engagement and happened to stumble across a couple of cracking dogs at a nearby kennels. Knowing that both CJ and the Brigadier were on the lookout – we were all dog-daft – I came back with a recommendation and directions for getting to the place.

Max was this beautiful black Labrador, fifteen months old, who had been trained as a gun dog but was just not quite up to the mark. He would make a cracking pet, and CJ recognised it too. He was dead keen and completed the deal there and then. In fact, he had only been back in the house a couple of hours when he decided to head off for the woods for Max's maiden walk. No sooner had he let him off the lead, however, than whoosh – off he went. Max was out of sight in seconds, and CJ simply could not find him anywhere. Trouble was, he used to have a tickle of whisky before he set off on a walk (CJ, not the dog), and somehow he managed to persuade himself that he had caught a glimpse of a black flash disappearing into the opening of this huge culvert. Yep, a big, stinking sewage pipe. So he set off in pursuit, through prickly hedges and into this stinking hole – to no avail, wriggling back out minutes later, covered in crap. Literally. He trudged back to the house, in this sorry state, feet dragging behind him like a schoolboy, with a lead but no dog, preparing to explain himself.

'Sorry, Anne,' he said. 'I've no idea where he's gone. I've lost the dog.'

'Don't be so silly,' she said, pointing over to the fire where the new arrival was lording it. 'He's here.' This was classic CJ. He was a comedy scriptwriter's dream.

One winter he turned up on a tour of Australia, and this led to me taking him to a barbecue at the house of a friend of mine, a senior lawyer, in Adelaide, whose lady friend was the deputy opposition leader in South Australia at the time. Mindful of his story-telling prowess, I pre-warned the rest of the party that he might just go off on a debatable tangent. 'If he does, just let him go,' I urged them. 'You'll have a ball.' I introduced him to everyone and, true to form, it was not long before he was telling them all he worked for the British government behind the Iron Curtain. Very dangerous, he said

– never went to bed without his Luger under the pillow, he said. 'Anyone for more wine?'

Later, he nipped out for a fag and came back agitated. 'I don't want to alarm anyone, but I think we're being watched,' he said.

'Yeah, no worries. They'll be with me,' the lady of the house reassured him. But CJ typically, without a crack in his expression, retorted: 'Thank goodness. I thought people knew that I was here.'

He was just a larger-than-life character. Any subject you broached in the golf club would be met with a CJism. 'The gas is going to run out in Aberdeen soon,' Tom might say to Dom. 'Yeah, that'll be a shame, that,' CJ would interject across locker room, 'because I put that gas in there when I was on the rigs.' Those of us who knew him would ask 'When?' Those who didn't would flex the muscles around the eyebrows. 'During my time as a deep-sea diving instructor,' he would reply. When people were talking about the luxurious palm developments in Dubai in the early Noughties, CJ would chime in: 'Yep, I've done a lot of work out there. We put a bank in for the Sultan, you know. He needed one set up and so I went across, what with my IT connections and all.' One day we will find out it was all true.

A hail-fellow-well-met character if ever there was one, CJ lured you in with his infectious, affectionate personality. You revelled in his fun. And his misfortune. He once got advised to buy some shares in a company called Knowledge, so he scraped together £1,000 by any means he could. It seemed to have been well worth it when, within a few months, his money had swelled tenfold, and within a few more the initial stake had rocketed into tens of thousands in value. I reckon at one stage his thousand smackers were worth £100,000. His new-found status led him to adopt the walk and cool air of a high-flyer. 'Yeah, I have just come into money from my investments,' he would mutter matter-of-factly, chomping on a big la-di-da like Harry Enfield's Loadsamoney man. But no sooner had the markets shot his shares up than they came right back down again.

Like a lot of the Cheshire set, he would trek to North Wales for family get-aways, heading for the picturesque Abersoch and Nefyn, little towns situated on a beautiful stretch of coast-line, featuring clean sand and lovely water. Thankfully for him, there is also a terrific pub called the Tycoch, a real fish-erman's haven, which can only be reached by foot. People congregate outside to drink and the kids can have a run around. He had a to-die-for cottage just up the road, and on arrival for a long weekend one time he settled in for a customary quenching session. Perhaps it was the alcoholic intake which stirred his sense of adventure. Whatever it was, he decided he was going to go fishing, despite being inappro-priately dressed in his work suit. Anyway, he clambered over the rocks, got tackled up and launched his rod … SHOOOM. He followed the lot in. Mobile phone ruined, the items in his wallet destroyed, he came out like a drowned rat. What a sight that would have been, and to quote the magnificent *Early Doors*: 'I wish I was there.' For him, we might as easily say: 'We wish he was here.' Everybody misses him terribly since he pegged out. What a top bloke.

Chapter 25

IN THE BAG

The Ashes winter

Touring is part and parcel of a life in cricket but this past winter I hit the road in a different way. Once started, the car didn't stop for a month as I took in 20 theatres up and down the land, bringing this very book to life on stage. What a trek it was, too, from Eastbourne to Gateshead, from Aberystwyth to Norwich, all via Crewe. We went four weeks without a square meal and during that time there was barely a service station in the country not temporary home to what the modern player might call our 'comfort breaks'. Comfort, indeed.

Comfortable is not something I generally feel when I get up on stage – put me in front of a camera and I'm fine, an audience is a different matter – but my sidekick Peter Hayter, the cricket correspondent of the *Mail on Sunday*, scripted the show perfectly. So despite the motorway madness, sleep deprivation and occasional spanner in the works, it was a very rewarding experience. One long chortle.

Let's just say the shows got off with a real bang on opening night at Leamington Spa. Quite literally, in fact, as the National Grid went down with 10 minutes left in the performance. It was my Elvis moment. The lights went out, there was a massive crash of noise and off went the microphones. There was no electricity. After a minute or so a fellow with a torch emerged from the back of the theatre and politely asked: 'Please could everyone leave the building.'

'No,' came the collective reply. At least that suggested folk had been enjoying it.

The management from the theatre came out to explain to me that it was a matter of health and safety that the building had to be evacuated. It wasn't just us in this scenario, half of Leamington Spa was without power and there was no sign of it coming back any time soon. I went onto the stage to convey this message to the crowd: 'Ladies and gentlemen, for your own safety would you please exit the building, and we will reconvene in the car park.'

Eager to please I gave them five more minutes out on the Tarmac before wishing one and all good night. It was bitterly cold, but as I have always been told by my thespian pals, 'the show must go on'. No matter what circumstances present themselves, whatever calamity befalls us *actors*, one should complete one's performance. What a load of old tosh I'm spinning you here. Our main concern, of course, was not that at all – it was to make sure no one asked for their money back!

During our travels we stayed in some of the dingiest hotels imaginable, but the one at Worthing was without equal – an absolute beauty. My partner in crime, Hayter, fondly referred to it as the Vile Madhouse. It was completely surrounded by scaffolding and, upon arrival, when I asked the whereabouts of the car park, I was told: 'it's just at the back, sir.' Turned out the lad was telling the truth. We later found it under rotting mattresses, sofas and various other remnants of the town's refuse.

In the guestrooms was a shower with an open door, which provided an unintentional wet room effect, the tiles slipping off the wall as you washed. Throughout the establishment wallpaper hung off the walls and ceiling-paint peeled, like they had seen enough and were desperate to escape their hellish existence. As you wandered around it was hard to tell the function of any of the rooms but the presence of a miniature pool table in one led to the assumption we were standing in the bar.

This particular hotel was positioned on the sea front, which you could imagine gave it some sort of quaint charm at the height of summer. Equally, because of its location it was in a permanent howling gale in the winter. Every single window in the building rattled for the duration of the day – and the entire night. There wasn't a moment when they were not bouncing around in their frames.

Not everything was down at heel, however, and the Richmond Theatre in south London provided an opportunity to mix with greatness. Well, we had our pictures taken with Sir Laurence Olivier. Yep, we were lording it in the same dressing room as dear Larry. Or should I say there was a photo on the wall commemorating his presence, so we had our picture taken next to him, on the very chaise longue upon which he used to recline. And the fact that we were booked for matinees in Norwich and Salford gave the tour a certain mystique. Well, before it became apparent that the matinee crowd had one of two purposes in life: to keep off the streets or keep warm.

That was not the only misjudgement on the tour and when we got to the Opera House in Buxton we were not alone in falling foul of the existence of *two* theatres in the town. The main one, which I thought we were playing, holds 1500 people. However, it turned out we were in the side theatre, which has a more modest capacity of 600. All my mates from the regiment piled down, typically making an all-dayer of it by arriving at 2pm and heading for the local boozers. They were absolutely steaming by 8 o'clock when I shoved them into some seats at the back, from where they could shout and barrack freely. They were far enough away for me to be as oblivious to their presence as that of the Hollies, who were on next door, churning out all their classic hits. It only became clear what was going on in a rather surreal second half of our gig. The format of the show offered the audience the chance to ask questions at half-time, to be answered by us during the final 45 minutes. Well, the funniest one we got the whole tour was that night at Buxton. 'This is the strangest Hollies event I've ever been to. When are you going to sing "Bus Stop"?' asked one disgruntled punter.

I thought touring was meant to be rock 'n' roll. Unfortunately that incident with the lost Hollies fan was as close as we got to a groupie. And we even forgot to smash up the chairs and screen projector, a la Pete Townshend, following the final show in Morecambe. Probably should have done because after one month of treading the boards that's it for me.

My next venue just a few days later was Brisbane, on the eve of the first Ashes Test, and as soon as I arrived I was subjected to the tub-thumping local press. 'Here come the Poms again, they're shit, they're hopeless,' I was informed. Former Australian players bagged our team and our chances of retaining the urn. But whenever I was asked to give my opinion, I was adamant: 'England will win 3–1. They're just a better team.'

You can live and die by your predictions but I was just convinced; nothing that happened during the course of the series altered my opinion. When they picked that bloke Xavier Doherty for the first Test it might as well have been Tommy Docherty. Doug 'the rug' Bollinger hit the wall before the series had really begun and Mitchell Johnson seemed more intent on publicising his new tattoos than getting our batsmen out. There he was at an early press conference, showing off what appeared to be a florists' window display on his arm. As he was introducing the lotus flower of summer, I thought: 'Aye, aye, this bloke is a bit fragile.' He seemed a bit lopsided, and he bowled like it too.

The two teams felt their way into the series at Brisbane, and the fag end of that Test presented one of the great crowd barracks. England got off to a tricky start with just 268, but it was such a flat pitch we racked up 517 for 1 the second time around. The final day had a pleasing inevitability about it from an English perspective, and the Australian public had already given up as their team showed no signs of getting anyone out. Nothing was happening in terms of a contest and when that kind of lull in the action occurs, cameramen naturally look for other things to show the viewers. When they panned round the ground it looked like fancy dress day. All the locals had turned up as plastic seats. A sea of purple, green and yellow.

At around 500 for one, Ricky Ponting positioned himself at silly, silly mid-on. To describe it, he was stood next to the non-striking batsman and the umpire, almost on the pitch itself, and being such a tiny chap, you couldn't actually see him behind the other two from certain angles. But with the silence deafening at this point, there was nowhere for him to hide as this lone voice boomed across the Gabba: 'Good thinking, Ricky! The last catch that went to silly mid-on was a hundred f***ing years ago. There's bound to be another one soon!'

The whole ground (well the well-populated English section) erupted, and even Ricky offered a smile. Everybody talks about how the players will cope with 90,000 people at Melbourne and when there are that many in you can't hear a thing because of the general drone. But this foghorn sledge reverberated all the way around the Gabba and was equal to one I remember in similar circumstances at the MCG when, after Ray Bright had bowled 16 consecutive overs of slow left-arm, this bloke piped up with: 'Give him the one that spins, Ray.'

It didn't take many days of that Ashes series to confirm that England were fitter, stronger and simply more talented than their opponents. Australia played the X man, Phillip Hughes, and 'Simon Smith and His Amazing Dancing Bear'. I actually expected the Alan Price Set to coming out crooning at one point. These blokes were nowhere near good enough for the job and the worry was that even one of their established, proven players, Michael Hussey, a man who has been around for a long time and whose dedication has been recognised with his Mr Cricket tag, could not see the parlous state his country's game was in. He was wonderful with his 195 in the first Test but his claim afterwards appeared miscalculated.

In the Bag

'We refuse to believe we are number five in the world,' he said. Well, you better get used to it, mate, because you are going further down than that.

As usual, knee-jerk inquiries have been set up but all they will find is a lack of talent. The way forward for Australia – and remember everyone has followed their lead for years – is a complete rethink. And I have a cunning solution. They need to get 18 states, 470 professional cricketers, 360 Twenty20 matches every season and send their players in their cars from pillar to post all over the country every single week of the summer. Meanwhile, get as many foreigners into each team as is possible, so hardly any at all are eligible to play for Australia. That, upon the evidence witnessed recently, is the template for a great side.

When England lost in Perth it felt like a total one-off. Johnson shifted from his preferred line of the boundary boards at fine leg and swung it back into the right-handers from off-stump at serious pace. But even after his series-levelling contribution of nine wickets there was no waving of fists and feistiness. Instead of the usual bombast associated with Australian pacemen, he conceded it was the conditions that did for 'em.

'The easterly doesn't usually blow,' he revealed. 'But it did and was perfect for me. It's not usually like that.' He was backing off when a stereotypical fast bowler would be falling over himself to declare: 'We are going to stick it up the Poms. Who do they think they are?' Australians shouldn't do kind and polite.

The jovial nature between the players was something Allan Border picked up on early in the five matches. He felt it was not as serious as it ought to have been. Subsequently, some of the players tried to get a bit nasty, with one or two unsavoury incidents unveiling themselves at the WACA – Peter Siddle offering Matt Prior outside being the one example that comes to mind. That one really riled me. As it happened, I did a breakfast Q&A in Melbourne in front of 500 people soon afterwards, with Peter as one of the other guests. When he was being interviewed (or egged on, more to the point) he was asked what it was all about with Matt and how close they came to a scrap behind the pavilion. 'Do you think you could take him?' he was asked. I considered the question obscene. What a shocking thing to say about a game of cricket.

'Oh yeah, I reckon I could take Prior if it came to that. I'd sort him out,' he boasted in front of his fellow Victorians.

Then it was my turn, and I was interviewed by this same bloke. 'How do you think the series has gone? Where's it going from here? You Poms will struggle here. Not in good shape now.' The usual stuff – as many statements as questions. With regards to my expectation of the outcome, I stuck to my guns. 'England will win the last two matches, that's my opinion, I've had a good bet on it and that's what's going to happen.' Not wanting to let the fighting talk pass, however, I added: 'By the way, I witnessed the on-field incident at Perth, and I know young Peter is still here in this room. But if he fancies a bit of that – let me advise everyone here that there's not one of the 22 players that could fight their way out of a paper bag. Next time you come into Manchester bring all your mates with you, get down the city centre and I will introduce you to four blokes who will have you shouting for your mummies!' I'd made my point.

Following years of being on the end of Australian taunts, the boot is now well and truly on the other foot. In my time as England coach I would bristle when I heard Australians say that the Ashes should comprise just three matches rather than be a five-match series. Call it what you will – arrogance, cockiness or overflowing self-confidence on their part – it is not nice to be kicked when you're down and we were going through a rough time back then. Now, with a set-up stumbled upon in the aftermath of the Kevin Pietersen–Peter Moores fiasco, everything appears to be in good shape.

When I did another Q&A, this time for the Australian board, I was naturally being asked questions about Australia. 'Here's a startling reality check for you,' I told the assembled guests. 'Nobody who has observed Test match cricket recently would argue with this, so hear me out. Tamim Iqbal is a better opening batsman than Phillip Hughes. Mohammad Ashraful is a better player than Steven Smith. Shakib Al Hasan is a better bowler than Michael Beer. Rubel Hossain is a better bowler than Ben Hilfenhaus. So that's four of the Bangladesh team that would walk into your side. It is my opinion and one shared by lots of other people in the game. Reality checks are not something you've previously had but you are in the same boat as other countries now.'

Australia had wonderful players, world-class performers in their team not so long ago – players of the ilk of Matthew Hayden, Justin Langer, Shane Warne, Glenn McGrath and Adam Gilchrist. But the reality is that they have now gone, and building a nucleus of great players always takes time because you don't get half a dozen turning up at once. Ricky Ponting was their great player for 2010–11 and England were fabulous against him. If you say you are hunting for the opposition captain then Andrew Strauss showed exactly how to do that. He was brilliant at getting to Ponting. And the usual rules applied: get to the captain and you get to the team.

In world cricket terms it is no bad thing that Australia have to start again. Meanwhile, England are gunning for the number one spot and going after current number ones India. The two teams meet this summer and I would have England down as raging favourites. Equally, if they were playing in India I would be favouring India – it is just a home and away situation for me – but if England pull it off as I think they should then they can be true to the word that was coming out of Australia this past winter. Namely that they believe they are on course to become the recognised best Test team in the world. What you have to do to get there is simple: keep beating the teams you are put up against.

The Ashes timeframe is fairly unforgiving, and the lack of respite in the itinerary meant I didn't get off the relentless treadmill until the one-day series began. Tasmania is a place where most folk are horizontal anyway due to their laidback disposition, and it was good to get to Hobart after the hurly burly of Melbourne and Sydney. (Don't mention the Hurley-burley to my mate Shane Warne, mind. Sore point.)

Every now and again it's good to depart from reality, and you certainly do so upon arrival in Tassie. The airport only has one baggage collection and getting to it is like a military operation. Sniffer dogs check your hand luggage and then have a wail of a time trotting round the carousel the wrong way. Work and play combined must be ticking some pen-pushers' boxes somewhere. Class A narcotics, firearms, bombs – these are the sinister things that these magnificently trained dogs are trying to uncover in other arrival halls around the world. But things are slightly different in Tasmania. What they are after is something higher on the contraband list: fruit.

In the Bag

It is a grave offence to bring apples and oranges, not to mention smuggling bananas and pears. If caught you are liable to death by scrotum hanging. Mark Lynch, aka DR Trumpington, one of our Sky Sports directors, was pulled aside to have his hand luggage wet-nosed by a Beagle. 'Are you concealing fruit in there?' a ginger-bearded operative – man, not dog – barked.

'No,' said the good doctor. 'But I do have a dog at home.'

'That will be it then, sir,' apologised the handler. 'Sorry to have troubled you.'

The very swish Henry Jones Hotel awaited. Now they offer the kind of comfort break I like. As I chilled out for what seemed like my first downtime since my British tour began, I picked up a pamphlet placed on the bedside table. It was a list of the convicts sent there two centuries ago. One David Lloyd preceded me in 1834, having arrived on the good ship John Barry, from London. Now I bet he was a rum bugger. Just hope he didn't have any fruit with him!